Understanding
AdobePhotoshopCS6

THE ESSENTIAL TECHNIQUES FOR IMAGING PROFESSIONALS

Richard Harrington

Understanding Adobe Photoshop CS6: The Essential Techniques for Imaging Professionals

Richard Harrington

Peachpit Press
1249 Eighth Street
Berkeley, CA 94710
510/524-2178

Find us on the Web at: www.peachpit.com
To report errors, please send a note to errata@peachpit.com

Peachpit Press is a division of Pearson Education

Project Editor: Nancy Peterson
Production Editor: Myrna Vladic
Development/Copy Editor: Anne Marie Walker, Robyn G. Thomas
Technical Editor: Wayne Palmer
Compositor: Kim Scott, Bumpy Design
Interior Design: Danielle Foster
Proofreader: Liz Welch
Cover Design: Mimi Heft
Indexer: Jack Lewis
Media Producer: Eric Geoffroy

ISBN-13: 978-0-321-83462-1

ISBN-10: 0-321-83462-3

9 8 7 6 5 4 3 2 1

Printed and bound in the United States of America

Dedication

To my wife Meghan, your patience and support fill my life with meaning. Thank you for your love and all that you do.

To my children Michael and Colleen, your curiosity and love inspire me. As you grow, you teach me what it means to be a better man.

To my family, thanks for your support and teaching me so much.

Acknowledgments

Several people have played an important role in this book coming to life:

- Ron Hansen and Michael Davidson, who gave me my first job teaching Adobe Photoshop at the Art Institute of Washington.

- Ben Kozuch, who believed in me enough to let me teach Photoshop to a room full of media professionals.

- Scott Kelby and the other instructors and staff of the National Association of Photoshop Professionals for their inspiration and support.

- Susan Rimerman and Nancy Peterson for challenging me to write the best book possible. Anne Marie Walker and Wayne Palmer for guiding me through the process and fixing my flaws.

- To James Ball, Jim Tierney, and Abba Shapiro, thank you for your generous gift of photos.

- To my many students through the years, thanks for the challenges and the motivation.

- To the staff of RHED Pixel for helping to bring the podcasts to life.

Richard Harrington, PMP

Richard has surrounded himself with media for his entire professional career. He's held such diverse jobs as directing television newscasts and publishing a music magazine to managing video production departments and consulting to nonprofit agencies. Currently, Richard is a founder of RHED Pixel (www.RHEDPixel.com), a visual communications company in the Washington, D.C. area.

RHED Pixel is a successful consultancy that provides technical and design services to clients such as the Community Health Charities, National Foundation of Credit Counseling, the Smithsonian Institution, Data Robotics, and the Children's National Medical Center. RHED Pixel creates everything from broadcast commercials to live events to interactive projects for a diverse clientele.

The Project Management Institute certifies Richard Harrington as a Project Management Professional. He holds a master's degree in project management as well. Additionally, Richard is an Adobe Certified Instructor and Apple Certified Trainer. He is a member of the National Association of Photoshop Professionals Instructor Dream Team.

His personal philosophy is communicate, motivate, create. Richard is a firm believer that media can have powerful results. You can follow his evolving interests in all things digital at www.RichardHarringtonBlog.com.

Contents

DVD Bonus Material

Introduction

The Role of Photoshop in Education

Learning Adobe Photoshop is essential to success in digital media industries. Photoshop is a gateway into several related technologies. From digital image acquisition and processing to typography and compositing, Photoshop is often your first introduction. If you can master this program, you can go on to success with several other technologies. With this in mind, it is important to learn Photoshop with one eye on the present and the other on the future.

The Role of Photoshop in Professional Industries

It's been said that if you know Photoshop, there's always work to be had. Photoshop is used by everyone from photographers to Web developers, video professionals to graphic designers. In fact, Photoshop is used in more places than you'd expect—including the medical, architectural, and legal fields. Adobe Photoshop is a portal to Adobe's other software applications, but it is also much more. Mastering the tools in Photoshop will teach you more about creative technology tools than any other program. With a solid knowledge of Photoshop, you'll be well on your way to being comfortable with an entire digital toolbox.

Purpose of This Book

When I decided to write this book, it was to fill a need. I have worked with Photoshop students of all levels, from the college classroom to working professionals across all industries. What I've heard time and time again is that people wanted an objective book that gave them everything they needed to truly understand Adobe Photoshop. Readers have grown tired of books that talk down to them or waste time promoting only the latest features.

It's not that there's a shortage of good books for the professional; I've read many of them and know several of their authors. But what has happened over the years, as Photoshop has become such an established program, is that we are left with two types of books: those for complete beginners and those for pros looking to dig deep on specific areas of the program. What was missing? A book that addresses the need of the learner who wants to understand the important features of Adobe Photoshop, as well as the core technology behind it, to build a solid foundation for future learning as well as immediate success.

This book is for learners who learn best by not just reading but by doing. Every chapter contains extensive hands-on exercises and all the files you need to practice. With the purchase of this book you also have immediate access to more than 100 videos that show you advanced skills and special techniques. In addition, interactive quizzes help you check your progress to ensure that the knowledge is "sticking." The accompanying DVD or digital download has everything you need. And you'll want to be sure to visit www.richardharringtonblog.com for updates and bonus downloads.

If you are learning Photoshop in a classroom, this book should combine with your instructor's knowledge to give you a rich, interactive learning experience. For those working professionals looking to fill in their understanding of Photoshop, this book answers and reinforces the essential information that you'll need. For both audiences, this book teaches you what you need to succeed in the professional workplace. As a teacher and a working pro, it's my goal to prepare you for professional success.

Suggestions on Learning

Photoshop is a very comprehensive program; don't try to learn it overnight. In fact, rushing to learn is often what causes problems. In an effort to learn quickly, skills don't have time to be absorbed. To combat this problem, I have eliminated nonessential topics from this book. I've also included a hands-on example or activity for every skill.

The truth is you'll learn best by doing. Don't skip the hands-on activities in a rush to make it through the book. I strongly encourage you to try each one. After completing the book's activities, you should repeat the techniques with your own photos. Nothing makes a topic as clear as you experiencing it interactively and achieving success. With practice—regular and thorough—you can understand and master Photoshop.

Understanding Adobe Photoshop DVD or Downloads

To help you get the most from Adobe Photoshop CS6, I've included several hands-on and interactive exercises.

Lesson Files

You'll find more than 250 images as well as Photoshop actions on the DVD or in the download to bring the lessons to life. The hands-on exercises are meant to be fun and informative, so be sure to use the lesson files as part of your learning process.

Interactive Quizzes

To help measure your progress, you'll find a Quizzes folder. Open the file Launch Quizzes. html with a Web browser and take a short quiz for each chapter. Just answer ten questions and see if you've learned the key concepts from each chapter. The quizzes use Adobe Flash Player 9 or later, so be sure that is loaded on your system.

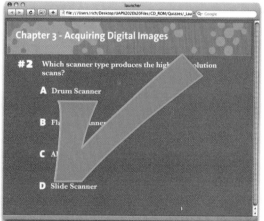

Video Training

Throughout the book you'll see Video Training icons that call out more than 100 additional modules you can watch. But what fun is just watching? You'll also find extra images in each lesson's folder to use with the videos.

Bonus Exercises

We've included ten additional Photoshop exercises to hone your skills. These projects include all the images you'll need, along with an outline on how to approach the project. These self-paced exercises help you refine your skills and gain important practice.

Resource Blog

The author maintains a resource blog at www.richardharringtonblog.com. Here you'll find news about graphics technology, tutorials, bonus videos, and great resources like free images. You can subscribe to the blog for free with an RSS reader or by email for notification of all posts.

Bonus Exercises

For additional hands-on practice, try these ten bonus exercises. You will find these exercises well suited for exploring the many features of Photoshop. Each exercise provides source images and general instructions to guide you in approaching the project. The exercises should be undertaken after you have completed the book's chapters.

Exercise #1: Digital Painting

A popular technique is to turn a photo into a painting-like image. There isn't a one-click answer, but a little experimentation can go a long way.

Exercise #2: Creating a Collage

You can combine multiple images into a new composite image. This can be for experimental or artistic purposes as well as to create an advertisement or cover image.

- **Photoshop is an essential program**
- **Can be used to create content for use with other programs**
- **Use of Layers and Styles can enhance appearance**
- **Never have more than seven bullets per page**

Exercise #3:
Designing Speaker Support

Creating a custom background or series of backgrounds is important when designing a custom electronic portfolio. It allows a designer to create a custom look for a client to use with Microsoft PowerPoint or Apple Keynote.

Exercise #4:
Designing a Magazine Cover

Designing a magazine cover is an excellent exercise for practicing with type and layout. Precise positioning of elements as well as creative use of color and design are important to capture the audience's attention.

Exercise #5:
Preparing Images for the Internet

Properly sizing and compressing images for the Internet is an essential skill. Finding the right balance of compression and image size is important to ensure that the end user can quickly download the images, yet still have them look good.

Exercise #6:
Designing a CD/DVD Label

Whether you're creating a music CD for a band or a DVD for a client, a professional-looking label is important. Use of text and effects are important to create a readable yet compelling design.

Exercise #7:
Creating a DVD Menu

Designing a DVD menu is an important task. More and more projects are being distributed on DVD, and it is the most quickly adopted format in consumer technology history. There are a lot of design options for a DVD menu (and it will depend on the DVD-authoring software used). But a lot of design work can happen in Photoshop, which allows you to fully explore design options.

Exercise #8: Artistic
Reinterpretations of a Photo

Working with a single image and processing in several ways is an excellent way to explore the power of filters. By creating unique looks through filter combinations, blending modes, and image adjustments, you have great design options.

Exercise #9: CD/DVD Package

In this project, you'll create a label for a DVD or CD using an Amaray-style case. A template for printing is provided from a DVD replicator (each replication facility usually uses a custom template). The design will include text and photos—a completed sample image is provided for reference.

Exercise #10: Preparing Images for CMYK Printing

Preparing images for CMYK printing requires special processing. Certain bright, saturated colors cannot be printed using the CMYK process. These out-of-gamut colors need to be reduced and brought into range.

Digital Imaging Essentials

1

Before you open your first image in Adobe Photoshop, it's very important that you understand how a digital image is built. Knowing how computers represent your digital image data is essential to your career. Being a "technical" person will not make you more creative, but it will make you faster and more confident. Let's take a quick look at what a working professional must understand.

VIDEO 1:
Pixels in Depth

Pixels: Digital Building Blocks

When it comes to digital cameras, most photographers (and salespeople) seem obsessed with megapixels—because "everybody knows" that having more pixels means better images (it doesn't by the way). What's lacking in all this hoopla is a clear understanding of what pixels are and just how many of them you need. The more pixels you have, the more RAM you'll need to open the images and the more hard drive space to store them all. So it's in your best interest to understand some of the technology behind the images you want to capture, manipulate, output, and store.

ISTOCKPHOTO/LORAN NICOLAS

In the Beginning...

Essentially, computers, cameras, and video devices use pixels to express image information. Each pixel is a small square of captured light. The pixel is the smallest portion of an image that a computer is capable of displaying or printing. Too few pixels and an image will appear "blocky" because there is not enough detail to work with. Too many pixels and the computer or output device slows down because it has to process more information.

A close-up of TV picture elements, or pixels.

The red circle shows an enlargement of the image. Notice how you can see actual pixels when you increase the magnification of an image. These squares of light are the building blocks of all digital photos.

Digital cameras use card-based storage, like this Secure Digital card, to hold the captured pixels.

But where did the term *pixel* come from? Pixel is an abbreviation for *picture element*. The word was coined to describe the photographic elements of a television image. In 1969, writers for *Variety* magazine took pix (a 1932 abbreviation of *pictures*) and combined it with *element* to describe how TV signals came together. There are even earlier reports of Fred C. Billingsley coining the word at NASA's Jet Propulsion Laboratory in 1965. Although the exact origins of the word may be disputed, its meaning is not. The word *pixel* quickly caught on, first in the scientific communities in the 1970s and then in the computer-art industry in the mid 1980s.

So What Are Megapixels?

When you shop for a digital camera, you are bombarded with talk of megapixels. Consumers are often misled about what megapixels are and how many are needed. A *megapixel* is simply a unit of storage, whether internal or on a removable card. A megapixel is one million pixels and is a term commonly used to describe how much data a digital camera can capture. As with your car, just because your tank can hold more gallons of gas doesn't mean it's more fuel efficient or better than your friend's car.

For example, if a camera can capture pictures at 3000×2400 pixels, it is referred to as having 7.2 megapixels ($3000 \times 2400 = 7{,}200{,}000$). If you were to print that picture on paper at 300 ppi (pixels per inch), it would roughly be a $10" \times 8"$ print. Professional photographers may need more pixels than this, but a consumer may not. It all depends on how the pixels are meant to be displayed or printed.

The more pixels you capture, the larger the image is (both in disk space and potential print size). Consumer usage (such as email or inkjet prints) is less demanding than professional usage (such as art books or magazines). Professionals need more megapixels than consumers; hence, high-end cameras cost more because they are targeted at people who make money by taking photos.

Understanding Resolution

OK, prepare to be temporarily confused (but not for long). A lot of terms are used to describe image resolution. The problem is that many people (and companies) use the wrong terms, which (understandably) leads to a great deal of confusion. Let's take a quick look at the most common terms and their accurate meanings. Knowing how to describe the resolution of images and output devices will help you make the right decisions when purchasing or choosing gear to use.

Dots per Inch (dpi)

The most common term used to describe image resolution is *dots per inch (dpi)*. Although you'll hear it used for digital cameras and scanners, it is really only appropriate for printers. As a measurement of output resolution, dpi is fairly straightforward.

To determine dpi, it is necessary to count the number of dots that can fit in a 1" × 1" area. A higher dpi can mean smoother photographs or line art; for example, newspapers tend to use around 150 dpi, whereas magazines can use up to 600 dpi. Consumer printers easily print at 600 dpi or even higher, which can produce extremely good results (when using the right paper). An increase in dpi can produce even better-looking images. You'll see (and hear about) dpi used a lot, but it solely refers to print and physical output.

Don't Believe the Megapixel Myth

More megapixels do not guarantee a better picture. Instead of picking a camera solely on how many pixels it will capture, investigate cameras with better lenses or options that are important to you. If you are shooting for large-format output, you'll need a larger megapixel-count camera, but if you're shooting for personal use, consider how you output most of your pictures.

A Fix for Those with Less Than Perfect Eyesight

Are you working with a high-resolution monitor and having a hard time seeing your menus in Photoshop? You can change the size of the display text. Press Command+K (Ctrl+K) to open the Preferences window and select Interface. From the UI Font Size menu, choose Medium or Large to give your eyes a break.

It's only in evaluating printers that the term dots per inch (dpi) makes sense. DPI is a function of the printer and can operate independently of the PPI settings of the file you send it.

In a commercial printing environment, very high-resolution images are required.

ISTOCKPHOTO/GMNICHOLAS

ISTOCKPHOTO/JOHNNYSCRIV

Detect Displays

Color LCD
✓ 1680 × 1050
1440 × 852
1280 × 1024 (stretched)
1280 × 1024
1280 × 800
1152 × 720
1024 × 768 (stretched)
1024 × 768
1024 × 640
800 × 600 (stretched)

Number of Recent Items   ▶
Open Displays Preferences...

Modern computer monitors support various screen resolutions. Changing the monitor resolution results in a different amount of pixels per inch displayed on your monitor. Do not run Photoshop at a screen resolution of less than 1024 x 768, or it will cause user interface problems (1280 x 800 or higher is recommended).

Pixels per Inch (ppi)

When you view your images on a computer monitor, you are seeing pixels displayed on your screen. Computer monitors use the concept of logical inches. Originally, the Mac OS most commonly used 72 *pixels per inch (ppi)* to match the concept of the printing idea of 72 points per real inch of paper. The Windows OS has traditionally used 96 ppi.

As computer monitors and portable devices have evolved, they've advanced to support variable resolution settings. As such, the actual ppi for a screen can vary greatly depending on the physical size of the screen and the resolution being used by the computer's graphics card. For example, modern laptops often use resolutions between 100 ppi and 140 ppi, and devices like an iPhone can jump all the way up to 326 ppi to make images crisper on the small screen.

Worry less about the ratio of pixels per inch on your screen and simply accept that the standard measurement of resolution in Photoshop (and most computer programs) is ppi. When talking about displayed graphics, its ppi, not dpi.

Samples per Inch (spi)

Although scanners are less common than they used to be, many professionals still use them to load sketches, photos, and original negatives. Manufacturers often tout the dpi capabilities of their scanner. This is inaccurate. Scanners don't use dots, they use samples. A *sample* is when a scanner captures part of an image. *Samples per inch (spi)* is a measurement of how many samples are captured in the space of one inch. In general, an increase in sampling leads to a file that is truer to its analog original. However, there is a threshold: Once a certain amount of information is surpassed, human senses (and electronic output devices) cannot tell the difference.

Consumer-level scanners can capture optical resolution ranging between 300 spi and 4800 spi. Professional devices can capture significantly higher optical resolution. If you're working with a large image, a lower number of samples is fine. If you're enlarging a very small image, a large number of samples is crucial. More samples per inch translates into more information available as pixels, which can then be harnessed in output when they are converted to dots in the printer. So if your scanner's software specifies dpi, it really means spi, but you can see how the two are closely related.

Lines per Inch (lpi)

In professional printing environments, you'll often hear the term *lines per inch (lpi)*. This is from the traditional process where images with gradiated tones (such as photographs) are screened for printing to create a *halftone*. This was originally performed by laying film with dots printed on it over the film before exposure. In the digital age, this process and these terms are used less often, but it is still good for you to have a basic understanding.

These days, the work of converting an image to lines is performed by an imagesetter. The dots are arranged in lines, and the lpi measurement refers to the number of lines per inch. An increase in lpi results in smoother images. **Table 1.1** shows the most common lpi settings for different output formats.

Table 1.1 **Common lpi Measurements**

Output Method	Typical lpi
Screen printing	35–65
Laser printer (matte paper)	50–90
Laser printer (coated paper)	75–110
Newsprint	60–85
Offset printing (uncoated paper)	85–133
Offset printing (coated paper)	120–150+
High-quality offset printing	150–300

STOCKPHOTO/PENFOLD

This image has been converted to a halftone, as is evident by the visible dot pattern.

Image Mode

Within Photoshop, you need to choose from one of eight image modes when working with a document. The mode you pick will depend on what you need to do with the image and how you intend to output it. For example, the mode used for web graphics will differ from those used for professional printing. The three most common modes used are RGB, Grayscale, and CMYK, but it's worth taking a quick look at all eight.

VIDEO 2:
Converting Image Modes

RGB Color

The most common mode for graphics in Photoshop is RGB. The RGB Color mode uses additive color theory to represent color (a 100% value of red, green, and blue light creates white light). Different intensity values of red (R), green (G), and blue (B) combine to form accurate colors. By mixing intensity values, virtually every color can be accurately represented.

When working in Photoshop, most designers choose RGB Color mode for its wider range of available color (also known as *gamut*) and extensive support for filters and adjustments. Additionally, computer monitors use RGB mode to display color, and this is the native color space for onscreen display. Because you'll most often be processing images on a computer, it is easiest to work in the same color space as your monitor.

CMYK Color

Professional printing uses a four-color process to simulate color. The four inks are cyan (C), magenta (M), yellow (Y), and black (K, for *key*). The CMYK Color mode uses the subtractive color model to re-create color. Subtractive color explains the theory of how ink or dye absorbs specific wavelengths of light and reflects others. The object's color is based on which part of the light spectrum is not absorbed. Although print designers use CMYK Color mode for professional printing, they will work in RGB mode throughout the design stage. CMYK Color mode has a smaller color gamut, so CMYK conversion is saved until the last stage of image preparation.

Grayscale

A grayscale image uses different shades of gray to represent image details. For example, an 8-bit image is represented by 256 levels of gray (see "Bit Depth" later in this chapter). Likewise, a 16-bit image would show 65,536 levels of gray (a substantial improvement, but it requires an output device that can utilize the data). When creating grayscale images, it is important to perform test prints with the output device and paper to see how contrast is maintained.

Duotone

A duotone image can actually be monotone, duotone, tritone, or quadtone. Grayscale images that use a single-colored ink are called *monotones*. *Duotones*, *tritones*, or *quadtones* are grayscale images printed with two, three, or four inks, respectively. Using both black and gray ink to represent the tonal values, duotones create better-quality printed grayscales. This mode should be used when you know the printer is set up specifically to handle the job. If you just want the look of a duotone, you can create that look by working in RGB mode and using the Black and White adjustment layer.

The most popular form of duotone is a sepia-tone image (often seen in historical prints). In modern times, a designer may use a duotone for style purposes or to save money by using fewer inks.

Bitmap

A bitmap image uses only one of two color values—black or white (no gray)—to represent the pixel data. These 1-bit images have a very small file size. To create a bitmap, you first must convert the image to an 8-bit grayscale formula, and then convert to the Bitmap image mode. Do not confuse Bitmap mode with a bitmap image, which is another name for *raster* (or pixel-based) images. Additionally, avoid confusion with the BMP file format, which is a standard Windows file format that dates back to the earliest version of Windows. An image in the Bitmap mode simply uses only black and white to represent image data.

Indexed Color

Indexed Color mode severely limits the number of colors used to represent an image. In Indexed Color mode, up to 256 colors are available. To reduce file sizes (and download times), some web designers use fewer colors in their graphics. They will turn to specialized formats like GIF and PNG-8. Although this mode reduces file size, it also visibly lowers the quality of the image. Indexed Color mode works well for illustrations or logos but not so well for photos on the Internet. Instead of converting your original image to Indexed Color mode via the Image menu, use the Save For Web command (File > Save For Web). This will convert the file to a GIF or PNG-8 (both use the Indexed Color mode), but leave the original image in its original mode.

Lab Color

L*a*b* Color is the most complete color mode used to describe the colors visible to the human eye. The three parameters of color are L for luminance of the color, a for the color's position between red and green, and b for its position between yellow and blue.

The Lab Color mode was created to serve as a device-independent, absolute model to be used for a reference. Lab attempts to simulate the full gamut of color; however, it is a three-dimensional model and can't be represented properly within Photoshop. Therefore, the * after the L, a, and b is used to signify that it is a derivative model. Lab images can only be printed on PostScript Level 2 and Level 3 printers; for all other professional printers, Lab images must first be converted to CMYK mode. The Lab Color mode is generally only used by imaging professionals seeking the truest color fidelity because it supports all the colors in both the RGB and CMYK Color modes.

Multichannel

Multichannel mode is a highly specialized mode used for complex separations for professional printing. You may never need to use it. Photoshop automatically converts to Multichannel mode when you delete a channel from an RGB or CMYK image. The color onscreen is no longer accurate because Photoshop cannot describe it. This is sometimes done for an effect or as part of the image repair process if one channel did not capture properly (such as from a malfunctioning digital camera). Most likely, you'll *never* want to work in Multichannel mode.

Bitmap
Grayscale
Duotone
Indexed Color...
✓ **RGB Color**
CMYK Color
Lab Color
Multichannel

✓ **8 Bits/Channel**
16 Bits/Channel
32 Bits/Channel

Color Table...

Bit Depth

Besides resolution (the number of pixels) and color mode (the way colors are processed), one other variable affects image quality. Bit depth measures how much color is available for display or printing of each pixel. A greater bit depth means each pixel contains more information for describing the color. A pixel with a bit depth of 1 can display the pixel as either black or white. The most common bit depth is 8-bit mode, which has a possible value of 256 intensity levels per color channel. However, depending on the version of Photoshop you are working with as well as the file type and image mode, you can access 8, 16, or 32 bits per channel. It's important to note that larger bit depth can limit image adjustment commands.

TIP

Shooting Raw

One of the major benefits of shooting images in a camera raw format is that you can often choose to work in 16 bits per channel in Photoshop. This offers superior options for manipulating color and exposure.

NOTE

32 bits per channel

You won't encounter 32 bits per channel images very often. They come into play when working with generated imagery (such as those from 3D modeling applications). They can also be created by merging multiple photos together into a high dynamic range (HDR) image. You'll learn about the HDR process later in the book.

Time to Move On

There's a lot more ground to cover, but you'll explore the topics discussed here and others in greater depth in each chapter. You'll feel a bit more comfortable with the language used to describe images and color as you read on. With the knowledge you've gained so far, you can jump into using Photoshop and start to navigate its interface.

Photoshop's Interface

2

Adobe Photoshop's interface can be pretty intimidating. Among all those panels, tools, and menu commands it's easy to get lost. However, it's worth it to master these components. Photoshop is by far the most-used image editing application on the planet, and knowing how to properly use it unlocks a world of design opportunities. Working professionals use it for a variety of tasks, from enhancing magazine photos to designing web animations and from creating television graphics to performing medical imaging.

Most important is to learn the essential features you need right away and then gradually learn the rest as needed. I frequently tell students of all levels that often there are three or more ways to perform the same task in Photoshop. Adobe's software engineers have tried their best to make the program intuitive (and everyone certainly doesn't think the same way). Additionally, new features are often unveiled with product updates, yet the old features frequently remain for those who resist change or prefer the older method.

Learning Photoshop is a very doable task, especially if you take a balanced and measured approach by matching learning new features with practical application. I've seen older professionals as well as young students become proficient Photoshop users. Just remember that a Photoshop expert is usually just someone who's mastered the skills to put three or four basic skills together in the right order to solve the task at hand.

VIDEO 3:
Setting Preferences
in CS6

Understanding the Interface

So let's start with a quick tour of the Photoshop interface. Adobe offers two versions of the application: Photoshop and Photoshop Extended. The standard version of Photoshop is suited for all users, whereas Photoshop Extended offers specialized features for medical researchers, 3D artists, architects, and engineers. This book shows the Photoshop Extended interface, because many users have access to that version of the software. But the book covers in depth only those features that are common to both versions of the application. Throughout this book you'll encounter a few bonus movies to help you understand Photoshop Extended's capabilities.

If you haven't done so already, launch Photoshop. Because many of Photoshop's panels will be new to you, we'll tackle them in the order in which you'll likely encounter them. The goal here is to get the "lay of the land" and just figure out what each panel is used for. Throughout the rest of the book you'll dig much deeper into how (and when) to use these specific panels and tools. As you learn Photoshop, you'll often need to use features before you've had a chance to learn about them in depth, so a basic knowledge right away is very important.

TIP

A Great Frame-up

Photoshop CS6 keeps all your documents and panels in an Application Frame to keep the interface clean. If you're using the Mac OS, you can toggle the frame off or on by choosing Window > Application Frame. Experiment to see which look you prefer.

1. Open the file Ch02_Eagle.psd from the Chapter 2 folder in the book's Lessons folder to explore Photoshop's interface. Many of the panels in Photoshop require an image to be open before they display any detail.

2. Choose Window > Workspace > Essentials (Default) to ensure that the application is in its default state.

3. Choose Window > Workspace > Reset Essentials to ensure that all the panels are in their default position.

VIDEO 4:
Switching Tools

Tools

All the hands-on tools are contained in the Photoshop Tools panel (typically displayed on the left edge of the screen). Photoshop groups similar tools together. You can access these hidden tools by clicking and holding on a particular tool. Whenever you see a triangle in Photoshop, click it to open additional nested options.

The first keyboard shortcuts you should master are those for the Tools panel because you'll use these the most. Frequently, the first letter of the tool is the keyboard shortcut. If you can't remember the shortcut, click the tool while holding down the Option (Alt) key to cycle through the available tools.

An alternative method to cycle through the tools is to press the keyboard shortcut multiple times while holding the Shift key (for example, Shift+M cycles between the Rectangular and Elliptical Marquee tools).

If you'd like to simplify the shortcuts even more, press Command+K (Ctrl+K) to call up the Preferences dialog box.

In the General category:

- Deselect the Use Shift Key for Tool Switch option. You can then press a shortcut key (such as G for the Gradient tool) and cycle through the tools contained in that tool's drawer. This speeds up your ability to switch tools.

- Select the Zoom with Scroll Wheel option if you have a three-button mouse. This makes it easier to zoom in or out of your working document.

In the Interface category:

- Make sure the Show Tool Tips feature is selected to assist you in learning common keyboard shortcuts. Tool tips teach you the proper name and the keyboard shortcut for each tool. Just hover over a user interface element to learn more about it.

- Set the UI Font Size to Medium or Large if you'd like to increase the size of screen elements so they are easier to read on high-resolution monitors.

Many tools are available, and each tool has multiple purposes (as well as strengths and weaknesses). Throughout this book you'll learn how to effectively use these tools. With patience, you'll get the most from Photoshop's powerful feature set.

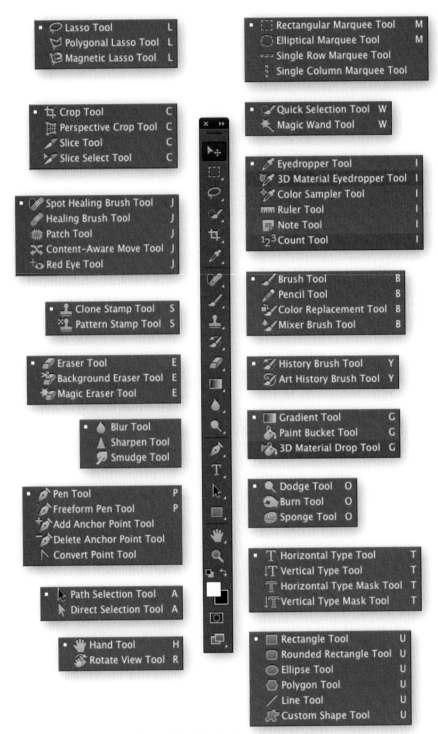

Lasso Tool L
Polygonal Lasso Tool L
Magnetic Lasso Tool L

Rectangular Marquee Tool M
Elliptical Marquee Tool M
Single Row Marquee Tool
Single Column Marquee Tool

Crop Tool C
Perspective Crop Tool C
Slice Tool C
Slice Select Tool C

Quick Selection Tool W
Magic Wand Tool W

Spot Healing Brush Tool J
Healing Brush Tool J
Patch Tool J
Content-Aware Move Tool J
Red Eye Tool J

Eyedropper Tool I
3D Material Eyedropper Tool I
Color Sampler Tool I
Ruler Tool I
Note Tool I
Count Tool I

Clone Stamp Tool S
Pattern Stamp Tool S

Brush Tool B
Pencil Tool B
Color Replacement Tool B
Mixer Brush Tool B

Eraser Tool E
Background Eraser Tool E
Magic Eraser Tool E

History Brush Tool Y
Art History Brush Tool Y

Blur Tool
Sharpen Tool
Smudge Tool

Gradient Tool G
Paint Bucket Tool G
3D Material Drop Tool G

Pen Tool P
Freeform Pen Tool P
Add Anchor Point Tool
Delete Anchor Point Tool
Convert Point Tool

Dodge Tool O
Burn Tool O
Sponge Tool O

Horizontal Type Tool T
Vertical Type Tool T
Horizontal Type Mask Tool T
Vertical Type Mask Tool T

Path Selection Tool A
Direct Selection Tool A

Hand Tool H
Rotate View Tool R

Rectangle Tool U
Rounded Rectangle Tool U
Ellipse Tool U
Polygon Tool U
Line Tool U
Custom Shape Tool U

Tools shaded in blue are only available in Photoshop CS6 Extended.

Options

The Options bar is essential because it contains the majority of controls for the currently active tool. It consolidates the most used (and useful) options for the active tool and moves them to the forefront for easy access. The Options bar is visible by default. It runs the length of your monitor across the top of the frame.

In the right corner you'll also find the Workspace switcher, which lets you switch between different arrangements of windows designed for specific tasks like Photography, Typography, Motion, and Painting. For the remainder of this chapter, you'll be using the Essentials workspace.

> **NOTE**
>
> **The Options Bar Is Essential**
>
> Be sure to keep the Options bar open because you'll always need it. If you accidentally close it, bring it back by choosing Window > Options.

VIDEO 5:
Managing Workspaces

A CUSTOM WORKSPACE

You'll find that the more you work with Photoshop, the more you'll want to use different tools for different situations. For example, you'll want Layer Styles and the Color Picker handy for text work, but you'll turn to the Histogram and Adjustment panels when doing image restoration.

You can save any combination and arrangement of panels that you want to reuse. Then you can access it in one click with Workspaces. Effectively, using Workspaces enables you to switch between different production tasks (such as image touchup and type work) with ease. Plus, it is a way to customize the application and make it feel more welcoming to your way of working. Try it out.

1. Open the windows you need and arrange them into the desired positions.

2. To save the current workspace layout, click the Workspace switcher menu (in the upper-right corner of the screen) and choose New Workspace.

3. Enter a unique name for the workspace and click OK.

To activate a workspace, choose it from the Workspace switcher in the Application bar. To update a workspace, resave it with the same name. To delete a workspace, click the Workspace switcher and choose Delete Workspace.

VIDEO 6:
Understanding Layers

Layers

In Photoshop, a layer can contain artwork and transparency information. This allows you to combine (or composite) multiple images into a new piece (such as a postcard or advertisement). Originally, Photoshop did not have layers. You could open a picture to process it, but that was about it. However, over time the demands placed on Photoshop by its users led to its evolution. As Photoshop moved beyond being a mere touchup tool, the flexibility of layers emerged to meet the demand. Photoshop now has several special layer types including adjustment layers, shape layers, and fill layers. By isolating discrete elements to their own layers, designers can make several changes and freely experiment with their design.

Without sounding like a zealot, layers in Photoshop mean everything to a designer. You will spend much of this book (and your early career using Photoshop) getting comfortable with layers. With that said, *always* leave your Layers panel open while you work (press F7 to open it); this is where most of the action takes place. The Layers panel is like the steering wheel of a car. You'll dig much deeper into layers in Chapter 7, "Layer Masking," and Chapter 8, "Compositing with Layers."

Channels

The previous chapter explained different image modes that a computer graphic could occupy. In the Channels panel you can view the individual components of color. The brighter the area in the individual channel, the more presence there is for that color. Let's look at a simple example of an RGB graphic.

1. Choose File > Open and navigate to the Chapter 2 folder in the book's Lessons folder.

2. Open the image file Ch02_RGB_Overlap.psd. You should see red, green, and blue circles overlapping one another. The overlap has also created new colors: red + green = yellow; blue + green = cyan; red + blue = magenta; and red + green + blue = white.

3. Activate the Channels panel. By default it is docked with the Layers panel (just click on its name and the panel will switch to display Channels). If you don't see it, choose Window > Channels.

4. Look at the individual channels; you'll see a definitive area for each color. Channels look like grayscale images when viewed independently. Notice how the full circles are visible (and white) where there is 100% value of each channel.

VIDEO 7:
Understanding Channels

5. Close the document by choosing File > Close.

Fully understanding Channels unlocks a wealth of image-processing power. Harnessing a color's individual components is difficult at first but well worth the effort. You'll delve much deeper into Channels in Chapter 10, "Color Correction and Enhancement."

Paths

Although Photoshop is known as a raster-editing tool (because of its several pixel-based functions), it does contain several vector tools as well. Vectors use lines that are defined by math equations; as such, they can be scaled indefinitely and always remain crisp. Several of Photoshop's vector tools can create paths, which are useful for complex selections. You can create a path with the Pen tool. By clicking around an image, anchor points are created, and then Photoshop connects the dots with vector lines. Paths can also be created using the vector Shape tools. Use the Paths panel to select the path you want to update. For more on complex selections, see Chapter 5, "Selection Tools and Techniques."

Adjustments

One of the most common tasks in Photoshop is making adjustments to images to fix tone and color. Photoshop offers an Adjustments panel to provide easy access to the most common, nondestructive adjustment commands. The adjustments are grouped into three categories:

- **Tonal controls.** Use these controls to adjust Brightness/Contrast, Levels, Curves, and Exposure in a nondestructive fashion.

- **Color controls.** Use these controls to adjust Vibrance, Hue/Saturation, Color Balance, Black & White conversion, Photo Filter, Channel Mixer, and Color Lookup properties.

- **Creative/Advanced controls.** These controls are special-purpose adjustments and include Invert, Posterize, Threshold, Gradient Map, and Selective Color.

NOTE

Future Learning Opportunity
You'll explore these adjustments more in later chapters.

Properties

If you're using an adjustment layer, you'll need to control how it affects your image. Additionally, adjustment layers (and optionally all layers) can have a mask applied to control the visibility of the layer. Photoshop uses masks to obscure parts of an associated item; transparency is defined by the use of white, black, and gray. In fact, you can apply a mask to a layer, a vector, or even a smart filter.

Photoshop CS6 offers precise control over masks, including the ability to adjust their density and edges. Masks are a useful way to erase parts of a layer nondestructively, which allows for future changes. They can also be used to isolate an adjustment to only parts of an image.

Both masks and adjustment layers are controlled using the Properties panel. To view the panel, just select an adjustment layer in an open image. Here you'll find buttons across the top to switch between the two. You'll see multiple masks in use in the sample document (Ch02_Eagle.psd) to isolate the effects of color correction. You'll explore masks in depth in Chapter 7.

Color

Don't confuse the Color panel with the color mode of the document. The Color panel allows you to modify and select colors using six different color models. You can choose colors using RGB sliders or the more intuitive Hue, Saturation, and Brightness (HSB) model. To adjust color, move the sliders for the corresponding value. Sliding the Red slider to the right increases the amount of red in the new color. Choosing colors is independent of image mode in that you can use a CMYK model for an RGB image. However, picking a color to use in a grayscale document will not introduce color into that image.

Spend some time exploring the Color panel and find a method that works best for you. Clicking on a color swatch opens the powerful Color Picker, which unlocks a larger visual interface for exploring color and enhances the use of the Eyedropper tool to sample color from a source image. You'll use color in several of the chapters in this book, and the Color panel and Color Picker are fairly easy to understand.

Swatches

The Swatches panel is like a painter's palette in that it holds several colors ready to use. Many colors are loaded by default, which are useful when painting or using filters that utilize those colors. If you click the panel's submenu, you'll discover many more swatch books to load for specialty purposes like web browser colors, spot color printing, or thematic color swatches (such as a blue saturated range). You can also store any custom colors you create for easy access by clicking on an empty space to store the swatch.

TEMPORARY BANISHMENT OF PANELS

If you want to hide your panels, you can quickly toggle them off and on:

- **Press the Tab key to hide all the panels.**
- **Press the Tab key again and they return.**
- **Press Shift+Tab to hide everything except the Options bar and Tools panel.**
- **To focus on only your image, press the F key once to go to Full Screen Mode With Menu Bar. Press the F key again to go to Full Screen and hide all the user interface elements. Press the F key once more to cycle to Standard Screen Mode. You'll also find the Screen Mode Switcher located at the bottom of the Tools panel.**

TIP

Docking Panels

To save space, any floating panel can be collapsed to an icon. Simply drag a panel to any new panel's edge or the edge of the screen, and a blue line will appear (which indicates where the panel will dock). The most common place to dock panels is on the right edge of the screen, but they can be docked on the left or bottom edges as well.

Styles

The Styles panel is where you can visually access Layer Styles, which are the combination of layer effects (they can also be applied singularly to create effects such as beveled edges, drop shadows, or glows). Effects are most useful in combination, and advanced photorealistic effects can be achieved. Photoshop ships with several built-in styles, and many more are available for download from Adobe's website (www.adobe.com/exchange) as well as many other Photoshop sites. Layer Styles are frequently used for text and image effects but can also be used for web rollover effects for buttons. For more on Layer Styles, be sure to read Chapter 13, "Layer Styles."

VIDEO 8:
Using the Navigator

Navigator

While working with photos, you'll often need to zoom in to touch up an image. It may sound cliché, but it's easy to lose your perspective when working in Photoshop. When you zoom in to a pixel level for image touchup, you often won't be able to see the entire image onscreen. This is where the Navigator comes in handy.

1. Open the photo Ch02_Bike.psd from the Chapter 2 folder.

2. Select the Zoom tool from the Tools panel or press Z (the tool looks like a magnifying glass). Make sure the Scrubby Zoom option is selected in the Options bar.

3. Click and drag near the bike tire head to zoom in.

4. Call up the Navigator panel by choosing Window > Navigator. Drag the corner of the Navigator panel to make it larger and easier to see.

5. You can now navigate within your photo:

   - Drag the red view box around the thumbnail to pan within the image.

   - Resize the Navigator panel for a larger image preview.

   - Move the Zoom slider to zoom in or out on the image.

   - Click the Zoom Out or Zoom In buttons to jump to a uniform magnification.

6. Close the document by choosing File > Close.

Histogram

When you are color correcting or adjusting exposure, the histogram can be a great help. This graph illustrates how the pixels in the image are distributed across brightness levels. To read a histogram, start at the left edge, which shows the shadow regions. The middle shows the midtones (where most adjustments to an image are made), and to the right are the highlights. Image touchup and enhancement are covered in Chapter 10. You may want to leave the Histogram panel open as you work, because it is an easy way to learn to read the graphical details of a digital image.

The Histogram panel has been set to Show All Channels view (click the triangle in the upper-right corner and choose All Channels view). The top histogram is a composite histogram for the Red, Green, and Blue channels combined; the next three show them individually.

Info

The Info panel is a useful place to find a plethora of image information, even when you're using the default options. You can get information about color values as well as precise details about the active tool. However, by customizing the panel you can make it truly useful.

1. Select the Info panel by choosing Window > Info or by pressing F8.

2. From the Info panel submenu (the triangle in the upper-right corner) choose Panel Options.

3. The resulting dialog box has several options; I recommend the following choices for a new user:

   - Leave Mode set to Actual Color.

   - Set Second Color Readout to CMYK if you're doing print work, or set it to RGB color if you are preparing images to use on the Internet or in video exclusively.

   - Set Mouse Coordinates to Pixels.

   - Enable the following choices under Status Information: Document Sizes, Document Profile, and Document Dimensions.

   - The last option, Show Tool Hints, provides a detailed explanation for each tool you select from the Tools panel.

4. Click OK.

History

The History panel will quickly become your best friend. It's here that Photoshop keeps a list of what you have done to the image since you opened it. By default Photoshop keeps track of the last 20 steps performed on an image, but you can modify this number. A higher number means more levels to undo.

1. Press Command+K (Ctrl+K) to call up the Photoshop Preferences dialog box.

2. In the Performance section, change History States to a higher number, such as 100. Note that more levels of undo require more RAM, so you may need to balance this number if your system is underequipped.

3. Click OK.

Actions

Actions are among the least-used features of Photoshop but offer huge time savings. Actions allow for visual scripting, which means you can record commands or adjustments that you need on one image and play them back on other images. For example, you could record an action that adjusts the size of an image, runs an adjustment to lighten the image, and then converts it to a TIFF for commercial printing. You could then play that series of commands back on another image or even batch process an entire folder of images (which can eliminate boring, repetitive work). Actions can be very useful for both design and production tasks.

You'll explore actions fully in Chapter 15, "Actions and Automation."

VIDEO 9:
Editing Video in
Photoshop CS6

 NOTE

Tools Meet Actions

Starting in Photoshop CS6, you can record the use of tools in an action. This means that you can record items like brush strokes to draw your signature and sign a photo. To enable the recording of tools not normally actionable, simply click the menu in the upper-right corner of the Actions panel and choose Allow Tool Recording.

Timeline

Photoshop CS6 adds an improved Timeline that allows for the editing of video files directly in Photoshop. A new video playback engine and essential trimming tools make it possible to perform basic video-editing tasks right in Photoshop CS6.

TIP

How Much RAM Do You Need?

With Photoshop CS6, Adobe has made the move to a 64-bit application (which requires a 64-bit operating system as well). A major advantage is the ability to address more memory. Although Photoshop needs a minimum of 1 GB to run, a better approach is to have 2–3 GB of memory per processor core in your computer. Memory has become much cheaper in recent years. Although you can run in a 32-bit mode under Windows, you should really upgrade for the best performance.

Character

Although Photoshop began its life as an image editor (essentially a digital darkroom), it has greatly evolved over the years to also include an extensive text tool. Many people start and finish their entire designs within Photoshop. These designs include advertisements, posters, packaging, and DVD menus. A close look at the Character panel reveals complex control over the size, style, and positioning of individual characters within a word. The Type tool is explained in depth in Chapter 12, "Using the Type Tool."

Paragraph

The Paragraph panel contains controls that impact paragraph text. When using the Type tool, you can click and type, which creates point type. Or, for more control, you can click and drag to create a text block and then access paragraph type. This causes the text to have boundaries and wrap when it hits a margin. Within a text block, you have a significant level of control over how your type is aligned and justified. For much more on text, see Chapter 12.

VIDEO 10:
Browsing in Mini Bridge

Mini Bridge

Mini Bridge is a useful panel in Photoshop that helps with tasks related to browsing and opening files. It lets you visually browse your files and makes it easy to manage files by ranking, sorting, and renaming them. Mini Bridge attempts to bring the core features of Adobe Bridge (a companion application) right into Photoshop. Choose File > Browse in Mini Bridge to open the panel. For you to use this panel, Adobe Bridge needs to be running in the background.

Acquiring Digital Images

3

Some of the core tasks of processing digital images involve sizing, manipulation, and processing. Even though their contents may vary, all digital images are essentially the same: They are composed of pixels that contain color and luminance information. Adobe Photoshop's powerful features allow you to adjust those pixels to better match your needs and desires.

And although the destination may be the same, the path your digital images take to get inside Photoshop will vary. Some may start out as digital images acquired with a still camera, whereas others may be archival images loaded via a scanner. You might also search online websites to find specialized images. Let's take a look at the many ways to acquire image files that can be loaded into Photoshop and manipulated.

Pixels in detail: When you zoom into an image at 1600% magnification, the pixels are very easy to see. You can open the photo CH03_Owl.tif from the Chapter 3 folder and use the Zoom tool (Z) to magnify the image. In fact, you can zoom up to 3200%, which makes pixel viewing quite easy. To toggle the visible grid at high magnifications, choose View > Show > Pixel Grid.

Digital Cameras

This book will not teach you how to use your digital camera. Many excellent books on that subject as well as classes are offered. What this book will address is how the pixels are converted, what file format you should choose to shoot your images, and how to transfer them to your computer.

IMAGE COURTESY NIKON INC.

Sensors in a digital camera acquire an image by converting light into pixel data.

Digital Camera Technology

Shooting a photo digitally produces a less accurate image than scanning a photo shot on film with a flatbed scanner using a high samples per inch setting. This is because digital cameras capture data using photosensitive electronic sensors. These sensors record brightness levels on a per-pixel basis. However, the sensors are usually covered with a patterned color filter that has red, green, and blue areas. Although the filter attempts to capture all detail that the lens sees, it is unable to completely do so due to its design.

The filter used is typically the Bayer filter arrangement, which contains a repeating pattern of two green pixels, one red pixel, and one blue pixel. The Bayer filter uses more green because the human eye has an increased sensitivity to green. This filter allows the image to record the brightness of a single primary color (red, green, or blue) because digital cameras work in the RGB color space. The RGB values combine using the additive color theory (which

A CMOS sensor (left), such as this one from Nikon, is the standard imaging device on a digital camera. The Bayer filter arrangement (right) uses red, green, and blue pixels, and is very common in digital cameras.

was briefly discussed in Chapter 1, "Digital Imaging Fundamentals") and form an image when viewed from a suitable distance.

Not all the properties of film can be fully imitated by the computer sensors in a digital camera, so the camera must interpolate the color information of neighboring pixels. This averaging produces an anti-aliased image, which can show visible softening. When anti-aliasing is present, hard edges are blended into one another. Sometimes this can be desirable (with low-resolution Internet graphics where you reduce file size by limiting color). Other times, anti-aliasing can produce an undesirable softness when you print an image. Depending on the colors in the original image, a digital camera might only capture as little as one-fourth of the color detail. For example, if you had a desert scene with lots of red detail and little green or blue, the sensor would rely on the red areas of the filter (which only cover a fourth of the sensor face).

TIP

Camera-specific Training

I highly recommend the *Snapshots to Great Shots* series from Peachpit Press to learn more about specific cameras. Several popular cameras are covered in depth in dedicated books to help you get the most from your camera.

Does this mean you should shoot film only? Of course not; it's getting awfully difficult to even buy film these days. Ultimately, film captures a high-quality image that can be optically enlarged using the negative. However, digital capture can be more convenient and affordable because you eliminate the time-consuming processes and costs associated with developing the film. Huge strides have made in the improvement of image quality in digital cameras, and the ability to experiment and shoot multiple exposures with real-time feedback makes them a much better learning tool.

It is important to shoot at a high pixel count (which can be accomplished by setting the camera to shoot in a high- or best-quality mode or choosing to shoot raw). You can always crop or shrink the image for output or display, but you should avoid enlarging the image if you don't have to. When a digital image is enlarged, it can create unwanted image softness or pixelization (a visible blockiness). Capture as much pixel data as possible to minimize digital upsampling (increasing the resolution of the image).

Shooting JPEG vs. Raw

When digital cameras became commercially available, the memory cards used to store pictures were very expensive. Many photographers couldn't afford multiple or high-capacity cards, so they wanted more images to fit on a single, smaller card. Many users also emailed their pictures to friends and family. Small file sizes enabled consumers who lacked an understanding of digital imaging to attach photos to emails with minimum technical headaches. With these two scenarios in mind, manufacturers turned to an Internet-friendly format, JPEG (Joint Photographic Experts Group). It was a proven technology and one that was familiar to many users.

IMAGE COURTESY NIKON INC.

The JPEG format is extremely common because most hardware and software manufacturers have built support for it into their products. The JPEG format is also extremely efficient at compressing images, and it is a good format for continuous tone images, such as photos. A JPEG file looks for areas where pixel detail is repeated, such as the color blue in a photo of the sky. The file then discards repeated information and tells the computer to repeat certain color values or data to re-create the image.

IMAGE COURTESY LEXAR.

The JPEG Options dialog box is available when you modify or first save a JPEG file with Photoshop. When saving, you can adjust the Quality slider to reduce file size. It is best to leave Quality set to maximum if you will be making future edits to the image: This applies the least compression that could damage the image's appearance.

Although JPEG is a good format for distributing images (due to their compatibility and small file size), it is not great for image acquisition or production. A JPEG file is lossy, meaning that every time you modify it in Photoshop and resave as a JPEG, additional compression is applied to the image. Over subsequent compressions, the image quality can noticeably deteriorate. This is similar to the act of making a photocopy of another photocopy: Additional image deterioration occurs with each processing step. The visible loss in image detail or accuracy is referred to as *compression artifacts*.

So, if JPEG is inferior, why do so many people use it? Money and resistance to change are the simple answers. It's cheaper to shoot JPEG images because you don't need to buy as many memory cards (however, the price of memory cards nowadays is so low that this is almost a moot argument). Certain scenarios like sports and photojournalism often rely on the speed associated with smaller files as well (but camera manufacturers are adding larger buffers

This image was captured as both a raw and a JPEG file when it was shot. The picture was taken with a Nikon D800, which can simultaneously write both files to the memory card when shooting. The raw file offers significantly greater latitude for post-processing and can recover more detail than the JPEG version.

in cameras to allow for high-speed raw shooting). Additionally, even many pros have been slow to abandon JPEGs due to fear of change. Learning how to use new technology requires time, something that many people are short of these days.

Newer digital cameras, generally the pro models, offer the ability to shoot raw (or native). The images are captured at a higher bit rate, which means that the pixels contain more information about the color values in the image. Most raw files have a bit depth of 10, 12, or even 16 bits per channel instead of the 8 used by JPEG. Raw formats also have a greater tonal range; hence, there is a better exposure for shadows and highlights. This extra information makes your work in Photoshop easier because it adds greater flexibility and control in image adjustments. You should have less work to do in Photoshop as well, because the image captured has more color information than a JPEG version.

Raw files can be four to ten times larger than JPEG files. This extra data is used to hold more image detail, which can reduce, or even eliminate, compression artifacts found in JPEG files. However, that extra data can increase the time it takes for the files to write to the memory card. As such, a memory card with a faster speed rating is a good investment and will help your camera keep up with the action you are shooting.

The raw file captures the unprocessed data from the camera's image sensor. Although your camera may contain settings for sharpness, exposure, or lighting conditions, the raw file stores that setting as modifiable information and captures the original (unmodified) data that came through your camera's sensors. This is very useful because it lets you easily adjust white balance within Photoshop. Each manufacturer treats the format differently, using a proprietary format. Fortunately, Photoshop frequently updates its raw technology to support the newest cameras on the market. To find out if you can access a particular camera format from within Photoshop, visit Adobe's website at www.adobe.com/products/photoshop/cameraraw.html.

Because the raw data is unprocessed, you must essentially "develop" the image data inside Photoshop. You'll be presented with several choices when opening a raw image. You can choose to adjust several options related to the image, as well as the lens and lighting conditions. All the adjustments made in the Camera Raw dialog box are nondestructive, meaning the original image is

TIP

Workaround for Unsupported Cameras

If Photoshop does not support a particular raw format used by your camera, use the software that shipped with the camera. The image can be converted into a 16-bit TIFF image (a high-quality file with no compression), which Photoshop can open.

TIP

Camera Raw for TIFF and JPEG?

Although the Camera Raw interface can be used for JPEG and TIFF files, those images have already had the camera's processing permanently applied to the image. Shooting raw has many benefits and should be fully explored by reading the documentation that accompanies your camera.

VIDEO 11:
Camera Raw Interface

VIDEO 12:
Localized Adjustments in Camera Raw

The Adobe Camera Raw dialog box is a versatile environment for "developing" your pictures. The image Cho3_Overhang.RAW is included on the DVD. Choose File > Open and navigate to the file in the Chapter 3 folder. In Photoshop CS6, you can even make localized adjustments by painting an area to select it and then use sliders to modify it.

preserved in pristine condition. You can "tweak" the image after shooting it, including being able to easily save those changes and apply them to similar exposures.

The Camera Raw dialog box has continued to evolve since it was first introduced as a purchased add-on to Photoshop 7. Subsequent versions of Photoshop have updated the user interface. Be sure to watch the detailed video tutorials to learn more about this powerful developing tool. Fortunately, the Camera Raw dialog box is fairly intuitive, especially once you understand the concepts of adjusting images. After you have completed Chapter 10, "Color Correction and Enhancement," you should feel much more confident using the options in the Camera Raw dialog box.

NOTE

Other Applications

Digital photographers who have large collections of digital images to manage will often use a library management application. Two of the most popular are Adobe Lightroom and Apple Aperture. Both have excellent integration with Adobe Photoshop.

IS DNG THE NEW RAW?

In 2004 Adobe released the **Digital Negative Specification (DNG) file format**. The code and specifications were made publicly available so manufacturers could build support for the format into their products.

The goal was to replace several proprietary raw file formats with a universal format. Despite initial optimism, camera manufacturers have been slow to adopt it (some even refusing). At this point, DNG files are a useful way to archive raw files and attach additional metadata. You can find out more about DNG by visiting Adobe's website at www.adobe.com/products/dng/main.html.

Acquiring Images from a Digital Camera

There are two major ways of downloading images from a digital camera. Which connection type you choose will depend on your work environment and budget for additional hardware.

The first method involves plugging the camera directly into the computer. Many cameras ship with a connecting cable (generally USB). The advantage of this approach is that it doesn't require an extra hardware purchase. The primary disadvantages of this method are that it ties up the camera, and it is hard on delicate ports built into the camera. If you break the USB port by constantly plugging in and unplugging a camera, it can lead to an expensive service bill. The data port is interconnected with several other systems on the camera; a break at one end can result in problems in other areas. Additionally, if the camera's battery were to be depleted during image transfer, the memory card and its contents can become corrupt.

A better option for downloading images from a digital camera is to purchase a stand-alone memory card reader. There are many options available, so consider these questions and choose wisely:

- Do you need only one card format, or do you need to read multiple formats?

- How fast do you want your files to transfer? Be wary of card readers that are USB 1, which can take a long time to transfer files. Look for USB 2, USB 3, FireWire, or eSATA for faster data rates. Laptop users with a card slot can purchase an effective card adapter for fast file transfers without tying up ports. Some laptops and desktops even ship with built-in card readers that tend to be reasonably fast.

- Do you want to transfer multiple cards at once? Some readers allow for two or even four cards to be mounted at one time so you can initiate a large transfer and walk away.

Transferring Files

The actual transfer of photos is not handled by Photoshop. Rather, you can use Adobe Bridge CS6, which includes a Photo Downloader (File > Get Photos from Camera). If you are not using Adobe Bridge, the files are handled natively by your computer's operating system. Just manually copy them to a folder on your computer.

Make Backup Copies

You may want to work with a copy of your transferred image, especially if you are just getting started in Photoshop. Many users will duplicate a folder of images and work with those. Others will burn a copy of the original images to a CD or DVD for backup. Preserving an original digital file is a good idea for future use.

But if you're shooting raw, there is no need to duplicate the raw file. The modifications to the image are stored in a separate sidecar file in the folder with your images. However, it is still a good idea to make sure your images are backed up to a second location in case your hard drive fails. For more on backup and image-management workflow, see www.dpbestflow.org.

VIDEO 13:
Importing Images
with Adobe Bridge

Need a Scanner?

Many all-in-one printers combine a printer and scanner, essentially creating a fax machine and photocopier in the process. Be sure to check if your printer offers scanning software to load your traditional photos. You can also rent scanners at many local photocopy shops.

VIDEO 14:
Crop and Straighten Command

Scanners

Many purists swear that shooting film adds richness in detail and color, as well as introduces subtle nuances like film grain, which cannot be replicated with a digital camera. Additionally, many pictures that you'll need to work with may only exist on traditional media (such as prints) or as a negative. You'll need to use a scanner to turn these optical formats into digital formats.

Choosing a Scanner

If you work in a computer lab or other work environment, your choice in scanners may have already been made for you. However, it is still important to understand the different types of scanners that are available to consumers.

Flatbed scanners

The most common scanner type is a flatbed scanner on which photos are loaded face down on a piece of glass. The scanner then moves a charge-coupled device (CCD) across the image to capture/digitize the image. High-quality scans can greatly increase the amount of data that is captured. So, be sure to look at high-speed scanner-to-computer connection options. For a modern computer, FireWire or USB 2 or 3 are the best options.

Be sure to pay close attention to the optical resolution of the scanner: This is the maximum size of the image before using software interpolation to enlarge it. Most users doing intermediate-level work or desktop publishing find a scanner capable of 600 to 1200 spi to be adequate. Remember, samples per inch can translate fairly well into pixels per inch. It is a good idea to have more pixels to start with, and then reduce the size of the image for delivery.

Film/slide scanners

Specialized scanners load in slides or film negatives. These scanners use a tray to hold the material, and then a motor pulls the tray slowly across an optical sensor. This process is relatively slow due to the resolution needed. The scanner must capture a lot of data from a very small surface area to produce a usable image. These scanners are slightly more expensive than flatbed scanners but are essential if you frequently work with slides or negatives.

Drum scanners

When top image quality is a must, pros turn to drum scanners. These units are expensive (starting at $5,000 and increase significantly). This is the oldest scanning technology. It calls for the image to be mounted on a drum. The drum is then rotated in front of a photomultiplier tube. The tube is much more sensitive than the CCDs used in flatbed scanners. Drum scanners' primary advantage is resolution, and they should be used when you need to significantly enlarge a scanned image (such as museum archival pieces or for magazine output). Because the machines are expensive and very complex (as well as potentially destructive), users will often send images to a service bureau for drum scanning.

A drum scanner is a highly specialized piece of equipment. These machines are expensive and are usually found only in high-end, service bureau facilities. ©iStockphoto

What Size to Scan? Think in Pixels

People often get confused when determining which settings to scan with. Too little information and the picture goes soft. Too much information and the scanner slows to a crawl. The answer is to know your intended output resolution as well as your device.

COMMON PPI REQUIREMENTS FOR FINAL FILES

Output Method	Typical ppi
Onscreen (web/slides)	72–96
Laser printing	150–250
Newsprint	120–170
Offset printing	250–300
High-quality offset printing	300–600

For example, if you need to create a 20-inch-wide poster that will be printed on a high-quality press requiring 300 ppi, use this calculation:

20 (inches) × 300 (ppi) × 1.25 (pad for flexibility) = 7500 pixels

Do not adjust your scanner's dpi (or ppi) settings. Rather, crop the image after running a preview scan. You can then adjust the scanner's resolution by looking at the output size of the scanned file. As you adjust the output file size, the scanning software will automatically determine the appropriate settings for samples per inch. All scanners tell you just how many samples you are about to capture. Looking at these numbers gives you a truer sense of the end result. Total pixel count is much more important than dpi, especially when scanning images of various original sizes.

More Advice on Scanning

On the DVD you'll find a bonus PDF called Scanner_Operation.pdf in the Chapter 3 folder.

Importing from CD/DVD/Blu-ray Disc

For many users, the practice of backing up images to optical discs has become very common. Additionally, many educational books (like this one) include media on their discs as well. This is a great way to distribute images because they are cheap to manufacture, are large-capacity discs, and are cross-platform compatible. You'll want to copy the images to your hard drive before you bring them into Photoshop. This will significantly increase the speed at which you can work on the images (hard drives transfer data faster than optical media drives). Additionally, you will be able to save your work in progress to your hard drive; you can't update a file once it's been burned to a disc.

NOTE

Royalty-free Does Not Equal Free

Don't confuse royalty-free and free. A royalty-free image must still be purchased. This is how the photographer and distributor make money. Royalty-free images can be a big savings because you can eliminate model releases, talent charges, location fees, travel, and many other costs associated with a photo shoot. However, keep in mind that someone had to pay those charges in the first place, and selling their pictures is their livelihood. Remember to pay for what you use. It's the professionally responsible way, as well as the law.

Stock Photo Services

Professionals find it is often necessary to purchase images to complete their projects. Whether it's a shot of a sports car for a magazine layout, a photo of a handshake for a Microsoft PowerPoint presentation, or the Chicago skyline for the cover of a DVD, stock photo services can help. But finding the right stock photo service is a balancing act. You must consider several factors when making a choice:

- **Cost.** There is a lot of competition out there, and photos are priced accordingly. Some services offer annual subscriptions; others charge per image.

- **Resolution.** Sites charge more for high-resolution images. Be sure to know how you'll use the image. Website designers will pay less for an image than someone designing an annual report. A website uses low-resolution images, whereas the report will be professionally printed and require high-resolution photos.

- **Exclusivity.** Does the image need to be yours and yours alone? Or is it OK if the photo is also used in someone else's project? Images that have their usage rights managed cost significantly more. A rights-managed image has restrictions placed on who can use the image for a certain time period. In contrast, a royalty-free image is purchased once and can be used as many times as the designer desires.

Public Domain Images

I'd say, "The best things in life are free," but that wouldn't be accurate here. More appropriately, "Why pay twice?" The United States has several federal agencies that document their work and make it available to the public. This work was paid for with tax dollars, and the people of the United States own the work. Fortunately, through the Internet, the U.S. government is willing to share it with most of the world.

I've created a portal page on my blog that points to the best government sites. These pages offer print-resolution images that you can use. Nearly every image is either copyright free or cleared for use, but you may be required to cite the source. Be sure to look at the terms of use posted on the site. Take the time to fully explore each site; you'll be surprised by the wealth (and diversity) of available images.

Visit www.richardharringtonblog.com/resources/freeimages.

THE FAIR-USE MYTH

A popular myth in academic cultures is *fair use*. The doctrine provides situations where copyrighted works can be used without paying. It places restrictions on:

1. The purpose and character of the use, including whether such use is of a commercial nature or is for nonprofit educational purposes

2. The nature of the copyrighted work

3. The amount and substantiality of the portion used in relation to the copyrighted work as a whole

4. The effect of the use on the potential market for or value of the copyrighted work

Students and teachers alike get caught up in exemption number one. It is true that in a classroom situation you can use virtually any image you want for practice or class exercises. However, here is the problem: As soon as a student wants to start looking for a job and builds a portfolio, those images are being used for financial gain. If you are a student, you need to build work samples that help you get a job. Use images that you have the rights to (or that you have photographed).

The other clause that is often seen as a loophole is number four. People often think that because their project was small or personal that damage cannot be claimed. It is relatively easy for a copyright holder to claim damages or lost revenue. Even though they may not go after you, why take the chance? As a content creator, you should respect the law and the welfare of your fellow designers and photographers. For more on copyright and fair-use doctrine, visit www.copyright.gov and www.asmp.org/content/registration-counts.

Sizing Digital Images

4

Once you've acquired your digital images, you'll need to size them for your project (as well as ultimate output). For many Photoshop users, such as photographers, this may be as straightforward as cropping and sizing. This chapter explores several techniques for sizing your images. You'll learn about the concept of resampling, which addresses how the computer adds or subtracts information from a digital image while trying to retain detail and clarity.

Resolution Revisited

Chapter 3 looked closely at the process of acquiring digital images. If you skipped ahead or just skimmed that chapter, go back—a solid understanding of those concepts is required to move forward. Quite simply, you must know the capabilities of your digital camera or scanner to process information.

Previous chapters also briefly discussed resolution requirements for different output formats. The second part of the image-sizing puzzle is a clear understanding of these output

This photo was scanned at two different resolutions. The image on the left was scanned at 300 spi, and the image on the right was scanned at 72 spi. Examine the detailed enlargements to see the impact of different scanner settings.

requirements. What resolution does your printer need? Are you sending the image to a service provider such as a commercial printer? You'll need to make lots of choices, but they should be based on where the image needs to end up. Know the destination of your image so you'll know which path to take.

Resampling

The process of resampling allows you to change the pixel dimensions of your image. This will affect the display and print size of your image. This part of the resizing process is important for several reasons:

- Images will print faster when they are sized properly for your output device.

- Images will print clearer when you size them to a target size and then run a sharpening filter to enhance the edge detail.

- Images appear crisper when they are displayed at 100 percent on a computer screen (such as for a PowerPoint presentation or website).

The process of resampling is often identified based on whether you are scaling the image smaller (downsampling) or larger (upsampling):

- **Downsampling.** If you decrease the number of pixels in an image, you are downsampling the image, which permanently discards data. You can specify an interpolation method (discussed in the next section) to determine how pixels are deleted.

- **Upsampling.** When upsampling, you create new pixels to expand the image. Again, you can specify an interpolation method to determine how pixels are added. When upsampling, you add information that did not previously exist, which generally just makes a larger image that may appear less sharp than the original.

Choose an Interpolation Method

When you resample an image, Photoshop creates new pixels. Those new pixels are created based on the neighboring pixels. How those new pixels are formed is determined by the interpolation method you specify. Photoshop offers up to six methods to resample your image.

Choose one of the following methods:

- **Nearest Neighbor.** This method is fast but not precise. It's useful for resizing illustrations but it can produce jagged edges.

- **Bilinear.** This approach uses pixel averaging. It is a balance of speed and quality, and produces medium-quality results.

- **Bicubic.** This method is slower but more precise than the first two (and more desirable). Photoshop spends more time examining surrounding pixels before interpolating new ones. The math at work is very complex, so this method will produce smoother results than Nearest Neighbor or Bilinear.

- **Bicubic Smoother.** This method is a refinement of Bicubic. It is specifically designed for upsampling (enlarging images).

- **Bicubic Sharper.** This is also a refinement of Bicubic. It's useful for downsampling (shrinking images). It does a better job of maintaining sharpness (when reducing) than other methods.

- **Bicubic Automatic.** Photoshop CS6 offers a new choice that automatically switches among the three bicubic methods based on the task at hand. For most, this is the best option.

Setting the Default Method

Photoshop allows you to choose a default interpolation method. This will be used when you invoke a sizing command, such as the Free Transform or Image Size command (more on both in the pages ahead). Choose the method that best matches your workflow.

1. Choose Edit > Preferences or press Command+K (Ctrl+K) to call up the Preferences dialog box.

2. From the Image Interpolation menu, choose your default method (Bicubic Automatic is the most flexible method and is highly recommended).

3. Click OK to store the setting.

VIDEO 15:
Changing Image Size

Resizing an Image

Most of your images will not be sized to the exact dimensions you need. You have several options at your disposal. To change the size of an image, you can use the Image Size or Canvas Size command. You can also use the Crop tool or Free Transform command to make an adjustment. You can use these choices individually or in combination to achieve the desired results.

Image Size

The Image Size command lets you permanently reassign the total pixel count, as well as resolution, for a particular image. You can also use this command to upsample or downsample an image. This is an easy way to size an image to a specific height or width. Let's put the command into action:

1. Open the file Ch04_Resize.tif from the Chapter 4 folder.

2. Choose Image > Image Size or press Command+Option+I (Ctrl+Alt+I).

   The Image Size dialog box offers several choices. You can choose to manipulate the pixel dimensions of the image (measured in pixels or percent). You can also modify the print size, which is the size of the image when printed. You can modify the print size based on percent, inches, centimeters, millimeters, points, picas, or columns. The most common choices are percent, inches, or centimeters, because most users easily understand these units of measure.

3. Set the Document Size to measure in inches. Specify a new height of **6** inches.

4. Be sure to select the Resample Image option if you want to change the pixel dimensions. Choose the method to Resample Image that is most appropriate for your image. Bicubic Automatic is the most common method, but you may have special circumstances. See "Choose an Interpolation Method" earlier in this chapter.

TIP

Return of Focus

You can avoid the need for upsampling by scanning or shooting the image at a sufficiently high resolution. If you want to preview the effects of changing pixel dimensions onscreen or to print proofs at different resolutions, resample a duplicate of your image.

5. Leave the Constrain Proportions check box selected,
   or you will introduce distortion. You generally want to
   keep the width and height
   constrained to the same
   ratio so the image resembles
   its original appearance.

6. Enter a resolution of **300**
   pixels per inch for professional printing.

7. Click OK.

Canvas Size

The canvas size is your work
area. When you create a new
document, you can specify the
size of your canvas. When you
scan a photo or import a digital image, the canvas size is automatically set to the edge of the image. You may need to change the
canvas size to crop or extend the canvas of your image to work on
specific areas of the image. Let's try it out:

VIDEO 16:
Changing Canvas Size

1. Open the file Ch04_Canvas.tif from the Chapter 4 folder.

2. Choose Image > Canvas Size or press Command+Option+C
   (Ctrl+Alt+C).

   In the Canvas Size dialog box you'll see the
   dimensions of your current canvas. You can
   specify a new canvas size using a variety of
   measurements. Pixels is a useful measurement if you're creating screen graphics,
   whereas inches or centimeters is easier to
   understand for print work. Using percentage
   is also good for incremental amounts.

   Let's place a uniform border around
   the image.

3. Select the Relative check box. This disregards the numerical values of the current canvas size and allows you to specify a new amount to be added to the existing image.

4. Ensure that the anchor point for the image is set to centered. This will expand the border in all directions around the center of the current image.

5. Add a half-inch border on all sides. Type *.5* inches into the Width and Height fields.

6. Specify a Canvas extension color. This is the color that Photoshop places around the image when you change the canvas size. You can choose to use the foreground or background colors that are loaded in the toolbox. You can also use white, black, gray, or other, which can be any color you specify. In this case, choose white.

7. Click OK.

Crop Tool

With the Crop tool you can change a viewer's perception of an image. You can choose to tighten the area of interest of an image, which allows you to de-emphasize (or even eliminate) parts of a photo and improve the image by better framing the subject.

You can invoke cropping in two ways. The first method involves making a selection with the Rectangular Marquee tool and then choosing Image > Crop. Although this works fine, it does not offer as much control as using the second method, the Crop tool. Let's put method two into action:

1. Open the image Ch04_Crop.tif from the Chapter 4 folder.

2. Select the Crop tool from the Tools panel or press C.

   Handles for the Crop tool automatically appear at the edges of the canvas. Let's crop to a specific ratio.

TIP

Use Overlays

Photoshop CS6 offers six different composition overlays when cropping. You can press the O key after you start a crop to cycle through the different guides. These overlays offer different theories for the placement of key subjects within a photo.

3. Click the Aspect Ratio menu and choose 1 x 1 (Square).

This automatically changes the shape of the crop to a 1:1 aspect ratio.

4. You can refine the crop selection after it is made.

Mouse over a corner of the crop until the pointer changes to a double-headed arrow, and then click and drag on the crop selection border to pull the crop tighter or to expand it.

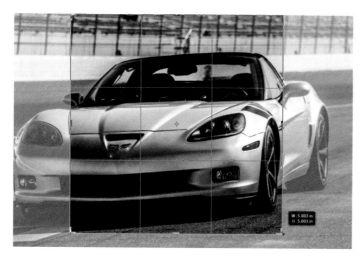

5. Examine the crop to determine if you like the composition.

If desired, you can click and drag inside the crop boundary to reposition the image within the crop box.

NOTE

Back in Time

If you don't like the new cropping mode, you can restore most of the previous functionality of cropping in Photoshop CS5. With the Crop tool active, just click the gear icon in the Options bar and choose the Use Classic Mode option.

TIP

Leave a Note

You can use Photoshop's Note tool to leave a comment that the image was cropped nondestructively to help you remember in the future.

6. In the Options bar, make sure the Delete Cropped Pixels option is deselected. This will simply hide the cropped pixels instead of deleting them.

7. When satisfied with the crop, press Return (Enter) or click the Commit button (check mark) in the Options bar. The shielded (darkened) areas will be cropped. To cancel, press the Esc key.

8. After applying the crop, you can still grab the crop handles at the edge the image and recompose the shot. You can also drag the image within the frame for a better composition.

Power crop

VIDEO 17:
Power Cropping

It is possible to crop and resize an image at the same time. I refer to this technique as a *power crop*, and it is a huge time-saver. Before cropping, you can choose the desired size of your final image in the Options bar. When you drag to crop the image, your box will constrain to the proper aspect ratio. Cropping will change the aspect ratio and the resolution setting, allowing you to resize and crop in one step.

Let's crop an image to a 5-inch by 7-inch shape at 300 ppi:

NOTE

Cropping Freely

If you want to crop to a custom aspect ratio, just use the default Unconstrained option.

1. Open the file Ch04_Power Crop.tif from the Chapter 4 folder.

2. In the Options bar, click the Aspect Ratio menu and choose Size & Resolution.

3. Enter a width of **5** inches, a height of **7** inches, and a resolution of **300** ppi.

TIP

Straighten and Crop

In the Options bar for the Crop tool is a Straighten button. Clicking this button switches to a measuring tool. Just find a straight line in the image (or choose your own reference), and then drag to rotate the image into a better orientation and remove any unwanted rotation.

4. Click OK to apply the initial crop.

The aspect ratio has likely been transposed with the image set to 7 × 5 inches.

5. Drag a corner to reset the orientation of the crop to portrait, and set the crop to a better composition for the elephant on the left. Use the figure as a guide.

6. Click the Commit button or press Return (Enter). When you're finished cropping, you may want to click Clear to reset the tool's default settings.

7. Press the V key to switch to the Move tool. You can drag the image within the canvas freely to reposition the crop as needed (as long as you didn't delete cropped pixels earlier).

TIP

Reduce Motion

In the Additional Options controls for the Crop tool (click the gear icon) you can toggle Auto Center Preview off. This disables the "image moving while resizing" behavior that attempts to keep the crop box centered.

TIP

Pixel Restoration

Because the cropped pixels were hidden (instead of deleted), details were preserved outside the cropped area. This allows for the image to be restored. You can choose Image > Reveal All to restore all hidden pixels after a crop (provided you left the Delete Cropped Pixels option deselected).

 VIDEO 18:
Nondestructive Cropping

VIDEO 19:
Perspective Cropping

Perspective cropping

Some images will have visible distortion, which is often caused by the camera not being square with the subject. If the photographer was higher (or lower) than the image or if the photo was taken at an angle, you will see distortion. In some cases, this distortion is part of the shot composition and is desirable. In others, the distortion can be distracting. Let's square off an image:

1. Open the file Ch04_Perspective.tif from the Chapter 4 folder.

2. Select the Perspective Crop tool by clicking the Crop tool in the Tools panel and choosing the second tool in the well.

3. Crop around the window in the photo as tight as you can to frame it.

Use the pixel grid to help position the initial crop. If it is not visible, select the option Show Grid in the Options bar.

TOOL PRESETS SAVE TIME

If you have a specific image size that you use often, harness the power of Photoshop's Preset Manager. You can create tool presets that already have the values for a tool loaded.

1. In the Options bar, click the Aspect Ratio menu and choose Size & Resolution.

2. Enter a desired size and resolution into the dialog box.

3. Select the Save as Crop Preset check box at the bottom of the dialog box and click OK.

4. When the Crop tool is selected, you'll see its icon in the upper-left corner of the Options bar. Click the triangle to access the menu.

5. You'll see several preset sizes that are stored in Photoshop. Select the Current Tool Only check box to narrow the presets. Photoshop stores the preset crop size in a temporary preferences file.

6. To permanently save cropping sizes, click the submenu icon in the menu (the small gear in the right corner of the panel) and choose Save Tool Presets to save them in a desired location.

4. Drag the upper-right and upper-left corners in toward the center to line up the crop borders parallel to the edge of the window.

   The crop selection will no longer look rectangular.

5. Click the Commit button or press Return (Enter). The result should appear as if the angle was squared and the camera was level.

   Depending on how you cropped the image, it may look slightly distorted. You can use the Image Size command with the Constrain Proportions option deselected or the Free Transform command to reshape the photo.

Rotate Canvas Command

Sometimes your image will need to be rotated or flipped. Loading your image upside down on the scanner, loading a slide backwards into a slide scanner, or turning the camera on its side when taking a portrait may cause inverted or reversed images. You may also want to make a change to your image for compositional purposes.

The Rotate Canvas command offers several choices: rotate the image 180° (half a rotation), 90° clockwise or counterclockwise, or an arbitrary amount (the user types in a number of degrees). Additionally, the entire canvas can be flipped (creating a mirrored image). You can flip the canvas horizontally or vertically:

1. Open the image Ch04_Rotate.tif from the Chapter 4 folder.

2. Choose Image > Rotate Canvas 90° CCW (counterclockwise). The image is now properly oriented.

VIDEO 20:
Adaptive Wide Angle
Correction and
Content-Aware Fill

There may be times when you want to freely rotate your view (just as you might angle a piece of paper to make it easier to draw). In this case, you are rotating just the view, not the actual image. Just press R to access the Rotate View tool. You can then click within the canvas and rotate the image for distortion-free viewing at any desired angle. This makes it really easy when painting or cloning to avoid having to crank your head or wrist in the middle of a brush stroke. Photoshop provides a compass to help you stay oriented, and you can click the Reset View button in the Options bar to return the canvas to its default orientation. You'll need a supported graphics card to use this feature.

VIDEO 21:
Free Transform
Command

Free Transform Command

The Free Transform command is another useful way to rotate and size an image. It works best when you have an object located on its own floating layer (not a *Background*) or if you have an active selection. You'll explore selections and layers in much greater detail in future chapters. For now, let's work with a simple layered image that has already been prepped:

1. Open the file Ch04_Free_Transform_ Basic.psd from the Chapter 4 folder.

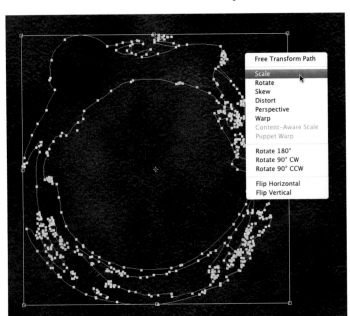

This image has two layers: a background, which is a pattern, and a vector shape layer. A vector layer is a special layer in Photoshop. It can be resized and transformed repeatedly with no degradation in quality. Vector layers use math to describe curved lines and can be freely manipulated.

2. If it's not visible, call up the Layers panel by choosing Windows > Layers.

3. Select the Vector Shape layer so it is active.

4. Choose Edit > Free Transform or press Command+T (Ctrl+T).

You can access several controls for the Free Transform command by Control-clicking/right-clicking. Try the following transformations on the Vector Shape layer. You can press the Esc key to cancel the transformation or Return (Enter) to apply it:

- **Scale.** You can scale by dragging a handle. Hold down the Shift key as you drag a corner handle to scale proportionately. Hold down the Option (Alt) key to scale in both directions simultaneously. To scale numerically, enter a value in the Options bar.

- **Rotate.** You can rotate a preset amount by selecting Rotate 180°, Rotate 90° CW, or Rotate 90° CCW. To rotate freely by dragging, move your mouse outside the Free Transform box. It will become a curved, two-headed arrow. Hold down the Shift key while rotating to constrain the rotation to 15° increments. Additionally, you can rotate numerically by entering degrees in the rotation box in the Options bar.

- **Skew.** Skewing an image creates a sense of distortion, as if the image were leaning. To skew the image, hold down Command+Shift (Ctrl+Shift) and drag a side handle (not a corner handle). The cursor will change to a white arrowhead with a small double arrow.

- **Distort.** If you want to distort an image freely, choose Distort. This allows you to move the corners of the image freely (a process also known as corner-pinning). You can also access this command by pressing Command (Ctrl) while dragging a corner point.

- **Perspective.** Transforming perspective creates the illusion that the image is being viewed from above or from the side. You can access this command by pressing Command+Option+Shift (Ctrl+Alt+Shift) or from the context menu. This is a useful command to fix perspective problems or to add perspective effects.

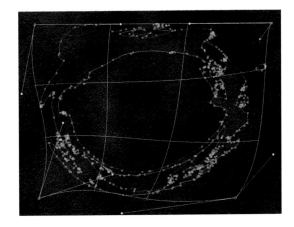

- **Warp.** The Warp command was first introduced in Photoshop CS2. It allows you to distort an image into a number of predefined shapes available in the Options bar (such as Arch, Flag, or Twist). When you choose Custom, several points can be freely dragged to distort the image as desired.

- **Flip Horizontal and Flip Vertical.** These simple commands let you flip an individual layer without flipping the entire canvas.

The Free Transform command has one major benefit over choosing individual transform commands from the Image menu: Free Transform lets you apply transformations in one continuous operation, which reduces quality loss in raster images.

Open the file Ch04_Free_Transform_Additional.psd. Using the Free Transform command, you can rotate, size, and flip the images to create a better layout.

Content-Aware Scaling

The Content-Aware scaling feature is a way to intelligently scale an image that allows for certain details to be preserved while others are distorted. It can be used to recompose an image. When used correctly, the image will automatically adapt to preserve vital areas during the scale.

VIDEO 22:
Advanced
Content-Aware Scale

1. From the Chapter 4 folder, open the image Ch04_Content_Aware_Scale.psd.

2. Select the layer called Headshot. The photo is not big enough to fill the entire canvas and needs to be resized.

3. Choose Edit > Content-Aware Scale.

4. In the Options bar, make sure the Protect Skin Tones button is pressed to tell Photoshop to attempt to preserve regions that contain skin tones.

5. Drag a resize handle on the bounding box to scale the image. Hold down the Shift key to scale proportionately. You can also hold down the Option (Alt) key to scale from the center of the image.

6. Size the image so it fits the width of the canvas. Notice that the face shows little to no distortion, but the background has been changed significantly.

7. Click the Commit button or press the Return (Enter) key to apply the change.

Puppet Warp

The Puppet Warp command is similar to the Free Transform command in that it allows for selective warping of a layer. The technology works by creating a geometric mesh that lets you dramatically warp specific regions of an image. The command takes a little getting used to in order to create natural results, but it can be quite useful because the image will automatically adapt so vital areas are preserved during scaling.

VIDEO 23:
Puppet Warp

1. From the Chapter 4 folder, open the image Ch04_Puppet.psd.

   This image has already been masked to isolate the elephant to its own layer; you'll learn more about masking in Chapter 7, "Layer Masking." The background has also been filled in using the Content-Aware fill command, which you'll learn about in Chapter 11, "Repairing and Improving Photos."

2. Select the layer named Elephant.

3. Choose Edit > Puppet Warp. Photoshop draws a polygonal mesh to allow the object to be distorted.

4. In the Options bar, adjust the mesh settings to create a refined mesh:

   Mode. Photoshop offers three levels of elasticity for the mesh. Normal is fine for this image.

   Density. Choose More Points to increase the precision of the warp (it will take more computer processing time).

   Expansion. If needed, you can contract or expand the mesh. The default value is usually best.

   Show Mesh. At times you may want to deselect this to see the image without the visible mesh applied.

5. Click on the image to add control pins. Add pins to areas you want to transform as well as points you want to anchor in place.

   Use the figure for guidance. Add pins to the trunk and in a few places on the elephant's body. Add additional points as needed as you manipulate the figure.

6. Experiment with dragging pins to warp the elephant. Try to curve her trunk and reposition her legs:

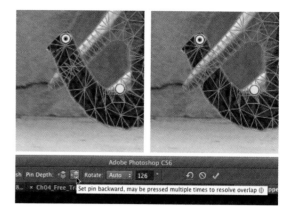

- Drag pins to warp the mesh.

- Try adding pins to keep nearby areas intact.

- If an area doesn't overlap properly, you can click the Pin Depth buttons in the Options bar. These can be used to control how much something overlaps.

- To remove a pin, right-click on it and choose Delete Pin.

- If unwanted warping occurs with a pin, select it, and then hold down the Option (Alt) key and drag.

7. When you're satisfied with your transformation, press Return (Enter) or click the Commit button in the Options bar.

Using Smart Objects Before Transforming

VIDEO 24:
Transforming
Smart Objects

Smart Objects are a bit of "under the hood" Photoshop magic. Essentially, this powerful command allows you to embed raster or vector data into a layer. The layer can then be transformed indefinitely because the embedded data remains editable and scalable. You can convert one or more layers into a new Smart Object or choose to add new content as a Smart Object.

A Smart Object is simply one file embedded inside another. This can be very useful because Smart Objects allow greater flexibility than simply applying the Free Transform command to a regular layer. With a Smart Object, you can perform multiple nondestructive transforms with no loss in quality (as long as you don't exceed the pixel dimensions of the original raster object).

TIP

Another Path to a Smart Object

Besides using the Place command to create a Smart Object, you can select one or more objects in the Layers panel and choose Layer > Smart Objects > Group into New Smart Object.

TIP

Smarter Smart Objects

In Photoshop, you can apply perspective transformations to Smart Objects as well. Simply follow the instructions in the "Free Transform Command" section earlier in this chapter.

1. Open the file Ch04_Smart_Object_BG.psd from the Chapter 4 folder. A background design for a multimedia presentation opens. Let's add a photo layer.

2. Choose File > Place to add a new document as a layer. Select the file Ch04_Smart_Object.tif from the Chapter 4 folder and click Place.

3. Size the image using the control handles. The controls are identical to those you used with the Free Transform command. Scale down the image to a very small size. Apply the transformation by clicking the Commit button.

4. Now, let's try scaling the image larger. Invoke the Free Transform command for the selected layer by pressing Command+T (Ctrl+T). Scale up the image to its original size. Apply the transformation. Notice that the image remains sharp. This is because the Smart Object contains a full resolution copy of the image embedded inside the layer.

Selection Tools and Techniques

5

If you really want to get things done in Photoshop, you have to be good at making selections. You might want to extract a subject from a photo or maybe change the sky to another shade of blue. Or, maybe the sweater in your advertisement needs to be orange instead of red, or you'd like to duplicate some of the background crowd so your photo doesn't look so empty. In each case, you'll need an accurate selection.

Why? You may be able to look at a digital image and clearly recognize that it's a shot of a rock outcropping in the desert. The scene has many similar colors for the red rock, as well as contrasting color in the sky. Unfortunately, your computer just sees a bunch of pixels. A little human intervention is necessary to distinguish which part of the image you want to manipulate or process. In Photoshop, this is called making a selection.

By selecting the rock outcropping, I applied a Curves and Vibrance adjustment to boost the contrast and color in the specified area.

Although this means extra effort, it also means that most digital imaging tasks require a human brain (which means jobs for designers and artists). Accurate selections are important, and there are several techniques you can employ to get them just right. Some are easier than others, and some are more accurate. You may in fact need to combine multiple techniques to get the job done. Knowing several different methods lets you make an accurate selection no matter what your source image looks like.

Basic Selection Tools

Photoshop's Tools panel contains three categories of tools that you can use to create a basic selection: Marquee tools, Lasso tools, and Wand tools. Although these three are very useful, many users forget that they are only starting points.

Marquee Tools

The Marquee tools (M) allow you to click and drag to define a selection. To toggle between the Rectangular and Elliptical Marquee tool, press Shift+M. Descriptions of the Marquee tools follow:

- **Rectangular Marquee tool.** Use this tool to make a rectangular selection. Press the Shift key to draw a square.

- **Elliptical Marquee tool.** Use this tool to make an elliptical selection. Press the Shift key to draw a circle.

- **Single Row or Single Column Marquee tool.** Creates a selection that is 1 pixel wide in the shape of a row or column. These two tools are not used often, which is why Adobe didn't assign the keyboard shortcut M to trigger them.

A FASTER TOOLS PANEL

There are a few ways to access tools from the Tools panel:

- You can click the tool icon.

- To access nested tools (those that share the same well), click and hold the mouse button on the tool icon.

- You can also hold down the Option (Alt) key and click an individual tool in the Tools panel to cycle tools.

- You can press the letter shortcut key. Hovering over a tool's icon will teach you the shortcut keys when the tool tip pops up.

- To switch to a nested tool, hold down the Shift key and press the tool's shortcut key.

- If the Shift key is an extra step you'd rather not use, modify your user preferences. Press Command+K (Ctrl+K) to call up your General Preferences screen. Deselect the check box next to Use Shift Key for Tool Switch.

Putting the Marquees into action

Let's give the Rectangular and Elliptical Marquee tools a try and make some selections.

1. Open the file Ch05_Marquee_Practice.tif from the Chapter 5 folder.

2. Practice selecting each of the four objects using both the Elliptical and Rectangular Marquee tools. Remember to use the Shift key to constrain proportions for the square and circle shapes. Don't worry about perfection; you'll learn lots of ways to tweak selections in the coming pages.

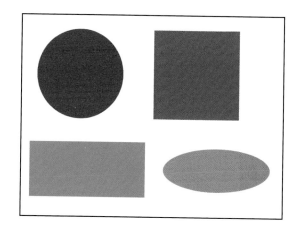

Selection options for Marquee tools

When using the Marquee tools, you have several options available in the Options bar. These modifiers can improve or alter your selection.

The first four icons specify the kind of selection:

A New selection. Creates a new selection.

B Add to selection. After you create one selection, you can click this button so subsequent selections are combined with the existing selection. You can also hold down the Shift key to add to a selection.

C Subtract from selection. After you create one selection, you can click this button so subsequent selections are subtracted from the existing selection. You can also hold down the Option (Alt) key to subtract from a selection.

D Intersect with selection. Requires you to make a first selection. When you draw a second selection, Photoshop creates a new selection where the two selections overlap.

A B C D   E   F   G   H

VIDEO 25:
Selection Basics

The following options modify the selection tool and must be chosen *before* making a selection:

E Feather. A normal selection has a crisp edge. Feathering a selection creates a gradual blend at the selection's edges. Think of it as the difference between a line drawn with a pencil and one drawn with a felt-tip marker. Feathered selections are useful when you want to extract objects.

F Anti-alias. When working with the Elliptical Marquee tool, you can select Anti-alias to create a smoother edge for curved lines (especially if your image is at a low resolution).

G Style. For the Rectangular Marquee tool and Elliptical Marquee tool, you can choose from three styles in the Options bar:

- **Normal.** This is the default option. Click to draw your marquee freehand.

- **Fixed Ratio.** You can set a width-to-height ratio. For example, to draw a marquee three times as wide as it is high, enter **3** for the width and **1** for the height.

- **Fixed Size.** You can specify an exact size for the marquee's height and width. You can enter the value in pixels (px), inches (in), or centimeters (cm).

H Refine Edge. This button refines any selection based on several criteria. You'll explore this functionality later in this chapter.

Moving a selection

There are a few ways to reposition a selection:

- While drawing a selection (with the mouse button still depressed) you can hold down the spacebar and move the selection.

- With an active selection, move the tool's cursor inside the selection border (marching ants). The icon changes to a triangle with a marquee border. You can then click inside and drag the selection to move it.

- To modify a selection using controls similar to the Free Transform command, choose Select > Transform Selection. All the options available to the Free Transform command can be applied to the selection border. For more on Free Transform, see Chapter 4, "Sizing Digital Images."

Selection Lassos

The Lasso tools allow you to draw freeform segments with your mouse to create a selection border. The Lasso tools are most often used to create a rough selection (which can then be refined using techniques such as Quick Mask mode (see the bonus article in the Chapter 5 folder). The keyboard shortcut for selecting the Lasso tool is the letter L. To select the next Lasso tool, press Shift+L. The following list describes each of the Lasso tools:

- **Lasso tool.** Use this tool to make a freehand selection. You must return to your starting point to close the selection loop. If you don't return to start and simply double-click, Photoshop will draw a straight line and close the selection point for you.

- **Polygonal Lasso tool.** Use this tool to draw straight-edged segments for a selection border. With every click, a part of the segment is drawn. Continue clicking to set endpoints for additional segments. Click your starting point to close the loop and create an active selection. To constrain the tool to 45-degree angles, hold down the Shift key while drawing.

- **Magnetic Lasso tool.** When you use the Magnetic Lasso tool, Photoshop attempts to snap the border to the edges of the image. If the anchor point doesn't snap accurately, click once to manually add a point.

Putting the Lasso tools into action

Let's give these tools a try.

1. Open the file Ch05_Channels.tif.

2. Try using both the Polygonal and Magnetic Lasso tools to select the boat. Make multiple attempts at practicing the selection.

   In the middle of making a selection with the Polygonal or Magnetic Lassos, you can press the Delete key to remove segments. Press and hold once, and then release and press subsequent times to remove segments (one per click). If you need to stop a selection, press the Esc key. If you need to deselect and start over, just press Command+D (Ctrl+D).

Selection options for Lasso tools

When using the Lasso tools, you have several options available in the Options bar to improve or alter your selection. These modifiers are very similar to those for the Marquee tools, so I'll just briefly mention them.

The first four icons specify the kind of selection:

A New selection

B Add to selection

C Subtract from selection

D Intersect with selection

The next three options create a smoother selection:

E Feather. This option creates a softer edge on your selection.

F Anti-alias. This creates a smoother edge for curved lines.

G Refine Edge. This button brings up a window with several sliders to adjust an active selection with intuitive controls.

Magnetic Lasso options

The Magnetic Lasso has a few additional options that mainly deal with its snapping behavior. You can change the following properties in the Options bar:

- **Width.** The width specifies how wide an area the Magnetic Lasso looks at when trying to detect edges. To see the width visually, activate the Caps Lock key before making a selection.

- **Edge Contrast.** This value determines the lasso's sensitivity to edges in the image. Higher values detect high-contrast edges, whereas lower values detect lower-contrast edges. On an image with well-defined edges, you should use a higher width and edge contrast setting.

- **Frequency.** The rate at which Photoshop adds anchor points is based on the Frequency setting. An anchor point is where the lasso attaches, so you can move the selection border in another direction. You can enter a value between 0 and 100. Higher values add more anchor points to your selection border.

- **Stylus Pressure.** Click the Stylus Pressure icon if you have a tablet connected. This lets you to use the pressure of the pen to affect edge width.

VIDEO 26:
Quick Selection Tool

Wand Tools

The Quick Selection and Magic Wand tools (W) allow you to click an area of color to create a selection based on adjacent pixels and your Tolerance setting. The Magic Wand is a much older tool that works reasonably well on photos with large areas of similar color. The Quick Selection tool is a significant improvement over the Magic Wand tool, however, and has quickly become a favorite tool of Photoshop pros.

Quick Selection tool

The Quick Selection tool allows you to create a selection that quickly forms based on color and contrast.

1. Open the file Ch05_Quick_Selection.tif from the Chapter 5 folder.

2. Select the Quick Selection tool by pressing W.

3. Choose the Auto-Enhance option in the Options bar.

4. Press the right bracket key (]) to make the selection brush larger; press the left bracket key ([) to make it smaller.

5. Click and drag in the flower to make an initial selection.

6. To add to the selection, click and drag again. If too much of a selection is made, hold down the Option (Alt) key to subtract from the selection.

TIP

Get Better Results Automatically

The Auto-Enhance option in the Options bar can quickly improve any selection made with the Quick Selection tool. You'll need to choose this option before you click. It automatically smooths out the edges of the generated selection.

TIP

A Better Wand

The Magic Wand tool works best if you turn on the pixel-averaging option. In the Options bar, use the Sample Size menu to change the Sample Size to a 5 by 5 Average (or 11 by 11 Average). The Magic Wand tool will then become less sensitive to erroneous clicks.

VIDEO 27:
Magic Wand Tool

Selection options for the Magic Wand tool

When using the Magic Wand tool, you have several options available in the Options bar that can improve or alter your selection. These modifiers are very similar to those for the Marquee and Lasso tools, so I'll cover them briefly.

The first four icons specify the kind of selection:

A New selection

B Add to selection

C Subtract from selection

D Intersect with selection

The remaining settings allow you to refine your selection parameters:

E Sample Size. This determines how additional pixels are selected. The targeted color value can be based on just the color you click on or an average of neighboring pixels.

F Tolerance. This setting determines how similar the pixels must be to your initial click in order to be selected. You can enter a value in pixels, ranging from 0 to 255. A higher value selects a broader range of colors.

G Anti-alias. This creates a smoother edge when you click.

H Contiguous. When Contiguous is selected, only adjacent areas with the same colors are selected. If deselected, all pixels in the entire image that use the same colors will be selected.

I Sample All Layers. If you have a multilayered document and want to select colors on all layers, select this check box.

J Refine Edge. This button brings up a window with several sliders to adjust an active selection with intuitive controls.

Putting the Magic Wand into action

Although the Magic Wand can be a little coarse at first, it is possible to get an accurate selection. Let's try out the Magic Wand tool.

1. Open the file Ch05_Magic_Wand.tif from the Chapter 5 folder.

2. Select the Magic Wand tool by pressing Shift+W for *wand*. You can press the keys multiple times to toggle between the Quick Selection and Magic Wand tools.

3. Set the Tolerance to **20** and select the Anti-alias check box.

4. Change the Sample Size menu to a 5 × 5 sample to average out the blue in the sky.

5. Click the sky in the upper-left corner to make an initial selection.

6. Part of the sky will be selected. Hold down the Shift key and click another area of the sky to add to the selection. Repeat as needed until the entire sky is selected.

Additional Selection Commands

A few more Selection commands are found on the Select menu or by choosing Select > Modify. For a sense of completion, let's take a quick look:

- **All.** The All command selects everything on the active layer or in your flattened document within the edges of the canvas. The keyboard shortcut is Command+A (Ctrl+A) when the canvas window is selected.

- **Deselect.** The Deselect command removes the active selection. You may need to do this when you're finished altering your selection to avoid accidentally modifying your image. The keyboard shortcut is Command+D (Ctrl+D) when the canvas window is selected.

- **Reselect.** The Reselect command is truly useful because it allows you to reactivate the last selection in your document. It only works with selections made since you've last opened the document. The keyboard shortcut is Shift+Command+D (Shift+Ctrl+D) when the canvas window is selected.

TIP

Actionable Detection

You'll learn about Photoshop actions later in this book. These macros let you record several steps for playback on an image (which can really save time for repetitive tasks). The Skin Tones and Face Detection options can be recorded into a custom action, which can really save you time when you're cleaning up several portraits.

- **Inverse.** The concept of inverse is very important. It is often far easier to select what you don't want, and then inverse the selection to get what you do want. The keyboard shortcut is Shift+Command+I (Shift+Ctrl+I) when the canvas window is selected.

- **Grow.** The Grow command selects adjacent pixels that fall within a certain tolerance range. To modify the range, adjust the Tolerance settings of the Magic Wand tool.

- **Similar.** The Similar command also selects pixels based on the Tolerance settings of the Magic Wand tool. However, the pixels do not need to be adjacent.

- **Transform Selection.** The Transform Selection command allows you to modify an existing selection. Invoking it gives you controls similar to the Free Transform command (see Chapter 4 for more on the Free Transform command).

The following commands appear on the Modify submenu:

- **Border.** If you have an existing selection, you can use the Border command. You can enter a value between 1 and 200 pixels. A new selection that frames the existing selection will be created.

- **Smooth.** The Smooth command simplifies the selection by adding more pixels to the selection to make it less jagged.

- **Expand.** The Expand command allows you to add pixels in an outward fashion to the selection. The border will get wider based on the number of pixels you add.

- **Contract.** The Contract command works the opposite of the Expand command. Specify the number of pixels that you want the selection to decrease.

- **Feather.** The Feather command blurs the edge of the selection. Although this creates a loss of detail at the edges, it can be very useful to create a blending transition (such as when extracting an object with a soft edge, like fabric or hair). The feather becomes apparent when you move, copy, or fill the selection. If you feather the edges too much, you might lose the selection border (marching ants), which is only visible above a 50% threshold. The keyboard shortcut is Shift+F6 when you have an active selection.

Let's try out the concept of Inverse, as well as some of the other commands.

1. Open the file Ch05_Inverse.tif from the Chapter 5 folder.

2. Select the Magic Wand tool.

3. Set the Tolerance to **32** and select the Anti-alias and Contiguous check boxes.

4. Click the sky to make an initial selection.

5. When most of the sky is active, choose Select > Grow. If needed, repeat the command.

6. Choose Select > Inverse to capture the castle.

Intermediate Selection Techniques

Simply put, don't stop now! Most Photoshop users develop an overdependence on the Magic Wand tool. Although the basic selection techniques are important, they are not necessarily the best solution.

Color Range Command

If you liked the Magic Wand tool, then prepare to love the Color Range command. The Color Range command allows you to select a specified color within the document. You can then easily add to the selection to refine it. All of its speed and power is complemented by a very intuitive user interface.

VIDEO 28:
Color Range Command

Let's experiment with the Color Range command.

1. Open the file Ch05_Color_Range.tif from the Chapter 5 folder.

2. Choose Select > Color Range. Set the Fuzziness to **25** to start and deselect Localized Color Clusters.

3. With the eyedropper, click a pink flower. You'll see an initial selection created in the dialog box. A black and white matte is shown to preview the selection. The white areas indicate the selection you are creating.

4. Hold down the Shift key and click more of the flower to build a larger selection.

5. Adjust the Fuzziness slider to your preference.

6. If too much of the image is selected, you can hold down the Option (Alt) key to subtract from the selection. You can also select the Localized Color Clusters option to require similar pixels to be closer together.

7. When you're satisfied, click OK.

8. Soften the selection further by choosing Select > Feather and entering a value of **5** pixels.

9. Let's use the selection to make an isolated image adjustment. One way to do this nondestructively is with an adjustment layer. Choose Layer > New Adjustment Layer > Hue/Saturation and Click OK.

10. Adjust the Hue slider to change the colors of the flowers (try a value of **–25** to make the flower more purple) and adjust the saturation to your preference.

Adjustment layers are covered in greater detail throughout the rest of the book.

Adjusting Skin Tones

The Color Range command has been expanded in Photoshop CS6 so it can intelligently recognize skin tones and human faces. These options make it easy to localize an adjustment to just the subject of a portrait and can be used to subtly improve the color and exposure of your subject.

VIDEO 29:
Adjusting Skin Tones

1. Open the file Ch05_Skintones.tif from the Chapter 5 folder.

2. Choose Select > Color Range.

3. From the Select menu choose Skin Tones.

4. Select the Detect Faces check box to further refine the skin tone selection using face detection.

NOTE

No 32-bit Support for Skin Tones

The Skin Tones and Detect Faces options will work with both 8-bit and 16-bit RGB images. For those of you working with 32-bit or HDR images, you'll need to first convert the image.

NOTE

Custom Choice for Skin Tones

You can still use the custom Sample Colors option to select the initial skin tone. Simply enable the Detect Faces option and adjust the Fuzziness slider to taste to refine the adjustment.

5. Adjust the Fuzziness slider to refine what is selected in the image.

   This slider lets you adjust the fuzziness based on the face detection point. The white areas are fully selected, and gray areas are partially selected.

6. When you're satisfied, click OK.

   Let's make a small adjustment to the face to boost the flesh tones.

7. Click the Vibrance button in the Adjustments panel to affect the skin tones with a color correction adjustment. You'll explore this adjustment and more in greater detail in later chapters.

VIDEO 30:
Quick Mask Mode

TIP

Saving and Reloading Selections

If you'd like to save your selection for later use, you need to create a channel. With an active selection made, choose Select > Save Selection. Name the selection and click OK to save the selection as an alpha channel. Alpha channels are simply saved selections that can be reloaded at a later time. They are also stored with your document when you close the file (unlike a quick mask, which is discarded when you exit the selection). Channels are covered in greater depth in Chapter 7, "Layer Masking."

Creating a Path with the Pen Tool

You can use the Pen tool to create paths (vector-based lines that you freely draw). Many users swear by the Pen tool, but be warned: It's not the easiest tool to use. The Pen tool allows you to click around the image, adding anchor points. Photoshop then connects those points with vector lines, which can be adjusted or resized. Those users coming to Photoshop from Adobe Illustrator generally find the Pen tool relatively easy to use. Reading about the Pen tool is very difficult; be sure to watch the video to see the tool in operation.

Let's give the Pen tool a try.

VIDEO 31:
Pen Tool

1. Open the file Ch05_Paths.tif from the Chapter 5 folder.

2. Choose the Pen tool from the Tools panel or press the keyboard shortcut P.

3. Choose the following options from the Options bar:

   • Choose Shape Layer from the Tool Mode menu to put a solid color over your image and make it easier to see if you are accurately tracing the object. You can click the color well and choose the color you want to use.

   • Change the shape stroke width slider to **0.00** pt to remove any stroke.

   • Select Auto Add/Delete so anchor points will automatically be added when you click a line segment. Likewise, Photoshop will automatically delete a previous anchor point if you click directly on the anchor point with the Pen tool.

   • Click the Settings menu (gear icon) in the Options bar to access the submenu. Select the Rubber Band option to make it easier to preview path segments while drawing.

4. Position the Pen tool in the lower-left corner of the extruded border and click and drag in the angle of the curved border. An initial anchor point is added.

5. You'll now need to draw curved paths. When you click at the top of the image to add a new point, keep the mouse button pressed. You can drag to create the curve: Remember that clicking adds a point and a straight line, whereas clicking and dragging produces a point with a curved line:

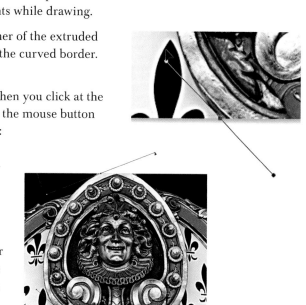

   • Drag away from the curve for the first point.

   • Try to minimize the number of anchor points added. Move forward along the object and pull to form the curve. You don't need a perfect shape yet.

6. When you reach the end of your path, click to close the shape. As with the Polygonal Lasso tool, you must click your starting point to close the path. The path for this photo can be created with only four points.

7. You can adjust the path by using the Direct Selection tool (A). This allows you to click an anchor point, or handle, and adjust the position or shape.

8. The Convert Point tool can be used to add a Curves handle to any path point that doesn't have one and allows you to curve any straight lines (just click and drag on a point).

9. When you're satisfied, Command-click (Ctrl-click) on the path's thumbnail in the Layers panel. You will see the marching ants, which indicate an active selection has been made.

And that is how paths work. Either you found that enjoyable (and if so, keep practicing–it gets easier) or you disliked it. Like many features in Photoshop, paths are optional and don't have to be part of your Photoshop workflow. They are worth learning, though, because they make it easier to select curved objects.

Refine Edge Command

Even though the Select menu offers several options, there is always room for improvement. Photoshop provides a powerful option for refining an existing selection—the Refine Edge command, which can be accessed in two ways. It is available in the Options bar for all selection tools. You can also access it by choosing Select > Refine Edge. This command is very intuitive, and its sliders provide quick feedback as you refine a selection. Let's try it out.

VIDEO 32:
Refine Edge Command

1. Open the file Ch05_Refine Edge.tif from the Chapter 5 folder.

2. Make an initial selection using a tool of your choice (the Quick Selection tool works well).

3. Click the Refine Edge button in the Options bar. A new dialog box opens with additional controls.

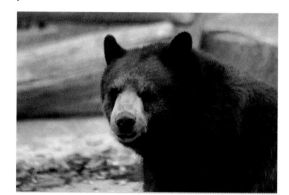

4. Click the View button to change the viewing mode for how the selection is displayed (or use the corresponding keyboard shortcut). Try the different modes to see the results:

- **Marching Ants (M).** Shows the selection with the started dashed line.

- **Overlay (V).** Behaves similarly to the Quick Mask mode.

- **On Black (B).** Previews the layer over black, which is good for light edges.

- **On White (W).** Shows the selected region over a white background.

- **Black & White (K).** Simulates a channel view where the selection displays as a black (transparent) and white (opaque) layer (with gray indicating partial transparency).

- **On Layers (L).** Composites the image over any other layers (or transparency if single-layer image). For this exercise, choose the On Layers option.

- **Reveal Layer (R).** Shows the entire, original layer contents.

TIP

Change Your Refined View

To cycle through the different viewing modes in the Refine Edge dialog box, just press the F key repeatedly. If you'd like to temporarily disable the view, press the X key.

5. Next you can use Edge Detection to clean up the edges further. These controls work best for areas of partial transparency. For this image, try to clean up some of the dark fringe and any of the edges of the hair that should be partially see-through:

TIP

Smarter Refinements

You can select the Show Radius or Show Original check box to make it easier to see the changes created with the Edge Detection options.

- **Radius.** Drag to refine the selection edge. Try a value of **8** for this image.

- **Smart Radius.** This option automatically evaluates contrast in the edges and attempts to correct for better transitions. If your object lacks uniform hardness and softness, use this option. Select this option for this image (and in most cases).

- **Refine Radius tool.** Use this brush-style tool to paint over any edges that need additional refinement. You can also hold the Option (Alt) key to switch to an erase mode to undo any unwanted refinements. Paint over the left edge of the skull.

6. The next group of sliders allows you to adjust the edge globally. Experiment with the following sliders:

- **Smooth.** Removes any jagged edges.

- **Feather.** Softens the edge of the selection.

- **Contrast.** Increases the contrast of a selection's edge. You'll get better results in most cases with the Smart Radius and refinement tools.

- **Shift Edge.** Grows or shrinks a selection. This is a quick way to tighten a rough selection and remove color spill.

7. The last category, Output, determines how the processed selection is treated.

   Decontaminate Colors applies color correction to remove any color spill from the background onto the selected object. For this image, select this option.

8. Finally, you'll need to determine what Photoshop does with the new selection. The choices are many (and useful):

   - **Selection.** Creates an active selection.

   - **Layer Mask.** Creates a nondestructive mask that produces transparency in the highlighted layer.

   - **New Layer.** Creates a new layer with only the selected area.

   - **New Layer with Layer Mask.** Creates a new layer with only the selected area masked. This is the most flexible option. Choose this option for this document.

   - **New Document.** Creates a new document with only the selected area.

   - **New Document with Layer Mask.** Creates a new document with the selected area masked.

9. Click OK to create the selection and masked image.

   The original image exists in the background with a new masked copy on top.

Advanced Selection Techniques

Two additional selection techniques–channels and Calculations–are advanced (in that they utilize channels). Remember, channels represent the components of color. The brighter the area in the individual channel, the more coverage there is for that color. By harnessing the black and white details of one (or more) channel you can create a mask. These two techniques won't be appropriate to use every time (they are image dependent), but they are pretty easy to use and should be part of your skill set.

VIDEO 33:
Selecting with a Channel

Using a Channel

In many images, there is often high contrast between the different elements. For example, a person framed by a bright blue sky may clearly stand out, since there are a lot of red values in skin and a lot of blue in the sky. You can make a quick decision whether the channel selection technique will work by looking at the Channels panel. Look for a single channel that is high contrast. It doesn't need to be perfect; you can use the Paintbrush tool to touch up the channel to make a more accurate selection.

Let's use the channel selection techniques to select and modify a logo on the side of a building. By isolating the logo, you can make a targeted selection to improve its appearance.

1. Open the image Ch05_Hotel.tif from the Chapter 5 folder.

2. Open the Channels panel. Click the Channels panel submenu (the triangle in the upper-right corner). Choose Palette Options and set the thumbnail to the largest size.

3. In the Channels panel, click the word *Red* to view just the red channel. Examine the channel for contrast detail. Repeat for the green and blue channels. Look for the channel with the cleanest separation of the motel's name. The blue channel should appear the cleanest.

4. Control-click/right-click on the blue channel and choose Duplicate Channel. Name it **Selection** and click OK to create a new (alpha) channel.

5. The new channel should automatically be selected; click its visibility icon (the small empty box next to its name). Turn off the visibility of the blue channel (click the eye icon next to its name).

6. Press Command+L (Ctrl+L) to invoke a Levels adjustment. This will allow you to adjust contrast on the mask. Make sure the Preview check box is selected.

7. Move the Black Input Levels slider to the right to increase contrast in the black areas.

8. Move the White Input Levels slider to the left to increase contrast in the white areas.

9. Move the middle (gray) input slider to the right to touch up the spotty areas.

10. Click OK to apply the adjustment to the channel.

11. To soften the edges of the channel, choose Filter > Blur > Gaussian Blur. Apply the filter with a value of **2** or **3** pixels to soften the edge.

12. To load the selection, Command-click (Ctrl-click) the Selection channel to create an active selection. By selecting the logo, you can make a controlled adjustment.

You now have a great selection that's ready to use for image adjustments or layer masking. Both topics will be covered in depth in the coming chapters.

Calculations Command

You can use the Calculations command to create a new selection based on the details in an image's channels. This technique is hit or miss, because it won't work with every image. But when it succeeds, it's a big success. The Calculations command works well when there is high contrast between the subject and the background. You should look at each channel independently until you find those with the highest contrast. Depending on the source photo, the selection you can generate will be anything from a great start to perfect.

Let's put the Calculations command into action to create an active selection and a saved alpha channel. You will first create a new channel based on the existing channels.

1. Open the file Ch05_Calculations.tif from the Chapter 5 folder.

2. Bring up the Channels panel (Windows > Channels) and look for the highest contrasting channels. Because you want to remove the background, look for the contrast between the foreground and background. The blue channel should stand out the most.

3. Choose Image > Calculations and make sure the Preview check box is selected. You'll now combine two of the color channels to create a new alpha channel. An alpha channel is simply a saved selection. You can Command-click (Ctrl-click) it to turn it into an active selection.

4. In the Source 1 area, set the Channel to Blue.

VIDEO 34:
Calculations Command

5. In the Source 2 area, you'll experiment to find the right combination. The red channel is a good place to start, because it looks very different than the blue channel. It's also a good idea to experiment by clicking the Invert button to reverse the channel. Calculations is all about trial and error, but since it works so well, taking a little time to experiment is worth it.

6. Combine the red and blue channels by using Blending. From the Blending menu, try different blending modes. Blending modes control how two different images or channels blend together based on their color and luminance values (for more on blending modes see Chapter 9, "Using Blending Modes"). Different source images will need different modes. Experiment by clicking through each mode on the list. You may also want to try deselecting the Invert check box when working with other images. In the Independence Hall image, the blue and red (inverted) channels combine most effectively using the Vivid Light blending mode. This will create a new channel that has a clean separation between the building and sky.

7. Click OK to create a new channel. The channel, called Alpha 1, should be selected in the Channels panel. Photoshop turned off the RGB channels for now.

8. Choose the Brush tool and set the foreground color to white.

9. Paint over the trees so the sky becomes pure white.

10. Run a Levels adjustment on the channel to adjust the contrast between black and white. Choose Image > Adjust > Levels or press Command+L (Ctrl+L). Move the Black Input Levels slider to the right to darken the gray areas to black. Move the White Input Levels slider to the left to brighten the whites in the image. Move the gray (gamma) input slider to the right to close up gray areas.

11. Click the OK button to apply the Levels adjustment.

12. Zoom in to 100% magnification to look for gaps in the alpha channel. You should see a few in the tower. With your Paintbrush set to black, paint out the spotting. You can also run a 1 pixel Gaussian Blur on the channel with the Filter command.

13. Command-click (Ctrl-click) on the alpha channel thumbnail to load the selection. You will need to choose Select > Inverse to choose Independence Hall.

14. Click the visibility icon next to the RGB composite channel to enable it.

15. Click the visibility icon next to the alpha channel to disable it.

Look closely at the selection; it should be pretty impressive. At this point, you could use the selection, copy the image, and add it to a different composite image, or you could run a filter or image-processing command on the building. With a little experimentation, you can generate a perfect alpha channel and turn it into a layer mask (you'll try this in Chapter 7). Calculations won't work every time, but it's a great solution that's worth a try when you have high-contrast channels.

Advice on Selections

No single technique is ideal for making the perfect selections. Every image is unique and will require you to analyze it. Knowing multiple techniques is very important, because it expands your options. Get comfortable with all the techniques in this chapter and be sure to practice. Practice really does make perfect.

Painting and Drawing Tools

6

Photoshop has a very rich set of painting and drawing tools. These tools have been in Photoshop since its first release, yet they have evolved greatly over time. The painting and drawing tools have many uses. To name a few:

- Fine artists can paint entire works into Photoshop with its realistic painting system. Using software can be an affordable alternative to traditional methods, which require more space and supplies.

- Comic book colorists can use Photoshop to paint the color into the inked drawings.

- FX designers can create background paintings for movie special effects work. In fact, the co-creator of Photoshop, John Knoll, is a lead visual effects supervisor at Industrial Light and Magic, the group behind the *Star Wars* franchise and many other well-known films.

- Commercial photographers can touch up and enhance photos using digital tools instead of a traditional airbrush. Nearly every photo you see in a fashion or entertainment magazine has undergone some digital touch-up in Photoshop to paint out imperfections.

These tools appear simple at first, and in fact they are. After all, the technology behind a paintbrush is pretty straightforward. It's the skill of the user holding the tool that determines results. A thorough understanding of the painting and drawing tools can come in handy while working in many areas of Photoshop. Whether you use Photoshop for image touch-up or to create original images from scratch, be sure to master these tools by practicing the exercises in this chapter.

Working with Color

Working with painting and drawing tools requires you to use color. Photoshop offers several flexible ways to choose colors. You can sample a color from an open image, choose a color from a library, or mix a new color by entering numerical values. Which method you use depends on a mixture of personal choice and the job at hand. Let's explore the different options.

Adobe Color Picker

The Adobe Color Picker is a consistent way to choose colors while using any Adobe software program. Both Macintosh and Windows systems have their own color pickers, but it's best to stick with the standardized Adobe Color Picker because it is a more full-featured and cross-platform tool.

You can choose a color from a spectrum or numerically. Use the Adobe Color Picker to set the Foreground color, Background color, and text color. Additionally, you can use the colors for gradients, filters, or layer styles.

Click the Foreground or Background color swatch in the Tools panel to open the Color Picker. In the Adobe Color Picker, you can select colors based on:

- Hue, Saturation, Brightness (HSB) color values

- Red, Green, Blue (RGB) color values

- Lab color values

- Cyan, Magenta, Yellow, Key (or Black) (CMYK) color values

- Hexadecimal color value

- Web-safe colors

Color Libraries

In some cases, designers need to access specific colors—those that come from a particular hue and brand of ink. This is most often to match colors used by a specific company. For example,

McDonald's always uses the same red on all its printed materials (PMS 485). This helps create a specific look or identity by branding based on color.

A designer can keep color consistent by specifying Pantone colors. The Pantone Matching System (PMS) is the most widely accepted color standard in the printing industry (www.pantone.com). Each color is assigned a PMS number, which corresponds to a specific ink or mixing standard, thus ensuring that a client will get consistent printing results. Accessing Pantone colors within Photoshop is easy:

1. Activate the Adobe Color Picker by clicking either the Foreground or Background color swatch.

2. Click the Color Libraries button to open the Color Libraries window.

3. From the Book menu you must choose among several options. Always ask your clients for specific color information. You can quickly jump to a specific color by typing in its number.

4. When you have a color selected, click OK.

5. Photoshop loads the closest equivalent color into your color picker. Essentially, the Pantone color will be simulated as accurately as possible by an RGB or CMYK equivalent.

6. If you need to have the exact color for printing, you will need to make a spot color channel (see the article "Creating Spot Color Channels" in the Chapter 6 folder or watch the video).

Color Libraries can also be loaded as color swatches. Just click the submenu (triangle) in the upper-right corner of the Swatches panel. Choose the library you need from the menu.

VIDEO 35:
Spot Color Channels

Kuler

Another tool that offers intuitive controls is Adobe Kuler. Originally an online-only tool, it lets you quickly create new color themes. Kuler began its life as a web-hosted application for experimenting with color variations and also allows for the sharing of color themes through an online community. To view the Kuler panel, choose Window > Extensions > Kuler.

TIP

Spot Color Channels

Are you doing professional printing? Learn how to assign specific colors to an area of an image. You'll find an exercise on creating spot color channels in this chapter's folder.

VIDEO 36:
Designing with Kuler

The Kuler panel is divided into three tabs:

- **About.** Introduces you to Kuler and links to the online community. You can create a free account to store themes as well as participate in Kuler forums and rate other users' themes.

- **Browse.** Allows you to browse thousands of color themes created by the Kuler community. Be sure to check back often because you can view by criteria such as the newest, highest rated, and most popular themes. You can also search for themes by tag word, title, creator, or hex color value.

- **Create.** Allows for the use of multiple color rules that are rooted in traditional design and is one of Kuler's best aspects. Kuler supports the following color rules: Analogous, Monochromatic, Triad, Complementary, Compound, and Shades–all are based on color theory.

To use a color you create, simply double-click its swatch to load it as the Foreground color in Photoshop. Across the bottom of the Kuler panel are additional options to save a theme, store it in the Photoshop Swatches panel, or upload it to the Kuler community.

TIP

Access Kuler Almost Anywhere

If you have web access, you've got Kuler. Just visit kuler.adobe.com to access the interactive design environment for color. You can even log in and sync your creations.

Eyedropper Tool

The Eyedropper tool lets you sample colors from any open document. This can be a useful way to choose colors that work well with an image. Let's try out the tool:

1. Open the file Ch06_Sampler.tif from the Chapter 6 folder.

2. Select the Eyedropper tool from the Tools panel or press the keyboard shortcut I.

3. Adjust the Sample Size in the Options bar:

- **Point Sample.** This method reads the value of a single pixel. It is very sensitive to clicking because you can have slight variations in color at the pixel level. For example, if you clicked on a blue sky, adjacent pixels could vary from each other.

- **3 by 3 Average.** This method reads the average value of a 3×3 pixel area. This is a more accurate method for selecting a color using the Eyedropper tool.

- **5 by 5 Average.** This method reads the average value of a 5×5 pixel area. It creates a more representative color sample.

  The remaining options simply use a larger sample area to produce an averaged color. The larger sample areas should be used on higher resolution images.

- 11 by 11 Average

- 31 by 31 Average

- 51 by 51 Average

- 101 by 101 Average

4. Click the reddish-brown feathers to set the foreground color.

5. Make sure the Show Sampling Ring option is selected in the Options bar. Click again to sample a new color. The ring shows you both the new color and the original for comparison.

6. Option-click (Alt-click) the grassy area to set the background color.

VIDEO 37:
Eyedropper Tool

TIP

More Precise Eyedropper

Be sure to open Photoshop's preferences by pressing Command+K (Ctrl+K), and then choose the Cursors category. Set the Other cursors option to Precise to see a useful sampler target.

NOTE

A Better Eyedropper

Adobe added a few useful features to the Eyedropper tool in Photoshop CS6. The Sample menu lets you choose from many new options, including the ability to ignore adjustment layers and to select layers current and below.

Using the Eyedropper tool, you can sample the color of the rooster's feathers. This can be useful for painting as well as color correction. For example, you can check the color details on two different shots of a rooster and then adjust color to make the images match more closely. For more on adjusting color, see Chapter 10, "Color Correction and Enhancement."

Color Panel

The Color panel is another way to access color without having to load the Adobe Color Picker. The Color panel shows you the values for the Foreground and Background colors. You can quickly mix or pick new colors from within the panel:

- You can adjust the sliders to mix a new color. To change color models, click the panel's submenu.

- You can click the spectrum across the bottom of the panel to pick a new color.

The Color panel might display two alerts when you select a color:

- An exclamation point inside a triangle means the color cannot be printed using CMYK printing.

- A cube means the color is not web-safe for color graphics viewed on a monitor set to 256 colors.

Swatches Panel

The Swatches panel holds color presets. You can quickly access frequently used colors by clicking their thumbnails. You can load preset swatches by clicking the Swatches panel submenu (top-right arrow). Additionally, **Table 6.1** shows several important shortcuts when working with the Swatches panel.

Table 6.1   Keyboard Shortcuts for the Swatches Panel

Result	Macintosh	Windows
Create new swatch from Foreground color	Click empty area of panel	Click empty area of panel
Select Foreground color	Click swatch	Click swatch
Select Background color	Command-click swatch	Ctrl-click swatch
Delete color swatch	Option-click swatch	Alt-click swatch

Painting Tools

Several tools are available in Photoshop for painting. Although these tools have subtle differences, they have one important component in common—the use of Photoshop's dynamic brush engine. Before exploring the unique tools, let's look at how to control your brushes.

Brushes Panel

The Brushes panel contains several options. Most of these will be well beyond what you'll need to get started. I'll briefly cover the options, but be sure to return to this panel as you increase your skills and confidence.

Brush presets

Photoshop has several brush presets to get you started right away. You access these presets from a panel that is docked with the Brushes panel; several are loaded and more are in the Photoshop Presets folder. Let's check them out.

1. Create a new document. Because this exercise is just for practice and you won't be printing the file, choose the 800 × 600 preset from the New Document dialog box.

2. Press D to load the default colors of black and white.

3. Select the standard Brush tool by pressing B.

4. Choose Window > Workspace > Painting to arrange the Photoshop interface so the most commonly used panels for painting tasks are visible.

5. Click the Brushes panel tab.

NOTE

Where Is?

A few of the less useful tools have been omitted in this chapter for space reasons or are covered with just a quick tip. If needed, you can look up these tools in the Photoshop Help menu for a quick overview. However, I doubt you'll miss the tools that have been omitted.

6. Click the button labeled Brush Presets. Photoshop displays a list and thumbnails of several brush styles in a new panel (it should be docked above the Layers panel).

7. Scroll through the list and choose a style.

8. Draw a stroke in your blank document to see the brush preset in action.

9. Repeat using different presets and create strokes to become familiar with your options.

10. Click the Brushes panel submenu (the triangle in the upper-right corner) and load a new Brush library.

11. Experiment with these brushes.

12. Load additional presets and continue to become familiar with your many options.

13. When done, you can restore the default set of brushes. Click the panel's submenu and choose Reset Brushes.

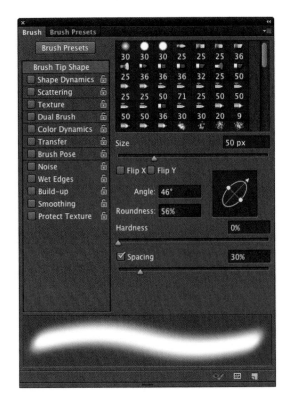

Brush Tip Shape

Although the brush presets are readily available and very diverse, they won't cover all your needs. Fortunately, Photoshop offers a flexible interface for customizing existing brushes as well as creating new ones.

1. Make sure you have the Brush tool selected.

2. Bring the Brushes panel to the forefront and make it active.

3. Choose a brush preset (from the thumbnail icons) that you'd like to modify. You can see the changes in the preview area or click your test canvas to try out the brush.

TIP

Dynamic Previews

Some brushes provide animated previews to show you how they interact with the canvas. Be sure to play with the Shape menu on the Brush Tip Shape tab to see the many different options.

You can modify the following brush tip shape options in the Brushes panel by clicking the words Brush Tip Shape:

- **Size.** Controls the size of the selected brush. You can enter a value in pixels (px) or drag the slider to a new size.

- **Use Sample Size.** Resets the brush to its original diameter. This is only visible if the brush was created by sampling pixels (such as part of a photo or a scanned brush stroke painted on paper or canvas).

- **Flip X.** Changes the direction of a brush by flipping it on its X-axis (essentially making a mirrored image). This is useful if the brush is asymmetrical.

- **Flip Y.** Flips the brush on its Y-axis.

- **Angle.** Specifies the angle of a brush. This works well for sampled or elliptical brushes. You can type in a number of degrees or visually change the angle of the brush by dragging the arrow in the brush preview interface. You can use angled brushes to create a chiseled stroke.

- **Roundness.** Specifies the ratio between the short and long axes. A value of 100% results in a rounder brush, whereas 0% creates a linear brush. Elliptical shapes can be used to create natural-looking strokes.

VIDEO 38:
Creating Custom Brushes

NOTE

How Big Can Brushes Be?

In Photoshop CS6, brush size diameter can go up to 5000 px. That's a lot bigger than you'll likely need, so be sure to pay attention to your brush size.

NOTE

Where Did My Brush Go?

Can't see a brush preview? Check if you've pressed the Caps Lock key.

CREATING CUSTOM SAMPLED BRUSHES

You can use an image to create a custom brush. This image can be a scan that you input or a stroke that you draw using other brushes. Let's give it a try:

1. Open the file Ch06_Brushes_to_Sample.tif from the Chapter 6 folder.

2. Select the first brush shape using the Rectangular Marquee tool. You can sample an image in size up to 2500 pixels x 2500 pixels.

3. Choose Edit > Define Brush Preset. A new box opens for naming the brush.

4. Name the brush and click OK. The brush is added to the set you currently have loaded in the Brushes panel.

5. Activate the new brush and paint in a new document to experiment with it. You might want to adjust the Spacing option to your preference.

6. Repeat for the other three brush shapes.

> **NOTE**
>
> **Brushes Can Be Recorded**
>
> If you want to create a complex series of brush strokes and reuse them, you can now record them as an action. For more, see Chapter 15, "Actions and Automation."

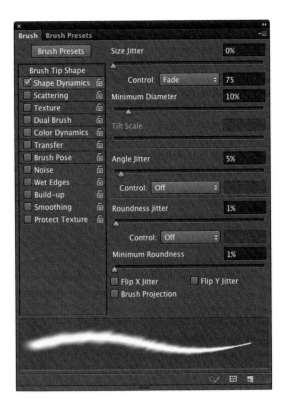

- **Hardness.** Creates brushes with soft edges. This can be useful to create more natural-looking strokes. You can adjust hardness between 0% (very soft) and 100% (no feathering). You cannot adjust hardness for sampled brushes.

- **Spacing.** Controls the distance between brush marks when you create a stroke. You can adjust spacing using the slider or type in a number. If you deselect the check box, the speed of your cursor will determine spacing.

Shape Dynamics

To create a more natural brush, you should adjust the Shape Dynamics of the brush. This can create natural variances that make the brush more realistic. The Shape Dynamics option adjusts the currently selected brush; therefore, be sure to choose a brush from the Brush Presets or Brush Tip Shape area.

- **Size Jitter and Control.** Specify how much variety Photoshop places in the size of the brush (trying to simulate the natural variation a real brush would produce). You can specify a total jitter size in percentage. Additionally, you can specify how to control the jitter from the Control menu:

  - **Off.** Select Off if you do not want to limit control over the size variance of brush marks. The jitter is random.

  - **Fade.** Allows the brush to taper off (like it ran out of ink or paint). The brush will get smaller based on a specified number of steps. Each step is one mark of the brush tip. If you specify 15, the brush will fade out in 15 steps.

- **Pen Pressure, Pen Tilt, Stylus Wheel, or Rotation.** Let you tie jitter to different features of a pen or stylus. Some Photoshop users unlock more features by connecting a stylus and graphics tablet. The most popular tablet manufacturer is Wacom (www.wacom.com).

- **Minimum Diameter.** Sets a limit on how much variation in scale can be introduced in the brush. A 0% value lets the brush shrink to a diameter of 0, whereas 25% allows the brush to range from full size to a quarter of its starting width.

- **Tilt Scale.** Ties the amount of scale to the tilt of the pen (or stylus). You must have a graphics tablet attached to utilize this feature.

- **Angle Jitter and Control.** Specify how much variety in the angle of the brush can occur. A larger number creates more variety. The control area ties the jitter to your pen.

- **Roundness Jitter and Control.** Introduce jitter into the roundness of the brush. Additionally, you can control the jitter with a pen.

- **Minimum Roundness.** Limits the amount of jitter.

Scattering

Enabling Scattering can add variation to the placement of strokes. This can simulate splattering or wilder strokes. There are a few options to work with:

- **Scatter and Control.** Distribute brush strokes from the center of the click. The Both Axes option distributes strokes radially. When the option is deselected, the strokes are distributed perpendicular to the stroke path.

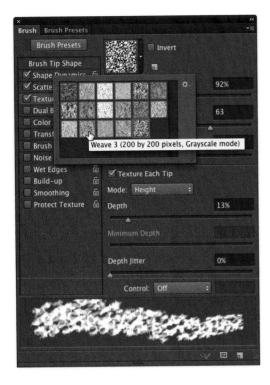

- **Count.** Specifies the quantity of brush marks applied at each spacing interval. This option works in conjunction with the Spacing option from Brush Tip Shape.

- **Count Jitter and Control.** Specify how much variety there is in the number of brush marks for each spacing interval. A high value will put more brush marks into the stroke. These properties are controlled in the same way as Shape jitter.

Texture

You can enable the Texture option to introduce a pattern into your strokes. This can help simulate canvas in your texture. Click the pattern sample to choose from one of the loaded patterns. Click the triangle menu to open the pattern picker to choose from the loaded textures. If you'd like to load additional textures, click the submenu in the pattern picker to load a built-in texture library. You can adjust several other options in the window and examine their effects in the preview area.

Dual Brush

What's better than one brush? Two, of course. By using a dual brush, you can use two brush tips to create a more dynamic brush. When selected, you'll have the option of choosing from a thumbnail list of presets for the second brush. You'll also see several options to modify the brush tip. You can modify the diameter of the second brush as well as specify spacing and scatter amounts.

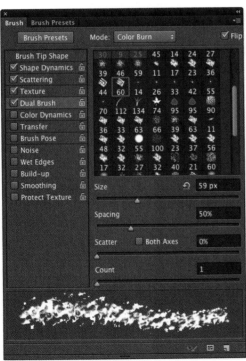

Color Dynamics

By now you might be thinking, those brushes are pretty dynamic, what else can Photoshop change? Well, color, of course. When you select Color Dynamics, you can enable several options that will produce subtle (or dynamic) variations in color:

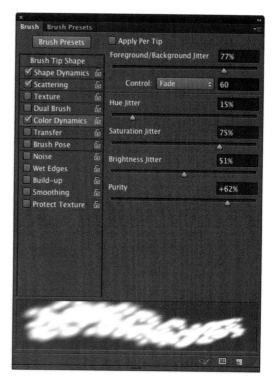

- **Foreground/Background Jitter and Control.** Allow the brush to utilize both the Foreground and Background colors that you have loaded. This can create a nice variation in color by loading lighter and darker shades of one color as your Foreground and Background color swatches.

- **Hue Jitter.** Allows you to specify how much variety of color can be introduced. Low values create a small change in color and higher values create greater variety.

- **Saturation Jitter.** Introduces variation in the intensity of the selected color.

- **Brightness Jitter.** Adds variety in brightness. A low value creates very little change in the brightness of the color. A higher value creates greater variations.

Transfer

The Transfer section offers additional styles of jitter that can be added:

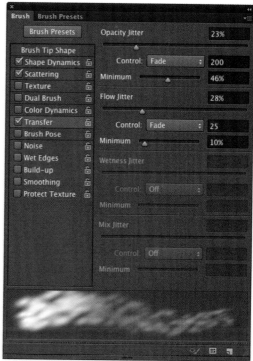

- **Opacity Jitter and Control.** Add variety to the brush so the opacity varies throughout the stroke. You can tie the opacity variation to a pen and tablet for greater control.

- **Flow Jitter and Control.** Affect how paint flows through the brush. A larger number means more paint flows through. The default value is 100%, which creates even strokes. A lower value causes less ink to be applied with each stroke.

Other brush options

A few other options can affect your active brush. These are either enabled (selected) or disabled (deselected); they have no modifiable properties:

- **Brush Pose.** Lets you specify a default tilt, rotation, and pressure for a brush. You can combine these with the dynamic settings of a stylus or choose the Override options to maintain a static pose.

- **Wet Edges.** Causes the paint to appear darker at the edge of the stroke. It simulates the effect of painting with watercolors.

- **Build Up.** Allows you to simulate a traditional airbrush (a device that uses pressurized air to spray paint out of a nozzle). Like an airbrush, this option applies gradual tones and allows the paint to build up. You can also access this option by clicking the Airbrush Build Up (Airbrush) option in the Options bar.

- **Smoothing.** Produces better curves in your brush strokes when painting.

- **Protect Texture.** Is a good option to enable if you are using Texture in your brush strokes. It keeps the pattern and scale consistent when switching between textured brushes. This will make your strokes more consistent.

Table 6.2 shows the frequently used Brushes panel keyboard shortcuts.

Table 6.2 Shortcut Keys for Using the Brushes Panel

Desired Result	Macintosh	Windows
Decrease/increase brush size	[or]	[or]
Decrease/increase brush softness/hardness in 25% increments	Shift + [or Shift +]	Shift + [or Shift +]
Select previous/next brush size	, (comma) or . (period)	, (comma) or . (period)
Display precise crosshair for brushes	Caps Lock	Caps Lock
Delete brush	Option-click brush	Alt-click brush
Rename brush	Double-click brush	Double-click brush
Toggle Airbrush option	Shift+Option+P	Shift+Alt+P

Brush Tool

After all this talk of brushes, there are still a few notable things to say about the Brush tool. Be sure to look in the Options bar for important brush controls. From left to right, these options are the most useful brush controls:

- **Tool Presets.** Stores frequently used brush configurations for convenient access.

- **Brush Preset Picker.** Displays a greatly reduced Brushes panel. You can access thumbnails of the loaded brushes as well as adjust diameter and hardness.

- **Mode.** Lets you change the blending mode of your painted strokes. Blending modes attempt to simulate real-world interactions between two elements. For example, Multiply allows the strokes to build up, much like a magic marker. You'll find much more on blending modes in Chapter 9, "Using Blending Modes."

- **Opacity.** Affects the opacity of your strokes.

- **Flow.** Reduces the amount of paint flowing to the brush.

- **Airbrush button.** Enables the Airbrush.

- **Brushes panel button.** Toggles visibility of the Brushes panel. Click it to open the Brushes panel, which gives you greater control over the brush shape and dynamics.

NOTE

The #2 Pencil

The Pencil tool is similar to the Brush tool. It shares many of the same options and controls. The fundamental difference is that it can only be used to create hard-edged strokes. Although there is a Hardness setting available for some brushes, it does little to change the stroke. The Pencil tool is fairly useless compared to the Brush tool and its many options.

NOTE

Color Replacement Tool

The Color Replacement tool can replace a selected color with a new, user-specified color. This tool was originally positioned as a way to remove "red eye" from photos. Photoshop CS2 added a new Red Eye tool specifically for that purpose.

TIP

New Bristle Tips

Be sure to check out the Bristle Tips options. These offer lifelike brush strokes. There are several customizable characteristics including Shape, Bristle density, Length, Thickness, and Stiffness. If you have a supported graphics card, you even get an interactive preview of the brush.

 VIDEO 39:
Using the Color
Replacement Tool

Mixer Brush Tool

The Mixer Brush tool was a new addition to Photoshop CS5 and goes a long way toward simulating realistic paint strokes. It mimics real-life brushes by allowing colors to mix on the canvas and simulating properties like stroke wetness.

1. Open the file Ch06_Color_Mixer.tif from the Chapter 6 folder.

2. Select the Mixer Brush tool (click and hold the Brush tool in the Tools panel to reveal the Mixer Brush).

VIDEO 40:
Using the Mixer Brush

3. Choose a soft brush and make sure it is a large size (25 px or greater). Set the Spacing to 5% for tighter strokes.

4. Click the Preset list in the Options bar to try different presets. For this image, use the Very Wet, Heavy Mix option.

    The Wet Controls affect how much paint the brush picks up from the canvas. A higher setting produces longer paint streaks.

5. Select the layer called Swatches in the Layers panel and try painting brush strokes near the intersection of different-colored squares to see the colors mix. Try painting circular stokes as well to see the color values mix.

6. Try changing the blending mode or opacity for the layer containing brush strokes to blend it with the original photo layer below.

Now that you see how the strokes can mix, let's explore a more realistic use for the tool. The Mixer Brush can be used effectively on a photograph to create paint strokes based on the colored image. This can produce an attractive effect, creating a painterly like image.

1. Turn off the visibility icon for the Swatches layer and select the layer Glass.

2. Choose the Moist, Heavy Mix preset. In the Options bar select the Sample All Layers check box.

3. Create a new, empty layer.

4. Select a brush preset. Option-click (Alt-click) on the image to sample a color, and then paint in the canvas.

> **TIP**
>
> **Clean Strokes**
>
> Be sure to experiment with the automatic Load or Clean options for the Mixer Brush. These make it easy to keep the brush clean and mix the color details in a picture.

5. Experiment with different brush strokes and Mixer Brush presets or settings to see the full depth of the tool. The bristle brushes work very well, especially if you trace some of the details in the underlying image.

History Brush Tool

The History Brush is easy to use but a little hard to understand at first. Essentially, it allows you to paint backward in time. This can be very useful because it enables you to combine the current state of an image with an earlier state. For example, you can process an image with a stylizing filter, and then restore part of the image to its original state.

The History Brush is directly tied to your History panel. This helpful panel shows you each action you have taken on an image. You can then move backward through your undos by clicking them. By default you have 20 levels of undo, but you can change this setting by increasing the number of History States in your general preferences.

Let's put the History panel and History Brush into action:

1. Choose Window > History to activate the History panel.

2. Open the file Ch06_History_Brush.tif from the Chapter 6 folder.

3. Press D to load the default colors of black and white.

The original image (top); the painted layer (center); Opacity of painted layer set to 80% and the Darken blending mode (bottom).

VIDEO 41:
History Brush

4. You'll now run a Brush Stroke filter to stylize part of the image. You can use Filters to create special effects in an image. (For more on filters, see Chapter 14, "Maximizing Filters.") Choose Filter > Filter Gallery.

5. In the Brush Strokes category choose the Sumi-e filter. Adjust the sliders to your preference. Click OK to apply the filter.

6. Clean up any areas in the dark background with the Brush or Mixer Brush tool.

7. Open the History panel and drag its resize handle to see more states (and snapshots). The History panel shows you all the actions you have performed on the open image.

   The image looks more like a painting at this point, but some key areas (like the text on the pump) are too heavily stylized.

8. Look at the top of the History panel to see a snapshot of the document. It was automatically created when the document was first opened. The brush icon next to it indicates that it has been set as the source for the History Brush.

9. Choose the History Brush from the Tools panel or press Y. Be sure to not choose the Art History Brush.

10. Select a soft-edged brush sized at approximately 70 pixels, and set the Opacity to 70% to restore 70% of the original details while preserving 30% of the new state.

11. Paint in the text to restore the original details.

NOTE

What About the Art History Brush?

Officially, you can use the Art History Brush tool to create stylized paintings. Unofficially, it doesn't work very well. A better option is to use the Color Mixer Brush tool or the new Oil Paint filter.

CONTROLLING SNAPSHOTS

Snapshots can also be used as "digital breadcrumbs" so you can find your way back to earlier versions of the image. You can add more snapshots so you can quickly jump back to specific points in time by:

- Clicking the Create new snapshot button (camera icon) at the bottom of the History panel.

- Changing the preferences for the History panel. Click the submenu icon for the History panel and choose History Options. You can choose to Automatically Create New Snapshot When Saving.

Remember, History States and snapshots are temporary. When you close the open document, they are discarded.

The original image (left); the filtered image (center); details restored with the History Brush (right).

12. Try lowering the Opacity to 25% and paint in additional details of the original image. You can combine multiple strokes as needed to build up an area.

The History Brush can be valuable when either filtering an image or performing color-correction tasks. It allows you to selectively paint back in time to restore lost or important details.

Working with Gradients

A gradient is a gradual blend between two or more colors. You can use gradients to create a photorealistic backdrop or to draw in areas like a blown-out sky. The Gradient tool is extremely flexible and offers the versatile Gradient Editor for creating custom gradients. Before you utilize the Gradient tool, let's explore how gradients are formed.

Gradient Editor

All gradients are edited using the Gradient Editor (which becomes available when you activate the Gradient tool). To access it, click the thumbnail of the gradient in the Options bar:

● **Presets.** You have several preset gradients to choose from, and you can browse them by thumbnail. Additionally, you can load other gradients by clicking the panel's submenu.

VIDEO 42:
Designing Custom Gradients

- **Name.** Naming each gradient can make gradients easier to sort through.

- **Gradient Type.** The two major categories of gradients are Solid and Noise. Solid gradients use color and opacity stops with gradual blends in between. Noise gradients contain randomly distributed colors within a user-specified range. Each has a unique interface.

Solid Editor

Solid gradients blend from one color to another, providing a traditional gradient type.

- **Smoothness.** This option controls the rate at which the colors blend. You can set it to be gradual or steep. The larger the number, the more Photoshop optimizes the appearance of the blend.

- **Opacity stops.** A gradient can contain blends between opacity values. To add a stop, click in an empty area on the top of the gradient spectrum. To adjust a stop, click it, and then modify the Opacity field.

- **Color stops.** A simple gradient contains only two colors. However, you might want to use a more complex gradient in your project. You can click below the gradient to add another color stop. Double-click a stop to edit its color with the Adobe Color Picker.

- **Stop Editor.** Selected gradient stops can be adjusted numerically. You can edit the opacity, color, and location (0–100%, read left to right.)

- **Midpoint.** Between stops are midpoints. By default the midpoint is halfway between two stops. You can adjust the midpoint to shift the balance of the gradient.

Noise Editor

Noise gradients use a specified range of color to create noise. These gradients do not blend smoothly between colors; rather, they create a new gradient each time you click the Randomize button:

- **Roughness.** Noise gradients use a roughness setting to determine how many different colors are used to create noise.

- **Color Model.** You can choose between three models: Red-Green-Blue, Hue-Saturation-Brightness, or Lab.

- **Color Range sliders.** Adjust the range of colors available to the gradient. Bring the black and white sliders closer together to limit the amount of color present in the noise gradient.

- **Options.** You can choose to further restrict colors as well as introduce random transparency. To create a new gradient, click the Randomize button. Every time you click, a new gradient is generated.

- **New button.** To add a gradient to the Presets window, type a name into the Name field, and then click the New button. This new gradient is not yet permanently saved but is stored temporarily in the Preferences file. You must click the Save button and navigate to your Presets folder (inside the Photoshop application folder) to save it. Be sure to append the filename with .grd to inform Photoshop that it is a gradient set.

Gradient Tool

You can use the Gradient tool to manually draw a gradient on a layer. To access the Gradient tool, select it from the Tools panel or press G. The Paint Bucket shares the same well as the Gradient tool, so if you don't find the Gradient tool, press Shift+G to cycle through your tools.

The Gradient tool can use any gradient you create in the Gradient Editor or from the Presets menu. To select a gradient, you can choose from those available in the Options bar. You can also load preset libraries or manually load gradients by accessing the panel's submenu.

You must choose one of these five methods to build your gradient:

- **Linear Gradient (A).** Blends from the starting point to the ending point in a straight line.

- **Radial Gradient (B).** Blends from the starting point to the ending point in a circular pattern.

- **Angle Gradient (C).** Blends in a counterclockwise sweep from the starting point.

- **Reflected Gradient (D).** Blends symmetrically on both sides of the starting point.

- **Diamond Gradient (E).** Blends in a diamond-shaped pattern outward from the starting point.

You have a few available options to further modify the gradient:

- You can specify a blending mode to affect how the gradient is applied to the layer. (For more on blending modes, see Chapter 9.)

- To reverse the direction of colors in the gradient, select the Reverse check box.

- To create a visually smoother blend by adding noise, select the Dither check box.

- To use a gradient's built-in transparency, select the Transparency check box.

Let's use the Gradient tool to fix a common problem, a washed-out sky:

1. Open the file Ch06_Grad_Sky.tif from the Chapter 6 folder.

2. Choose Select > Color Range to create an active selection in the sky area. Adjust Fuzziness to get a gentle selection.

3. Load a dark blue as your Foreground color and a lighter blue as your Background color. You can try to select colors from the existing sky to make your gradient believable.

4. Choose the Gradient tool and select a Linear Gradient. Set the mode to Multiply and set Opacity to 40%.

5. Select the Foreground to Background gradient from your pre-set list (it's the first one).

6. Click at the top of the sky and drag down toward the buildings.

The first click is where the foreground color will start; where you release the mouse is where the second color will be placed. Photoshop will blend the colors in between using the settings in the Gradient Editor.

The sky should look more natural now with greater variation in colors. If your sky has a lot of texture in it, try setting the Gradient tool to Color mode before drawing.

Eraser Tools

Photoshop offers three kinds of Eraser tools to complement your drawing tools. These tools can be useful for cleaning up a brush stroke, but that's about it. They often produce crude edges in the erased area that lower the quality of your project.

The three tool options include:

- **Eraser tool.** This tool deletes pixels as you drag over them. On a layer they are replaced with transparency. On a Background, the pixels are replaced with your Background color. To use, just drag through the area you want to erase.

NOTE

Mask, Don't Erase

From years of personal experience, I strongly suggest avoiding the Eraser tools. These three tools are relatively primitive in their approach to selecting pixels for deletion. Additionally, the erasers are permanent—the discarded pixels are gone for good. It bears repeating: If you have anything beyond a basic image that you need to extract from its background, the answer is layer masking, which is covered in depth in Chapter 7.

VIDEO 43:
Gradient Maps

- **Background Eraser tool.** This tool is designed to help erase the background from an image. The difference between foreground and background in the image must be very clear and high contrast. This tool is significantly less flexible than the technique of layer masking, which is covered in Chapter 7, "Layer Masking."

- **Magic Eraser tool.** This tool is most similar to the Paint Bucket tool in that it attempts to select and modify similar pixels under your click point. Instead of filling those pixels with a color, however, the Magic Eraser tool deletes them.

GRADIENT MAPS OFFER UNIQUE COLOR

Gradient Maps are another way to harness the power of gradients to enhance an image. The Gradient Map can be applied as an adjustment layer or image adjustment command (stick with the adjustment layer for greater flexibility). You can create a new Gradient Map by choosing Layer > New Adjustment Layer > Gradient Map.

The Gradient Map will map a new gradient to the grayscale range of an image. A two-color gradient produces a nice duotone effect. Shadows map to one of the color stops of the gradient fill; highlights map to the other. The midtones map to the gradations in between. A multicolored gradient or noise gradient can add interesting colors to an image. This is an effective technique for colorizing textures or photos.

Open the file Ch06_Gradient_ Map_Demo1.psd and Ch06_ Gradient_Map_Demo2 to see Gradient Maps in action. Turn on each map one at a time to see the effect. By using blending modes in conjunction with the Gradient Map, you can get a more pleasant effect.

PHOTO BY ABBA SHAPIRO

You'll find a great new set of Gradient Maps included with Photoshop CS6. In the Gradient Map dialog box just click the gear icon to access its settings. Load the Photographic Toning set to experience a wealth of toning options, including sepia and duotones. These can also be combined with blending modes to produce all new results.

Vector Drawing Tools

Even though Photoshop is best known as a pixel-based (or raster) program, it does have a respectable set of vector drawing tools. Vector graphics are made up of mathematically defined lines and curves. Vector graphics are resolution-independent, because they can be scaled and repositioned with no loss of quality. Vector graphics are a good choice for creating shapes (such as rectangles, circles, or polygons) within your Photoshop document. The added benefit to using the drawing tools is that you can then scale the shapes and modify the design while still maintaining a crisp image. With Photoshop CS6, vectors have become more robust and include the ability to assign custom fills and strokes (much like Adobe Illustrator).

VIDEO 44:
Vector Drawing Tools

Choosing the Right Drawing Tool

Photoshop offers six Shape tools. They can be used to create vector shapes, vector paths (which can be used to make a selection), or raster shapes. The following list explains how to change how the Shape tools work:

- **Rectangle tool.** The Rectangle tool draws rectangles; if you hold down the Shift key, it draws squares.

- **Rounded Rectangle tool.** The Rounded Rectangle tool is well suited for drawing buttons for websites. Adjust the Radius setting to modify the amount of curvature.

- **Ellipse tool.** The Ellipse tool draws ellipses; if you hold down the Shift key, it draws circles.

- **Polygon tool.** The Polygon tool creates polygons. The fewest number of sides a polygon can have is three (which is a triangle). The most complex polygon you can create is a hectagon (a 100-sided figure). Enter the number of sides in the Options bar. Additionally, the Polygon tool can be used to create stars by clicking the Geometry Options button in the Options bar.

- **Line tool.** The Line tool draws lines. Specify a thickness in the Options bar. The line can be between 1 and 1000 pixels in width. You can also choose to add arrowheads by clicking the Geometry Options button in the Options bar.

CREATING CUSTOM SHAPES

You can create custom shapes and save them for future use:

1. **Create a shape with the Pen tool or paste one into Photoshop from Adobe Illustrator.**

2. **Select the Paths panel, and then select a path. It can be a vector mask from a shape layer, a work path, or a saved path.**

3. **Choose Edit > Define Custom Shape.**

4. **Enter a descriptive name for the new custom shape in the Shape Name dialog box. The new shape now appears in the Shape pop-up panel, which can be quickly accessed from the Options bar.**

5. **If you'd like to permanently save the shape by adding it to a library, choose Save Shapes from the submenu in the Custom Shape Picker.**

- **Custom Shape tool.** The Custom Shape tool is *very* versatile. There are several shapes built into Photoshop. These can be extremely useful during the design process. To view your loaded shapes, click the Custom Shape pop-up panel in the Options bar. Additional shapes can be loaded by clicking the submenu in the Custom Shape panel. Choose from the built-in libraries or load more.

Loading Custom Shapes

Thousands of free shapes are available to download for Photoshop. An Internet search using the keywords "Photoshop," "Free," and "Custom Shapes" returns plenty of great results. You can choose to load these custom shapes temporarily or add them to your preset list.

For a temporary load of shapes:

1. From the Custom Shape pop-up panel in the Options bar, click the submenu.

2. Choose Load Shapes.

3. Navigate to the desired shape library (it should end in the extension .csh).

4. Select the shape and click OK.

5. You can choose to Replace the current shapes or Append the new shapes to the end of the old list.

To permanently store shapes, load them into Presets:

1. Navigate to your Photoshop application folder.

2. Open the Presets folder.

3. Open the Custom Shapes folder.

4. Copy the custom shapes files into the Custom Shapes folder. Be sure the shapes are not compressed (such as a .sit or .zip file).

5. Restart Photoshop; the presets will be loaded into the submenu in the Custom Shape Picker.

Drawing Shapes

Using the Shape tools is very similar to using the Marquee tools. In fact, the same shortcut keys apply: Holding down the Option (Alt) key after you start drawing causes the shape to draw from the center of the initial click, whereas holding down the Shift key constrains the width and height to preserve a constant ratio.

Let's try using the Shape tools.

1. Create a new RGB document sized at 1024 × 768 pixels. Set the Background Contents to Transparent. Name the document **Playing Card**.

2. Select the Rounded Rectangular Shape tool. Set the Radius to 10 pixels.

3. In the Options bar, make sure the tool mode is set to Shape to create a Shape Layer and set the fill to White.

4. Click and draw a rectangle in the vector shape of a playing card.

5. With the vector shape layer selected, click the stroke width menu and change it to 10 pixels.

6. Click the well next to the Stroke type and choose a textured stroke.

 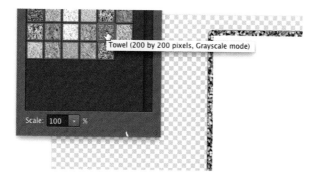

7. Choose the Custom Shape tool. Open the Custom Shape Picker and select the Heart shape. If it is not visible, choose Reset Shapes to load the default set.

8. In the Options bar, set the fill color to a custom red gradient. Go from a darker red to a brighter red.

9. Draw a large heart in the center of the card (hold down the Shift key to constrain its proportions).

10. Use the Alignment tools to center the heart in the middle of the card. Select both layers in the Layers panel. Activate the Move tool and choose the Horizontal and Vertical Alignment buttons in the Options bar.

11. Draw a heart icon near the upper-left corner of the card. Leave room for a letter A (for *Ace*).

12. Press Command+J (Ctrl+J) to duplicate the current heart layer. Move it to the lower-right corner. Invoke the Free Transform command and rotate the heart 180°.

13. Press T to select the Type tool. In the Options bar choose a font such as New York or Palatino. Set the style to Bold, the size to 100 pt, and the color to Red.

14. Click in the upper-left corner and add the letter A.

15. Press Command+J (Ctrl+J) to duplicate the current "A" layer. Move it to the lower-right corner. Invoke the Free Transform command and rotate the A 180°.

THREE KINDS OF SHAPES

You can use the Shape tools to create shapes in three different ways:

- **SHAPE LAYERS.** Creates a shape on a separate layer. A shape layer has a fill layer that defines the color and a linked vector mask that defines the shape.

- **PATHS.** Draws a work path on the current layer. This path can then be used to make a selection. It can also be used to create a vector mask, or it can be filled or stroked. Paths appear in the Paths panel.

- **FILL PIXELS.** Paints directly on the active layer. It makes the Shape tools perform like Paint tools. In this mode you create raster, not vector, graphics.

If you'd like to look at the completed project, open the file Ch06_Playing_Card.psd and check it out.

Layer Masking

7

When you're working in Photoshop, you'll often need to combine multiple images together into a new composite image. Those original images, however, may have backgrounds or objects that you no longer want. This is where Layer Masks come in. Far superior to erasing pixels, Layer Masks allow you to hide (or mask) part of a layer using powerful painting and selection tools. The more you work on combining multiple images, the more you'll use masks.

In this chapter, you'll revisit several techniques that you learned in Chapter 5, "Selection Tools and Techniques," but here you'll convert them into Layer Masks.

The mask is the black-and-white area attached to the layer thumbnail. It contains all the transparency information that the layer needs to isolate the bird from the background.

Layer Mask Essentials

Masks generally start as a selection, which is then attached to a layer. The mask can be refined by adding to it with black or subtracting from it with white. Learning to create and modify masks is an important skill that becomes significantly easier with a little practice.

Adding Layer Masks

The best way to learn about Layer Masks is to jump right in and create one. You'll start with an easy image, but one that will help illustrate the important concepts. Let's get started.

1. Open the file Ch07_Mask_Start.tif from the Chapter 7 folder.

2. To mask the image, you'll need to convert the *Background* layer into a floating layer. Double-click the layer name in the Layers panel. Name the layer **Tower**.

3. Select the Quick Selection tool from the Tools panel.

4. Make a selection of the blue sky.

5. Reverse the selection by choosing Select > Inverse. The building is now selected.

6. Click the Refine Edge button in the Options bar.

   The Refine Edge dialog box opens. Here you can adjust the selection as well as create a mask.

7. Select the Smart Radius check box and adjust the Radius slider to refine the edge of the selection.

8. From the Output To menu, choose Layer Mask and click OK.

   A new mask is added to the layer.

9. To make it easier to see the edges of the border, place a solid color layer behind the Tower layer. Choose Layer > New Fill Layer > Solid Color and click OK. Choose a color that is not in the image, such as green.

10. Drag the fill layer below the Tower layer in the Layers panel.

11. Depending on the accuracy of your initial selection, your mask may be usable as is. If needed, you can quickly touch it up using the Brush tool.

12. In the Layers panel, click the Layer Mask thumbnail to select it.

13. Activate the Brush tool by pressing B or by choosing it from the Tools panel. Press D to load the default colors of black and white.

14. Zoom in to better see your edges. You can use the Zoom tool or the Navigator panel to get a better look at your edges.

15. Paint with a soft-edged brush to refine the mask. Paint with black to add to the mask (to add transparency) or white to make an area opaque.

   If you add too much to the mask, press X to toggle the mask colors and paint with the opposite color you were just using.

16. Delete the solid color fill layer.

Disabling Layer Masks

The primary benefit of masks is their flexibility. In the previous section you explored that flexibility by adding and subtracting to a mask. This flexibility can also be used to temporarily disable a mask, which can be useful if you want to check your progress or if you need to restore the original image to use on another project.

1. Work with the Tower image from the previous exercise or open the file Ch07_Mask_End.tif from the Chapter 7 folder.

2. Select the Layers panel so it is active.

3. Shift-click the Layer Mask thumbnail to disable it. Alternately, you can Ctrl-click (right-click) the mask's thumbnail to access more options, such as deleting it and permanently applying it.

4. To reenable the mask, Shift-click its thumbnail again.

Shift-clicking a Layer Mask's thumbnail will temporarily disable the mask.

VIDEO 45:
Layer Masking

Deleting Layer Masks

After going through the effort of creating a mask, you are unlikely to want to permanently discard it. But if you change your mind and are certain you want to delete it, doing so is easy.

1. Work with the Tower image from the previous exercise or open the file Ch07_Mask_End.tif from the Chapter 7 folder.

2. Select the Layers panel so it is active.

3. Click the Layer Mask thumbnail. Drag it to the trash icon in the Layers panel.

4. A dialog window appears asking you to decide what to do with the mask:

   • **Delete.** Discards the mask and restores the image to its pre-masked state.

   • **Cancel.** Allows you to cancel the command and return the image to its masked state.

   • **Apply.** Permanently applies the mask and deletes the pixels that were originally masked.

5. Click Apply to permanently apply the mask. The mask is used to permanently discard portions of the masked layer in a destructive edit.

VIDEO 46:
Alpha Channels

Mask Creation Strategies

There are many different approaches to creating Layer Masks. The approach you should take will vary based on your source image. Let's try using four different images and techniques to perfect your Layer Masking ability.

Using a Gradient as a Mask

When you're designing, you may need to gradually blend the edges of an image. This can be easily accomplished by combining a Layer Mask and a gradient. Let's give it a try.

1. Open the file Ch07_Gradient_Mask.tif from the Chapter 7 folder.

2. Duplicate the *Background* layer by pressing Command+J (Ctrl+J).

3. Select the top layer and choose Image > Adjustments > Desaturate.

4. With the topmost layer active, click the Add layer mask button at the bottom of the Layers panel (it looks like a rectangle with a circle inside). A new, empty Layer Mask is added to the layer.

5. Press G to select the Gradient tool.

6. Press D to load the default colors of black and white.

7. From the Options bar, choose the black-to-white gradient. If it's not available, choose Reset Gradients from the Gradient Picker's submenu.

8. With the Layer Mask selected, click and drag to create a new linear gradient going from top to bottom in the document window.

9. The new Layer Mask creates a gradual blend from the grayscale version to the colored version.

This technique of adding a mask can also be used on one layer to create a gradual fade to transparency or to a different layer stacked beneath.

The gradient mask allows the image to blend between the grayscale and color image.

Using a Channel

Often, a channel will get you very close to a perfect Layer Mask. This technique works particularly well when the subject is against a high-contrast background (such as a sky or a wall), and it works very well with fine details like hair. The image can be masked so it is ready for integration into a composite image. For example, a masked image could be used to add a palm tree to another photo. Let's give it a try.

1. Open the file Ch07_Channel_Mask.tif from the Chapter 7 folder.

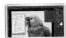

VIDEO 47:
Refine Edge Command
for Fine Edges

2. Switch to the Channels panel and examine the Red, Green, and Blue channels.

Look for one with high contrast from the background. Although all three channels are fairly high contrast, the Blue channel stands out the most.

3. Duplicate the Blue channel by dragging it onto the New Channel icon at the bottom of the Channels panel (it looks like a pad of paper).

4. Rename the new channel **Selection** by double-clicking its name.

5. With the Selection channel selected, press Command+L (Ctrl+L) to invoke a Levels adjustment. Levels is a powerful command that allows you to adjust the gamma (gray) point as well as the black and white points.

6. Move the black slider to the right, setting the Input Level to around **60**. The black in the channel should get crisper.

7. Move the white slider to the left, setting the Input Level to around **190**. The gray areas in the channel should switch to pure white.

8. Move the middle (gray) slider to refine any gray spots in the channel. A value of **1.5** should be approximately correct.

9. Click OK to apply the Levels adjustment.

10. Command-click (Ctrl-click) on the Selection channel's thumbnail to load the selection (you'll see the marching ants).

11. Choose Select > Inverse to reverse the selected area from the sky to the palm tree.

12. Turn on the visibility for the RGB channels by clicking the RGB composite channel's visibility icon. Turn off visibility for the Selection channel.

13. Switch to the Layers panel.

14. Click the Add layer mask button at the bottom of the Layers panel to turn the palm tree into a layer with a mask added.

VIDEO 48:
Color Range Command
and Masking

Using Calculations

You explored the Calculations command to create an advanced selection in Chapter 5. This command uses channel data to create a new alpha channel. You can then refine the channel to create an accurate selection. You can also take this one step further to make a high-quality Layer Mask. Let's give it a try.

VIDEO 49:
Calculations for Masking

1. Open the file Ch07_Calculations.tif from the Chapter 7 folder.

2. Turn the *Background* layer into a floating layer by double-clicking its name in the Layers panel. Name the layer **Banana Tree**.

3. Call up the Channels panel and closely examine the channels for a high contrast between the tree and the background. Although all three channels have contrast between the sky and the tree, the Blue channel has the best.

4. Invoke the Calculations command by choosing Image > Calculations.

5. Set Source 1 to the Blue channel, set Source 2 to the Red channel, and select the Invert check box. The Red channel differs most from the Blue channel in this image, so it will create a good matte.

6. Experiment with different blending modes so you get a clearer separation between the tree and the sky. In this case, the Vivid Light mode works best to create a new channel. Click OK.

7. The new channel will need a little touch-up. You can get the channel near perfect with a Levels adjustment. Press Command+L (Ctrl+L) to invoke the Levels dialog box.

8. Adjust the black, white, and gray points for Input Levels to improve the matte. Click OK when you're satisfied.

NOTE

Using CS4 or CS5?

In earlier versions of Photoshop is a dedicated panel called the Masks panel to adjust a mask's properties. It behaves exactly like the Properties panel.

9. You then need to reverse the channel so the area you want to discard is black. Press Command+I (Ctrl+I) to invert the channel.

10. Soften the selection by blurring it. Choose Filter > Blur > Gaussian Blur, set it to a value of **1** pixel, and click OK.

11. Load the channel as a selection by Command-clicking (Ctrl-clicking) the channel's thumbnail.

12. Turn on the visibility icon for the RGB channels and turn it off for the alpha channel.

13. Switch to the Layers panel and select the Banana Tree layer.

14. Click the Add layer mask button to apply a mask to the selected layer.

TIP

The Masks Panel Is Essential

The Masks panel offers several other useful commands. You can load a mask as a selection, apply a mask, disable its visibility, or discard it. Additionally, you can use the Color Range or Invert command to further refine the selection. The Masks panel consolidates all the masking commands into a single location, which can save you valuable time.

Refining Masks

By now you should be feeling more comfortable making Layer Masks. However, there's always room for improvement (at least where masks are concerned). Let's take a look at three ways to refine or adjust a mask.

Using the Properties Panel

If you need to refine an existing mask, one of the easiest ways is to use the options in the Properties panel. The panel combines several tools and commands into one location and makes it very easy to adjust a mask (even after first adding it). In fact, the Mask Edge and Color Range options are identical to the selection commands you've previously explored.

1. Open the file Ch07_Masks_Panel.psd from the Chapter 7 folder.

2. Select the Panda layer's mask.

3. In the Properties panel, experiment with the Density and Feather sliders to see their effects (if the panel is not visible, choose Window > Properties):

   - **Density.** Reduces the overall impact of the mask by essentially lowering the opacity of the Layer Mask.

   - **Feather.** Creates a gentle edge to the mask.

4. Set Density to **100**% and Feather to **0** px.

5. Click the Mask Edge button to open the Refine Mask dialog box. The controls are identical to the Refine Edge dialog box except here they are used to modify the Layer Mask.

6. Adjust the Mask Edge properties to remove fringe from around the image. Use the same techniques you learned in the previous chapter for the Refine Edge command.

Setting the View option to On Layer makes it easier to see the fine edge details over the solid color layer.

7. Experiment with the Smart Radius option and the Refine Radius tool to enhance the edge and get a better processing for the fur.

8. Click OK to apply the change to the Layer Mask.

Using Smudge and Blur

Sometimes a mask is close to being ready to apply but needs a little touch-up. What better way to do this than to paint? By using the Blur and Smudge tools you can polish problem edges:

- **Blur.** Choose the Blur tool to soften a hard edge that looks unnatural. Just be sure the mask is selected before blurring.

- **Smudge (Lighten).** Choose the Smudge tool and set its mode to Lighten in the Options bar. This is useful for gently expanding the matte. Leave the Strength set to a low value to make subtle changes.

- **Smudge (Darken).** Choose the Smudge tool and set its mode to Darken in the Options bar. This is useful for gently contracting the matte. Leave the Strength set to a low value to make subtle changes.

Open the file Ch07_Bird_Mask.psd to experiment with the Smudge and Blur tools.

Adjusting Content Within a Mask

By default, Layer Masks are linked to their respective layers. Applying a transformation (such as a Free Transform command) affects a layer and its Layer Mask. However, there are times when you won't want this default behavior to occur. Sometimes it is useful to adjust the contents of a masked layer without repositioning the mask. Let's give it a try.

VIDEO 50:
Adjusting Content Within a Mask

1. Open the file Ch07_Mask_Content.psd from the Chapter 7 folder. Even though the Layer Mask is accurate, too much of the layer's content is obscured.

NEWSPAPER IMAGE ISTOCKPHOTO

2. Click the chain icon between the layer thumbnail and Layer Mask icons for the Newspaper layer. You can now manipulate the layer content or its mask independently.

3. Select the Newspaper layer's thumbnail to modify the visible pixels of the layer.

4. Press Command+T (Ctrl+T) to invoke the Free Transform command. Scale the Newspaper layer smaller and move it slightly to better fit the opening in the newspaper stand. Click the Commit button to apply the transformation.

Advice on Masks

Layer masking and advanced selections go hand in hand. The more you practice one, the easier both will get. New users often lapse into bad habits and are drawn back to features like the Eraser tools or Copy and Paste commands. Although these may seem easier, in the long run they are not. Learn to work like a professional, and you'll achieve professional results.

Compositing with Layers

When Photoshop debuted, it did not have layers. Its original purpose was to touch up frames of motion picture and photography film. It was, as its name implied, a photo shop that provided a digital darkroom where photos could be enhanced, color corrected, and repaired. Over time, people wanted to do more with Photoshop, such as create print advertisements and television graphics. As people expected Photoshop to do more, Adobe responded with the introduction of layers. In this chapter you'll learn how to combine multiple layers together to create complex image composites.

What Are Layers?

In traditional cel animation, artists would paint their animations onto clear sheets of acetate. These clear sheets would often contain a single character or element. They could then be laid together with sheets containing other characters and backgrounds to create a composited scene.

Layers work the same way. Each layer can contain discrete elements of your design. You then combine them to create the finished product. Layers can contain photos, text, logos, shapes, and even textures. There are lots of ways to create and manage layers, but it all comes back to having an organized design. Every layer should have a clear, descriptive name to make your design workflow easier.

Why You Need Layers

If you plan to create complex designs in Photoshop, layers are a must for a few reasons:

- **Easy modification.** Layers make it simple to modify your design. Separate elements can be easily accessed and edited.

- **Easy manipulation.** If you are using Photoshop to create web or video animation as well as multimedia elements like slides or DVD menus, individual elements can be animated, highlighted, or revealed.

- **Interface with other programs.** Many other software programs rely on Photoshop layers as a content creation tool because these other programs lack Photoshop's drawing and painting tools. By supporting the layered Photoshop format, these software programs cleanly interface with the best-selling, image-editing tool.

Dissecting a Composite Image

Let's examine a practical example of how layers work by analyzing a menu from a DVD. Open the file Ch08_Layered_DVD.psd from the Chapter 8 folder. This nine-layer document is a good example of using the general features of the Layers panel. To start, all layers are turned off; don't be surprised to see an empty screen or checkerboard pattern. (The checkerboard is Photoshop's default way of showing transparency.)

1. Begin turning layers on from the bottom up, starting with Texture.

   The bottommost layer is a simple pattern that adds a sense of depth to the piece. This pattern was made by painting a physical canvas with traditional media. A digital photo was taken and tinted using Photoshop.

2. Turn on the next layer, Water, and click its name to select the layer.

At the top of the Layers panel, you should notice that the layer is set to 60% opacity. Opacity is the opposite of transparency. A layer or image that is 60% opaque is 40% transparent.

There's a great shortcut for changing opacity of a layer, but you must have a tool selected that does not have its own transparency settings (such as the Move or Marquee tools). To change the opacity of a layer, type the corresponding number on the numeric keypad. For example, press the 2 key for 20%, the 5 key for 50%, and so on. If you want to be even more specific, you can quickly type a number such as 23 for 23%, and Photoshop will adjust the layer accordingly.

3. Turn on and select the third layer, Skyline. This layer introduces another layer feature: blending modes. This layer is set to the Overlay blending mode.

In this case a grayscale image is used to add a silhouette of a building. Blending modes combine the contents of one layer with another based on the luminosity or colors of the layer.

4. Turn on and select the fourth layer, Vignette, and you'll see a similar technique employed to add an area of focus to the image.

A good technique is to try changing the blending mode before you make an opacity change. This subtle change to your working style will give you dramatic results.

5. Turn on and select the fifth layer, which looks different than the rest. It is an adjustment layer.

   A Levels adjustment (used to control balance and contrast) is being applied to multiple layers simultaneously. A Levels adjustment affects the overall balance of lights and darks in an image. The key benefit of the adjustment layer is that it is non-destructive; the effect is "live" in that you can alter or disable it at any time.

6. Locate or open the Properties panel. Try adjusting the middle slider and note the resulting changes.

   You will likely make a Levels adjustment on every image; it is the key to maintaining proper image contrast.

7. Turn on the next layer, Bars.

   These borders will be used to create an edge effect. The empty area between the bars is transparent and allows other layers to show through.

8. Turn on and select the Logo layer (which is vector based).

   This logo is a Smart Object as indicated by its special icon on the layer thumbnail. Smart Objects can add flexibility to the design process because they allow for the ability to scale and transform a vector object repeatedly without losing quality. This layer also has layer effects applied to create a slight beveled edge with a drop shadow.

9. Turn on the final layer, Text.

Photoshop has a robust text engine that is useful for creating screen-ready text (such as for television or Internet use). You will fully explore the robust text capabilities of Photoshop in Chapter 12, "Using the Type Tool."

By employing proper use of layers, you've generated a professional-looking DVD menu that you can use as is or import the layers into another application to animate. Proper naming makes it easy to find each layer. To name a layer, double-click on the name in the Layers panel.

Creating Layers

You can create a new layer easily in several ways. You can click the Create new layer icon (looks like a notepad) at the bottom of the Layers panel. If menus are your thing, choose Layer > New > Layer or press Shift+Command+N (Shift+Ctrl+N).

Additionally, you can drag layers up or down the layer stack or from one document to another, if you are so inclined. You can move layers or reorder them with keyboard shortcuts to change your image. **Table 8.1** shows a few keyboard shortcuts for just this purpose.

Table 8.1   Layer Mobility

Layer Movement	Mac	Windows
Move current layer down one position	Command+[	Ctrl+[
Move current layer up one position	Command+]	Ctrl+]
Move current layer to bottom of Layers panel	Shift+Command+[	Shift+Ctrl+[
Move current layer to top of Layers panel	Shift+Command+]	Shift+Ctrl+]

Duplicating Layers

When you need to duplicate a layer, you have a few choices. You can choose Layer > Duplicate Layer or right-click (Ctrl-click) the layer's name in the Layers panel and choose Duplicate Layer. Another method is to drag one layer onto the Create new layer icon at the bottom of the Layers panel. My favorite method is to press Command+J (Ctrl+J)—think *jump*—to create a copy of a layer immediately above itself.

Deleting Layers

If you decide you don't need a layer, you can throw it away. This reduces the size of your file, which means it'll take up less disk space and require less memory to work with. To throw away layers, drag them into the trash icon at the bottom of the Layers panel. You can also right-click (Ctrl-click) a layer's name and choose Delete Layer to throw it away or choose Layer > Delete > Layer. If you are in a hurry, you don't have to throw away layers one at a time. Just Command-click (Ctrl-click) on multiple layers, and then delete the layers using one of the previously mentioned methods.

Delete layer

Adjustment Layers

While clicking through your Layers menu, you likely noticed Adjustment Layers (like Levels or Hue/Saturation). These important layers are for image enhancement and color correction. They offer a nondestructive way to fix image problems. These special layers can contain one of 15 image manipulations. Unlike normal image adjustments, these can be enabled or disabled as well as modified with no loss in image quality. For now, be patient—you'll tackle these in depth in Chapter 10, "Color Correction and Enhancement."

Fill Layers

Photoshop allows you to create specialty Fill Layers, which let you quickly create graphical content for your designs. Choose Layer > New Fill Layer, and then choose Solid Color, Gradient, or Pattern (alternatively, click the black and white circle icon on the bottom of the Layers panel). Create a new document (sized 1024 × 768) and try out these new layers:

VIDEO 51:
Using Random Fills

- **Solid Color.** Choose Layer > New Fill Layer > Solid Color. Pick from any color using the Color Picker or Color Libraries. To edit the color layer, just double-click its thumbnail in the Layers panel.

- **Gradient.** Choose Layer > New Fill Layer > Gradient. A *gradient* is a gradual blend between two or more colors. You can use gradients as backgrounds or blend them over an image to perform the same function as a camera filter. Photoshop supports five types of gradients: Linear, Radial, Angle, Reflected, and Diamond. You can double-click the gradient in the Gradient Fill window to launch the Gradient Editor. Within the editor you can modify the gradient or click the submenu to load addition gradient presets. For more on gradients, be sure to read Chapter 6, "Painting and Drawing Tools."

- **Pattern.** Choose Layer > New Fill Layer > Pattern. Photoshop comes with a variety of built-in seamless patterns, which you can access from the Pattern Fill window. To choose a different pattern, click the drop-down menu to see the active patterns. To load even more patterns, click the triangular submenu on the right edge of the drop-down panel.

Working with Multiple Layers

As Photoshop has continued to evolve, so has its ability to offer powerful layer management. When creating complex designs, such as website mock-ups or print advertisements, it is important to maintain control over your design. This includes naming all your layers, as well as creating relationships or linking between them. Depending on which version of Photoshop you are using, you may find slight differences in layer behavior.

To get some practice, open Ch08_Layer_Organization.psd from the Chapter 8 folder. This file contains several color-coded layers that you will manipulate (the color coding identifies layers that will interact with each other). You might want to change the color of layers in your own documents to better organize them. To change the label color of a layer, right-click it and choose the new color. You can also choose from a list of default colors to label the layer.

Selecting Multiple Layers

One of the first skills to learn is how to select multiple layers. In the Ch08_Layer_Organization.psd file, select the Right Foot and Left Foot layers (which are color-coded red). Hold down the Shift key and click to select multiple contiguous layers or hold down the Command (Ctrl) key to select noncontiguous layers.

Linking Layers

Link layers

Linking layers creates a family relationship. When one of the family moves, the others move along with it (the same goes for scale and rotation). You link two layers together to create a relationship of particular elements that need to react to one another. For example, if you had a logo and text that you wanted to scale at the same time, you'd link them together.

1. Link the Right Foot to its companion Left Foot. You can click multiple layers to select them using the techniques mentioned in the preceding section.

2. With both layers selected, they are temporarily linked; simply use the Move tool to reposition both layers.

3. To make the connection persist when you deselect the layers, click the link (chain) icon at the bottom of the Layers panel.

Aligning Layers

A design can look sloppy if the designer relies solely on his or her eyes for a precise layout. Alignment is the process of positioning multiple objects on a straight line. This line is usually determined by one of the edges of the selected objects. This is useful to create a professional-looking design where the objects appear precise and organized. Align the two layers you are working with.

1. Make sure the Right Foot and Left Foot layers are selected or linked.

2. Press V to activate the Move tool.

3. In the Options bar you will see the alignment options. Hover your pointer over each to become familiar with their names.

4. Select the object that you want to use as a reference point for the alignment. In this case let's use Left Foot.

5. Click the Align bottom edges button. Notice that the feet shapes are aligned along their bottom edge.

Distributing Layers

Distribution places an identical amount of space between multiple objects. This can be an important step in creating a professional-looking design. Distribution is similar to alignment in how it is accessed. However, the intent is slightly different. You will need three or more objects to distribute them. Let's distribute a few layers.

1. Turn off the visibility icons for all layers except *Background*, Spring, Summer, Fall, and Winter. Click the eye icon to make a layer invisible.

2. Select the Spring, Summer, Fall, and Winter layers.

3. Choose the Move tool by pressing V.

VIDEO 52:
Layer Organization

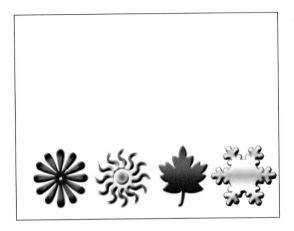

4. In the Options bar you will see distribution options (to the right of the alignment options). Roll over each to become familiar with their names.

5. Click the Distribute horizontal centers button to spread the images apart evenly.

6. Click the Align bottom edges button. Your image will now be evenly aligned and distributed.

Grouping Layers

Sometimes you'll want to take several layers and treat them as if they were one layer. This is useful for aligning a design composed of multiple images or just general cleanup for organizational purposes. The process of nondestructively joining layers is called grouping. A permanent technique is called *merging* (see "Merging Layers" later in this chapter), but that is pretty decisive. Let's group some layers together so they still retain their individual identity, yet behave as a group.

1. Select the Spring, Summer, Fall, and Winter layers using the Command-click (Ctrl-click) technique.

2. Press Command+G (Ctrl+G) or choose Layer > Group to place these layers into a new group (which looks like a folder). If you'd like to name the group, double-click the folder's name in the Layers panel.

3. You can now move these elements together. For example, select both the *Background* and Group 1, and then use the horizontal center and vertical center alignment commands to center these images on the page.

TIP

Multiple Locks

If you've selected multiple layers, clicking a lock button will apply that state to all of the selected layers.

Locking Layers

Sometimes you need to protect yourself from your own worst enemy (you). Photoshop gives you the option of locking properties of a layer to prevent accidental modification. Just click the icons next to the word Lock in the Layers panel. You can lock three separate properties (or a combination of the three):

- **Lock transparent pixels.** The grid icon locks all transparent areas of an image, but you can still modify any data that was on the layer prior to locking.

- **Lock image pixels.** The paintbrush icon locks all image pixels in the layer.

- **Lock position.** The arrow icon prevents you from accidentally moving a layer out of alignment or changing its position.

- **Lock all.** The padlock icon locks all three properties in one click.

Let's try locking a layer.

1. Turn off the visibility icons for all layers except *Background* and Key.

2. Select the Key layer.

3. In the upper-left corner of the Layers panel, click the Lock transparent pixels and Lock position icons.

4. Press B to select the Brush tool.

5. Click the foreground swatch and load a color of your choice.

6. Paint on the Key layer. Notice that the paint stays "inside the lines."

7. Choose the Move tool (V) and try to move the layer. (A dialog box should pop up indicating that Photoshop "Could not complete your request because the layer is locked.")

Clipping Mask

Sometimes you'll want to place the contents of one layer inside those of another. Designers often use this technique to fill text with a pattern or to constrain a photo to fit inside a shape. The concept is called a Clipping Mask (earlier versions of Photoshop called it Group with Previous), and it's fairly easy and flexible. All you need to do is place the content layer above the container layer (the one you want to "fill") and choose Layer > Create Clipping Mask.

1. Turn off the visibility icons for all layers except *Background*, Ribbon, and Texture.

2. Select the Texture layer.

3. Choose Layer > Create Clipping Mask or press Command+ Option+G (Ctrl+Alt+G). In the Layers panel, you'll see that the layer indents and fills the opaque areas in the Ribbon layer below. Notice that the layer style applied to the layer is still visible.

4. Choose Layer > Release Clipping Mask or press Command+Option+G (Ctrl+Alt+G) to toggle the mask on and off.

TIP

Quick Clip

You can create a clipping group quickly by Option-clicking (Alt-clicking) between two layers in the Layers panel.

Filtering the View of Layers

As you build a complex layered graphic, the Layers panel can get pretty cluttered. Photoshop CS6 introduces the ability to filter which layers appear in the list based on user-specified criteria. To change which type of filter is used, click the Filter Type menu. These criteria make it easier to find a specific layer or layer type based on the following filter types:

- **Kind.** You can choose to see one or more category of layers by clicking on the associated icon type.

- **Name.** You can enter text into the field to search by a layer's name.

- **Effect.** Once the Effect filter is chosen, a second pop-up menu lets you choose a specific type of layer effect.

- **Mode.** This method lets you choose from any one of Photoshop's blending modes.

NOTE

Filtering Your View

When you filter the visibility of layers, it only impacts what appears in the Layers panel list. The visibility of a layer in the canvas is determined by the layer visibility switch (eye icon) next to each layer's name.

- **Attribute.** Filtering by attribute type lets you find very specific types of layers. For example, you can choose to look for Empty layers to discard them or to find all locked layers at once.

- **Color.** If you've used colored labels to organize your layers, this filter will show you a specific color, which makes it easier to find layers you've marked for review.

Merging Layers

Sometimes you'll want to permanently merge layers together to commit to a design. This can be useful to reduce file size or to improve compatibility when importing a layered Photoshop document (PSD) file into another application (such as Apple Final Cut Pro, Adobe Premiere Pro, or Adobe After Effects). This process is destructive (in that it permanently joins the layers, which limits future changes).

To merge layers, follow these steps.

1. Select two or more layers by Command-clicking (Ctrl-clicking) on their names in the Layers panel. For practice, select the Texture and Ribbon layers.

2. Choose Layer > Merge Layers or press Command+E (Ctrl+E).

Flattening an Image

If you want to merge all your visible layers and discard all the layers with visibility disabled, choose Layer > Flatten Image. However, flattening an image is a permanent change. You work hard for those layers—*keep them!* Here are some alternatives to flattening that will preserve future flexibility:

- Save a copy of your image in a flattened format. By choosing File > Save As (with the As a Copy check box selected) or File > Save for Web, you can save another version of your image.

- If you need a flattened copy to paste into another document (or within your current document), use the Copy Merged command. Select an active, visible layer, and then choose Select > All. You can copy all visible items to your clipboard as a single layer by then choosing Edit > Copy Merged or by pressing Shift+Command+C (Shift+Ctrl+C).

NOTE

One Type of Filter at a Time

You can only use one category of filters at a time. When you switch categories, the filtering of the list will switch to unfiltered.

NOTE

Not a Permanent Filter

The filter state that you've applied to a layer is not saved with the document when you close it. When you open the document again, the filtered view is reset.

NOTE

Flattening Images

Remember that flattening is permanent. Be 100 percent positive before you discard your layers permanently. If you need a flattened image, choose to save a flattened copy (File > Save As and select the As a Copy check box). You can also group multiple layers into a Smart Object by selecting the layers and then choosing Layer > Smart Object > Convert to Smart Object. You can always edit the Smart Object and extract the layered file.

VIDEO 53:
Create a Panorama

Creating a Panorama

By using layers, you can take several photos from one location and merge them together to create a large panoramic photo. Many people take an assortment of photos of a subject while holding the camera, but it's best to use a tripod. It's important to ensure that you have some overlap between each frame; that is to say, the adjacent photos share some common subject matter—about 25 percent overlap is usually enough.

Let's try piecing together some photos using the Automation command called Photomerge.

1. Choose File > Automate > Photomerge. Photomerge is a specialized "mini-application" within Photoshop that assists in combining multiple images into a single photo.

2. Click the Browse button and navigate to the Chapter 8 folder.

TIP

Professional Panoramic Photography

Pros know that it's best to use a tripod and slightly move the camera to create overlap. There are even specialized tripod heads that you can purchase from companies like Kaidan (www.kaidan.com), Manfrotto (www.manfrotto.com), and Really Right Stuff (www.reallyrightstuff.com) that make leveling and rotation more precise.

TIP

Want to Know More About Panos?

Be sure to check out a website I contribute to called Triple Exposure (www.3exposure.com). It covers panoramic, time-lapse, and HDR photography.

3. Select the folder Ch08_Pano, and then select all the files within the folder (hold down the Shift key to select a range of images). Once selected, click Open.

4. Several Layout options are available that attempt to fix problems (such as distortion) caused by panoramic photography. A good place to start is Auto, which attempts to align the images but will bend them as needed.

5. Select the check boxes next to Blend Images Together and Vignette Removal. These two options attempt to blend the edges of the photos together and can hide subtle differences in exposure.

Photoshop attempts to straighten the image. Although this photo was shot with a tripod, the wall was not level. Photoshop attempts to compensate and corrects the image using the horizon automatically.

6. Click OK to build the panoramic image. Photoshop attempts to assemble the panorama based on your choices in the dialog box. Because layers are preserved, however, you can still tweak the position of individual layers.

VIDEO 54:
Repairing Panoramic Images with the Adaptive Wide Angle Command

7. Although unlikely, you can nudge any layers with the Move tool if your alignment is off. You may need to adjust the Layer Masks.

8. The Layer Masks help to blend the photos together. They can be modified as needed using the techniques you learned in the previous chapter.

9. Choose Layer > Flatten Image.

10. Crop the image to a clean rectangular shape using the Crop tool (C). You may need to fill in some additional areas of the image if there are holes in the panorama. If so, you could use the Clone Stamp and Content-Aware Fill options, which you'll learn about in Chapter 11, "Repairing and Improving Photos."

Be sure to check out the file Ch08_Pano_Complete.psd to see how the image was further enhanced with adjustment layers.

Auto-Aligning Layers

VIDEO 55:
Auto-Align Command

The technology that powers the Photomerge command can also be harnessed to stitch together nonpanoramic shots or scans that take multiple images to capture a larger print. The Auto-Align Layers command is a useful way to stitch together multiple shots or scans of a large object or a group photo. The command is very easy to use and produces impressive results.

1. Choose File > Scripts > Load Files into Stack to combine two or more files into one document.

2. In the Load Layers dialog box, click the Browse button to navigate to the files you need.

3. Open the folder Ch08_Cyborg, select both images inside, and click Open.

4. In the Load Layers dialog box, select the check box next to Attempt to Automatically Align Source Images.

5. Click OK. Photoshop opens both images and aligns them, and does a good job (especially since the top layer was taken at such an angle). This alignment can be refined even further.

6. Make sure both layers are selected in the Layers panel.

7. Choose Edit > Auto-Align Layers.

8. Select the Auto option to enable both Vignette Removal and Geometric Distortion options for Lens Correction.

9. Click OK. Photoshop removes some of the distortion in the glass case, giving it a more rectangular shape.

The layers can be seamlessly blended together using the Auto-Blend Layers command. This applies Layer Masks as needed to each layer to mask out exposure issues and create a seamless composite.

10. Choose Edit > Auto-Blend Layers, specify the Panorama method, and click OK (be sure the Seamless Tones and Colors check box is also selected).

11. Crop the image as needed, adjust Levels, and flatten.

LAYER COMPS

Photoshop CS introduced Layer Comps, which allows Photoshop to memorize combinations of layer visibility, opacity, and position. This can be useful for storing multiple designs inside one document. When experimenting with layouts, you'll often use several options in one document. You might set the headline in three different typefaces and try the main photo in two different positions. Using Layer Comps allows you to set up different options within one document (instead of having to save and keep track of several).

VIDEO 56:
Layer Comps

1. Open the file Cho8_Layer_Comps.psd. If you get any font warnings, dismiss them.

2. Make sure the Layer Comps window is visible. If not, choose Windows > Layer Comps.

3. Click the forward triangle to Apply Next Selected Layer Comp. Click through and examine the different layer comps.

4. For Layer Comp 1, move the words around onscreen to a new position.

5. Click the Update layer comp icon at the bottom of the Layer Comps panel (it looks like two arrows in a circle).

6. Switch to Layer Comp 2. On the layer called This is, click the visibility icon next to the Layer Style Outer Glow. A black glow should be added.

7. Click the Create new layer comp icon (it looks like a pad of paper) on the bottom edge of the Layer Comps window. Name it Comp 2 Alternate.

8. Save a copy of each layer comp to send to a client. Choose File > Scripts > Layer Comps to PDF. Photoshop creates a new PDF with all four layer comps in one document. This is a convenient way to email a project to a client for review.

Layer Comps are a bit confusing at first, but as you master what layers can do, you'll turn to Layer Comps for flexibility. Be sure to check out the Adobe Help Center for more on Layer Comps.

Using Blending Modes

Blending modes are both a mystery and a source of great design power. Each blending mode controls how one layer's pixels are affected by those in another layer (or by a tool from the Tools panel). Most users give up on blending modes because the technical definitions of each mode get very tricky. The secret is to not worry too much about the technical issues and to learn how to experiment. Although you'll explore the technology and the creativity behind blending modes in this chapter, there are only a few basics that you must know to make blending modes part of your design toolbox.

About Blending Modes

There are 27 different blending options available from the Layers panel and a few additional blending options that work with specific tools. How do they work? The simple answer is, it depends. Your response is likely, depends on what? Simply put, the effect achieved by blending two layers varies with the contents of those two layers. A blending mode compares the content of two layers and enacts changes based on the content of both layers. You'll find blending modes in many of the tools, and they can be combined with every filter.

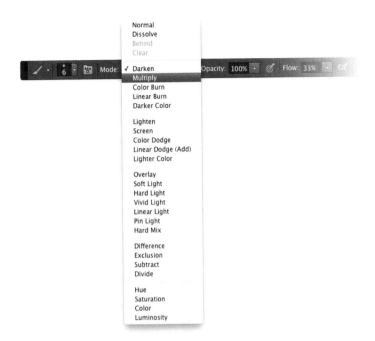

The blending mode specified in the Options bar controls how pixels are affected by a painting or editing tool. Additionally, you can set the blending mode of a layer to control how it interacts with those below it. A clear understanding of the following terms will better help you understand blending modes:

- **Base color.** The original color in the image

- **Blend color.** The color being applied with the painting or editing tool (or the color in the top layer)

- **Result color.** The color resulting from the blend

List of Blending Modes

With 27 blending modes to choose from, keeping them straight can be tough. Fortunately, the modes are grouped together by similar function. Here are clear and simple definitions as well as a sample of how each blending mode behaves:

The colored swirl will be blended with the underlying photo to illustrate each mode. Open the file Cho9_Blended_Overlay.psd from the Chapter 9 folder to experiment with blending modes.

Normal.
The default mode performs no additional change to how layer contents interact.

Dissolve.
Creates a random replacement of the pixels with the base or blend color.

Darken.
Pixels lighter than blend are replaced; darker ones are not.

Multiply.
Is similar to drawing strokes on the image with magic markers.

Color Burn.
Evaluates each channel; darkens base by increasing contrast.

Linear Burn.
Evaluates each channel; darkens base by decreasing brightness.

Darker Color.
Uses the lowest value from both layers to create resulting color.

Lighten.
Evaluates each channel; it then uses base or blend color (whichever is lighter).

Screen.
Use a lighter color. It is useful for "knocking" black out of a layer.

Color Dodge.
Evaluates color information and brightens base by decreasing contrast.

Linear Dodge (Add). *Evaluates color information and brightens base by increasing brightness.*

Lighter Color.
Uses highest value from both layers to create resulting color.

Overlay.
Overlays existing pixels while preserving highlights and shadows of base.

Soft Light.
Effect is similar to shining a diffused spotlight on the image.

Hard Light.
Effect is similar to shining a harsh spotlight on the image.

Vivid Light.
Burns or dodges by increasing or decreasing the contrast.

Linear Light.
Burns or dodges by decreasing or increasing the brightness.

Pin Light.
Is useful for adding special effects to an image.

Hard Mix.
Enhances the contrast of the underlying layers.

Difference.
Evaluates each channel and subtracts or inverts depending on brightness.

Exclusion.
Is similar to the Difference mode but lower in contrast.

Subtract.
Looks at the color in each channel and subtracts the blend from the base.

Divide.
Looks at the color in each channel and divides the blend from the base.

Hue.
Uses luminance and saturation of the base and the hue of the blend.

Saturation.
Creates color with luminance and hue of base and saturation of blend.

Color.
Preserves gray levels. It's very useful for coloring and tinting.

Luminosity.
Is the inverse effect from the Color mode.

Blending Modes in Practice

So far you've looked at blending modes in a strictly technical sense. Although it's useful to have a clear understanding of the technology, don't lose sight of the design possibilities. Blending modes are a great way to mix layers together. Let's take a look at a stylized photo that uses blending modes to enhance its look.

1. Open the file Ch09_Butterfly.psd from the Chapter 9 folder. This five-layer document uses blending modes to create a colorful image.

2. Turn on the visibility of the Gradient Fill layer. Set its blending mode to Multiply, and adjust its opacity to 60% to create a vignette effect.

3. Turn on the visibility of the Pattern Fill layer. Set its blending mode to Divide, and adjust its opacity to 25% to create a distressed texture.

4. Turn on the visibility of the Vibrance adjustment layer. This adjustment selectively boosts the saturation in the image. Set it to Overlay mode to dramatically increase the saturation of the image.

5. Turn on the visibility of the Gradient Map adjustment layer. This adjustment tints the image. Set it to Hue mode to shift the colors in a gentle way.

Feel free to experiment with different combinations of blending modes and Opacity settings. This sample image provides just a quick glimpse into the power and flexibility of blending modes.

Blending Modes in Action

Now that you have a little practice with blending modes, it's time to explore their creative and production side in greater depth. Blending modes are part of a professional's workflow. The next three sections showcase a few different ways to better integrate blending modes for professional results.

VIDEO 57:
Blending Modes
in Action

DESIGN "RULES" FOR BLENDING MODES

RULE #1—DON'T TRY TO MEMORIZE HOW EACH BLENDING MODE WORKS. The good news is that they are grouped by similar traits. As you make your way through the list, you will notice a gradual progression through styles. The first group darkens your underlying image, whereas the second lightens it. The third set adds contrast, and the last two generate dramatic results by comparing or mapping values. Depending on your sources, some blending modes will generate little or no results. Sound confusing? Keep reading.

RULE #2—EXPERIMENT. The best way to use blending modes is to just try them out. Clicking through a long menu is boring. A much better alternative is to select the Move tool and then use the Shift++ keyboard shortcut.

RULE #3—EXPLOIT THEM. Do you need to tint an image? Place a solid or gradient on top of the image and change to Hue or Color mode. Need to drop out white in a layer? Just set it to Multiply mode. Blending modes are available for every filter (choose Fade Filter from the Edit menu) and all the Brush tools.

VIDEO 58:
Adding Spice with
Blending Modes

Instant Spice

One way to improve a washed-out or flat image is through blending modes. By blending a blurred copy of an image on top of itself, you can quickly create a visual pop. Let's give it a try.

1. Open the file Ch09_Spice1.psd from the Chapter 9 folder.

2. Select the *Background* layer in the Layers panel.

3. Duplicate the *Background* layer by pressing Command+J (Ctrl+J).

4. Significantly blur the new layer by choosing Filter > Blur > Gaussian Blur. A value of 25 pixels should do the trick.

5. Select the Move tool by pressing V.

6. Cycle blending modes by pressing Shift+=. Look for modes (such as Multiply or Soft Light) that increase saturation and add visual "pop" to the image. Adjust the layer's opacity to deemphasize the effect if needed.

7. If needed, adjust the opacity of the layer as desired. You can quickly change opacity by typing in the first number of an Opacity setting, such as 4 for 40% opacity. You can type 25 to quickly switch to 25% opacity, for example, if a more specific adjustment is required.

Original

Gaussian Blur | 25 Pixels

Soft Light | 80% Opacity

Multiply | 40% Opacity

Fixing a Shadowed Image

If an image is completely thrown into the shadows, you can turn to blending modes to shed a little light. In fact, this technique is often used by law enforcement to enhance security photos or footage.

1. Open the file Ch09_Shadow1.tif from the Chapter 9 folder.

2. Duplicate the *Background* layer by pressing Command+J (Ctrl+J).

3. Set the top layer to Screen mode. You can choose it from the menu in the Layers panel or press Shift+Option+S (Shift+Alt+S). The image should appear significantly lighter.

4. You can further lighten the image by placing another duplicate copy on top. Press Command+J (Ctrl+J) as many times as needed. Each will lighten the image further.

Applying a Rubber Stamp

You can also use blending modes to make one image appear as if it were applied to another. If you add the Free Transform command, you can make that stamp match the perspective of the photo. Let's give it a try.

VIDEO 59:
Filters and Blending Modes

1. Open the files Ch09_Boxes.tif and Ch09_Logo.psd from the Chapter 9 folder.

2. Select the Logo.psd file so it is active.

3. Choose Select > All and then Edit Copy to add it to your clipboard.

4. Switch back to the Boxes file and choose Edit > Paste.

5. Press Command+T (Ctrl+T) to invoke the Free Transform command.

   To use additional transformations, right-click.

VIDEO 60:
Corner Pinning an Image

6. Choose Distort: This allows you to corner pin the logo and match its angle to that of the box. Adjust the position so the corners of the image match up to the edge of the box.

7. You now need to scale the logo smaller. Right-click (Ctrl-click) and choose Scale. Shrink the logo so it fits better on the side of the box.

8. Set the Logo layer to the Multiply blending mode and lower its opacity to 85% to make the Logo layer appear to be stamped on the crate.

Table 9.1 provides the keyboard shortcuts to make it easier for you to use blending modes.

Table 9.1 Blending Shortcuts

Result	Mac OS	Windows
Normal	Shift+Option+N	Shift+Alt+N
Dissolve	Shift+Option+I	Shift+Alt+I
Darken	Shift+Option+K	Shift+Alt+K
Multiply	Shift+Option+M	Shift+Alt+M
Color Burn	Shift+Option+B	Shift+Alt+B
Linear Burn	Shift+Option+A	Shift+Alt+A
Lighten	Shift+Option+G	Shift+Alt+G
Screen	Shift+Option+S	Shift+Alt+S
Color Dodge	Shift+Option+D	Shift+Alt+D
Linear Dodge	Shift+Option+W	Shift+Alt+W
Overlay	Shift+Option+O	Shift+Alt+O
Soft Light	Shift+Option+F	Shift+Alt+F
Hard Light	Shift+Option+H	Shift+Alt+H
Vivid Light	Shift+Option+V	Shift + Alt+V
Linear Light	Shift+Option+J	Shift + Alt+J
Pin Light	Shift+Option+Z	Shift + Alt+Z
Hard Mix	Shift+Option+L	Shift + Alt+L
Difference	Shift+Option+E	Shift + Alt+E
Exclusion	Shift+Option+X	Shift + Alt+X
Hue	Shift+Option+U	Shift+Alt+U
Saturation	Shift+Option+T	Shift+Alt+T
Color	Shift+Option+C	Shift+Alt+C
Luminosity	Shift+Option+Y	Shift+Alt+Y

Color Correction and Enhancement 10

The primary purpose of Photoshop is to act as a digital darkroom where images can be corrected, enhanced, and refined. How do you know an image needs touch-up? You can pretty much assume every image can look a little (or even a lot) better than how the camera captured it. Whether it's adjusting the exposure, increasing contrast, or boosting saturation, Photoshop is the place to improve an image.

Learning how to spot problems and then choosing the right correction technique is an essential part of mastering Photoshop.

The left image is as shot by the camera. The right image has been refined using the Camera Raw plugin. You can open the Ch10_Major_Fix.NEF file to experiment.

Several different tools are available, some more useful than others. By analyzing the most important tools and determining in which situations they might help you, you can achieve a more thorough understanding of color correction.

Approach to Color Correction

New users often have a difficult time when color correcting or enhancing images. They generally lose sight of the goal: making the image look better while still being believable. Many users go "too far" in their quest to fix images. If the image starts to look fake or too altered, it will be distracting. Although getting it "right" requires some practice, here's some general advice to get you started:

- **Identify what's wrong.** Before you can fix a picture, be sure you have decided on what's wrong. Is it too dark? Is the sky washed out? Has the picture faded over time? Make a list and prioritize the issues you find in each image. It's easiest to fix one problem at a time, and if you identify those problems, you'll know when to stop twiddling with the image.

- **Work with a copy of the image.** Before you start to color correct an image, you should duplicate it. This way you can return to an original version if you make a mistake or go too far in your image touch-up. After opening your file, choose File > Save As and name the duplicate version that will be corrected. Color correction can be a *destructive* process, meaning that you cannot revert to the original state at a later time. By preserving an original version of the image or employing adjustment layers, you make *nondestructive* editing possible. Some users also choose to duplicate the *Background* layer at the bottom of the layer stack.

- **Edit with adjustment layers.** Adjustment layers allow you to apply most of the image correction commands as nondestructive effects. They are added as a layer above the actual image; the adjustment layer can be blended, masked, or deleted at any time. Additionally, if you select the adjustment layer, you can modify its properties in the Adjustments panel. The same modifications are available in both the Adjustments menu and Adjustments panel. You should work with an adjustment layer whenever possible because its flexibility will be important for future revisions.

- **Get a fresh opinion.** It's not a bad idea to step back and examine your work. Open the backup copy of the original image and compare it to the image you've been working on. This before-and-after comparison can be very useful. If you have a fresh set of eyes nearby, ask that person for his or her opinion.

- **Use Smart Filters.** This will open up most of the filters and several of the image adjustments including the Shadows/ Highlights command and Variations. Just choose Filter > Convert for Smart Filters.

Primary Image Adjustments

Photoshop offers several image adjustments, but only a few are used most often. Commands such as Levels and Curves are used by professionals to achieve outstanding results. These professional imaging techniques may take a little time to get comfortable with, but the power they offer is worth your investment.

Levels

The Levels command corrects tonal ranges and color balance issues. With this command you can fix poor exposure. Additionally, you can perform color correction by manually identifying a white point and black point in the image. Nearly every image can benefit from making a Levels adjustment.

To understand Levels, you must be able to read a histogram. This graph works as a visual guide for adjusting the image. The Levels adjustment has its own histogram that is visible when working in the Adjustments panel. You may also want to call up the Histogram panel (Window > Histogram) and leave it open while color correcting to help you spot issues in color and contrast. You can also expand the Histogram panel by clicking the submenu and choosing All Channels View. Let's give the command a try.

NOTE

Levels Beats Brightness/Contrast

A Brightness/Contrast command does exist, but the Levels adjustment lets you perform several improvements with one command. Using a single image process cuts down on the loss of quality introduced from multiple image-processing steps.

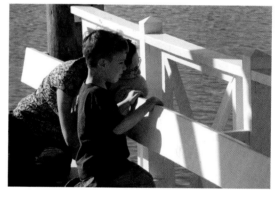

1. Close any open files, and then open the file Ch10_Levels.tif from the Chapter 10 folder.

2. Add a Levels adjustment layer by clicking the Levels icon in the Adjustments panel. Levels is also available from the Adjustments menu (Image > Adjustments), but the adjustment layer is more flexible for future modifications.

3. This photo was shot under mixed light, but you can reset the black and white points of the image to fix the exposure. In the Adjustments panel, move the white Input Levels slider to the left. This affects the image's white point and allows you to reassign where white should begin in the image.

4. Move the black Input Levels slider slowly to the right. The more you move the black slider to the right, the more contrast is introduced into the image.

5. The true power lies in the middle (gray) Input Levels slider. By moving this slider, you can modify the gamma setting. Effectively, you can use the middle Input Levels slider to change the intensity of the midtones. This adjustment can be made without making dramatic changes to the highlights and shadows, and lets you better expose an image. Move the slider to the left to add light; move the slider to the right to subtract light.

6. In the future if you need to edit the adjustment, simply select the adjustment layer in the Layers panel and manipulate the controls in the Adjustments panel.

TIP

Rinse and Repeat

If you have several images from the same camera or shoot, they may need the same Levels adjustment. The Save button allows you to save a Levels adjustment (to the folder that contains the image is a good place). You can then click the Load button to apply that adjustment to another image.

VIDEO 61:
Levels Command

Auto-Levels

When working with the Levels adjustment layer, you may have noticed the Auto button. This command button triggers an analysis of the histogram data by Photoshop that is then used to modify the individual controls of the Levels adjustment. In many cases this results in an image that is properly adjusted for color balance and exposure issues. In others it will get you closer to a corrected image.

1. Close any open files, and then Open the file Ch10_Auto_Levels1.tif from the Chapter 10 folder.

2. Add a Levels adjustment layer by clicking the Levels icon in the Adjustments panel.

3. Click the Auto button to perform an automated adjustment for the image. The image's levels and color are adjusted.

4. To refine how the automatic adjustment works, hold down the Option (Alt) key and click the Auto button again. A new dialog box opens.

5. Select Enhance Per Channel Contrast and Snap Neutral Midtones to create a very natural balance of colors for the image.

6. Click OK to close the dialog box.

7. Adjust the middle slider (gray) to refine the Levels adjustment to taste.

VIDEO 62:
Correcting Color Cast
with Levels

VIDEO 63:
Adjusting Levels
per Channel

Color cast

In the first Levels example you made a Levels adjustment to all the channels evenly. In the Auto-Levels example, you let Photoshop adjust the levels and remove color cast using an automated algorithm. The Levels command can be further isolated to a specific channel by clicking the drop-down list in the center of the Levels dialog box. This allows you to tackle color cast issues, such as spill from a background, a bad white balance, or a photo shot under mixed or colored lighting.

PHOTO BY JAMES BALL

1. Close any open files, and then open the file Ch10_Levels_Color_Balance.tif from the Chapter 10 folder. Notice how the image has a greenish tint.

2. Add a Levels adjustment layer using the Adjustments panel. You will use the Levels command to fix color and exposure issues.

3. Select the Set White Point (white eyedropper) in the Levels dialog box. Click an area that should be pure white. For this image, click a bright area in the white pillar. If you click an area that is not bright enough, the whites in the image will overexpose. (You can click the Reset button—it looks like a circular arrow—at the bottom of the Adjustments panel to reset the Levels command, if needed.) After you click, you'll see that some of the color spill has been removed.

4. Select the Set Black Point (black eyedropper) in the Levels dialog box. Click an area that should be pure black. Choose an area such as a jacket or a dark shadow. This will adjust the color balance and the exposure.

5. The image's color balance should now be better. Adjust the middle Input Levels slider to brighten the image.

Curves

VIDEO 64:
Working with Curves

Most users will either use Curves a lot or they won't use it at all. The Curves interface is more complex than Levels, which scares away many users. Although Levels gives you three control points (highlights, midtones, and shadows), the Curves adjustment allows for up to 16 control points. This can significantly open up more options when adjusting color and exposure.

Let's try the Curves command on a practice image.

1. Close any open files, and then open the file Ch10_ Curves_Practice.tif from the Chapter 10 folder.

2. Add a Curves adjustment layer by clicking the Curves button in the Adjustments panel. When you first open the Curves interface, there are two points (one for white and one for black).

3. Add a single control point in the middle of the line (click at an Input Value of 50%).

4. Pull this new control point down to lighten the image (toward the lighter area on the Y axis). You can pull the point up to darken the image. Notice that the Input and Output values update as you drag.

5. The adjustment is applied gradually throughout the entire image. Multiple points can be employed for contrast adjustments based on tonal range.

The primary advantage of Curves is that you have precise control over which points get mapped (whereas in Levels you do not). Another benefit is that Curves adjustments can use several points

NOTE

RGB Reverse

You're about to work with an RGB image; the direction of darks and lights will be reversed from the Grayscale image.

connected by a curved line (as opposed to Levels, which uses only three control points) to make adjustments. So, color correction can be applied in a more gradual manner (without the hard clipping that can be associated with Levels).

1. Close any open files, and then open the image Ch10_Curves.tif from the Chapter 10 folder.

2. Add a Curves adjustment layer by clicking the Curves icon in the Adjustments panel. The curve has only two points on it—one representing the black point; the other, the white point.

3. It's now time to add more control points to refine the curve. To do this, you'll use a Curves preset. Click the menu to select a Curves preset in the Adjustments panel. Choose the Strong Contrast (RGB) preset. Notice that the image now has more contrast in the shadows and highlights, and more visual "pop."

4. Experiment by adjusting the five control points. Try to further emphasize the shadows in the image. Continue to experiment by moving the control points (you can use the up and down arrow keys for precise control).

TIP

Easy Curves

When the Curves Editor is open, you can easily add control points. Click the icon that looks like a pointing finger, and then just click and drag in the image to modify the curve. The control points will appear in the editor.

NOTE

Pay Attention to Your Axes

When working with a grayscale or CMYK file, the axes go from light to dark. When working with RGB images, the scales are reversed. This means that pulling a control point up or down may have a different effect.

Hue/Saturation

The Hue/Saturation command lets you adjust the hue, saturation, and lightness of color components in an image. Additionally, you can simultaneously adjust all the colors in an image. This command can work in two ways:

- To adjust colors in an image that appears slightly out of phase or skewed toward a color, such as an image that appears to have a blue overcast

- To create stylistic changes by dramatically changing colors in an object, such as trying out different combinations of colors in a logo

When combined with a selection command (such as Color Range), the Hue/Saturation command can be used to selectively enhance colors in an image.

Let's give the command a try.

1. Close any open files, and then open the file Ch10_Hue_Saturation.tif from the Chapter 10 folder. You'll subtly tweak the color in the motorcycle.

2. Choose Select > Color Range and click the motorcycle body to make an initial selection. Hold down the Shift key to add to the selection. Adjust the Fuzziness slider to soften the selection. Use the Localized Color Clusters to further constrain the selection. Click OK when you have a suitable selection.

3. Click the Hue/Saturation button in the Adjustments panel to add an adjustment layer.

TIP

The Five Most Useful Image Adjustments

- Levels
- Curves
- Black & White
- Vibrance
- Shadow/Highlights

4. The two color bars at the bottom of the dialog box represent the colors in the color wheel. The upper bar shows the initial color; the lower bar shows the new color. Drag the Hue slider to the left until maroon appears under red.

5. Additionally, you can adjust Saturation (which is the intensity of the color) and adjust Lightness (which adds white or black to the image). Increase Saturation to **+15** and decrease Lightness to **−20**.

NOTE

A Better Saturation

If you need a more robust saturation control, be sure to try out the Vibrance adjustment. It offers its own saturation control that uses a different method to control saturation. It tends to produce better changes, but doesn't offer Hue or Lightness controls.

Recolor

A Hue/Saturation adjustment can be a fast way to experiment with color options. You can use it to quickly change the fill colors of an object by making a global adjustment. This works well when you are experimenting with different color combinations. Let's try it out.

1. Close any open files, and then open the file Ch10_Logo_ Adjustments.psd from the Chapter 10 folder.

2. Select the layer thumbnail of the Hue/Saturation adjustment layer to access its controls in the Adjustments panel.

3. Adjust the Hue slider to try out different color combinations.

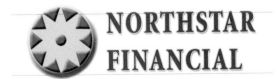

Tinting a photo

You can also use the Hue/Saturation command to tint an image. If you are working with a grayscale image, you need to convert it to an RGB image first.

VIDEO 65:
Tinting a Photo

1. Close any open files, and then open the file Ch10_Tint.tif from the Chapter 10 folder.

2. Add a Hue/Saturation adjustment layer.

3. Click the Colorize box to tint the image.

4. Adjust the Hue slider to try out different color combinations. Adjust Saturation and Lightness to refine the tint.

   The adjustment layer automatically has a Layer Mask attached, which allows you to mask the effect.

5. Click the Layer Mask icon for the Hue/Saturation adjustment layer.

6. Select your Brush tool and press D to load the default colors of black and white.

7. With a small black brush, paint the flowers so the original red shows through. If you make a mistake, you can press X to toggle back to white for touch-up.

VIDEO 66:
Vibrance

Vibrance

When working with photos, many choose to have very saturated and rich colors. The problem with too much saturation is that it can cause clipping (a flattening of the range of colors). To help with this, Photoshop offers the Vibrance command. Unlike Saturation, Vibrance only boosts those parts of a photo that are less saturated. It also respects skin tones, which means photos look more natural when pumping up the intensity of color.

Original image.

1. From the Chapter 10 folder, open the image Ch10_Vibrance1.tif.

2. You'll first add a Saturation adjustment layer for comparison. In the Adjustments panel, click Saturation icon to add a new adjustment layer.

3. Drag the Saturation slider to the right until the colors in the image start to clip.

4. Discard the Saturation adjustment layer by clicking the trash icon at the bottom of the Adjustments panel. Click Yes in the dialog box that appears.

5. In the Adjustments panel, click the Vibrance icon to add a new adjustment layer.

Hue/Saturation begins to posterize the reddish areas of the image.

6. Drag the Vibrance slider to the right to increase saturation without color clipping.

7. To add a little more saturation overall (in a gentler fashion than the Saturation adjustment layer), use the Saturation slider in the Vibrance adjustment layer.

A Vibrance adjustment increased saturation selectively.

Useful Image Adjustments

Although a Levels or Curves command can usually get the color-correction job done, there are often atypical problems that require particular commands. Let's explore some other commands that have special purposes and should generally be reserved for the unique problems they address. Let's take a look at the specialty commands.

Black & White

If you want to create a dramatic grayscale or duotone effect, the most effective way is to use a Black & White adjustment layer. Unlike a simple saturation adjustment, you maintain full control over how individual colors are converted. This allows you to emphasize or deemphasize specific colors and tonal ranges. Additionally, you can tint the grayscale by applying a color tone to the image (such as a sepia tone).

VIDEO 67:
Black and White Adjustments

1. Close any open files, and then open the file Ch10_Black White Conversion.tif from the Chapter 10 folder.

2. Click the Black & White icon in the Adjustments panel.

3. Photoshop performs a default grayscale conversion. You'll want to adjust the conversion using the color sliders. You can also apply an Auto conversion or use a saved custom mix.

You can adjust the color sliders to emphasize gray tones of specific colors in an image. Each image is unique, so you'll need to find the right balance. Drag a slider to the left to darken or to the right to lighten. Be sure to select the Preview check box so you can see the results of your changes.

TIP

Black & White Auto—A Good Start

Normally, I recommend avoiding the Auto buttons, but with the Black & White adjustment layer it works well. Auto sets a grayscale mix based on the image's color values. It attempts to maximize the distribution of gray values. The Auto mix often produces excellent results and can serve as the starting point for tweaking gray values using the color sliders.

TIP

Blended Black and White

Be sure to try out blending modes with your adjustment layers. The Black & White adjustments look great blended. Try Multiply or Overlay for this exercise.

VIDEO 68:
Creative Sepia Tones

4. With the Black & White command window open, click the icon in the Adjustments panel that looks like a pointing finger.

5. You can click on the image to sample a target. The mouse pointer changes to an eyedropper if you move it over the image. Just click and hold on an image area to target the right color slider for the strongest color at that location. You can then drag to shift the color slider for that color, thus making it lighter or darker.

6. To create a duotone effect, select the Tint option. To change the tint color, click its swatch and use the Color Picker to choose a new color that matches your needs.

Gradient Map

You can use the Gradient Map to dramatically or subtly stylize images. The effect works best when used as an adjustment layer. The command works by mapping the colors of a gradient to the image based on the luminance values of the source image. Let's give the technique a try.

1. Close any open files, and then open the image Ch10_Gradient_Map1.tif from the Chapter 10 folder.

2. Click the Gradient Map icon in the Adjustments panel.

3. In the Properties panel, click the gradient to open the Gradient Editor.

4. In the Gradient Editor, choose a loaded gradient or load a new set to taste. For more on gradients, see Chapter 6, "Painting and Drawing Tools." Click OK when you're satisfied.

5. To soften the effect, you can change the adjustment layer's blending mode. Setting it to Hue or Color creates a nice tint effect.

Photo Filter

Professional photographers often place glass filters in front of the camera lens. These can be used to "cool" or "warm" a picture, or to add special effects. Since Photoshop often tries to simulate or correct for steps not taken in the field, the addition of Photo Filters was a logical evolution for Photoshop.

Adobe added to the "real-time," color-correction options with the addition of 20 different adjustments. These layers simulate the traditional colored glass filters. Besides the built-in presets, you can also choose custom colors from the Photo Filter interface using the standard Color Picker.

There are three main groupings for color effects:

- **Warming Filter (85 and LBA) and Cooling Filter (80 and LBB).** These adjustment layers are meant to even out photos that were not properly white balanced. The Cooling Filter (80 or LBB) makes images bluer to simulate cooler ambient light. The Warming Filter (85 or LBA) makes images warmer to simulate hotter ambient light.

- **Warming Filter (81) and Cooling Filter (82).** These adjustment layers are similar to the previous filters but cast a more pronounced color. The Warming Filter (81) makes the photo more yellow, and the Cooling Filter (82) makes the photo bluer.

- **Individual Colors.** The Photo Filter also has 14 preset colors to choose from. These can be used for two primary purposes: to add a complementary color to a scene to remove color cast or for stylistic reasons.

VIDEO 69:
Stealing Sunsets

Let's try applying a Photo Filter adjustment layer.

1. Close any open files, and then open the file Ch10_Photo_Filter.tif from the Chapter 10 folder.

2. Click the Photo Filter icon in the Adjustments panel.

3. In the Filter area, choose Warming Filter (85) to adjust the temperature of the photo.

4. Deselect the Preserve Luminosity option to allow the image to darken.

5. Adjust the slider to taste.

   The sky and the image should be "warmer." You can adjust the Density slider to control the intensity of the effect.

Shadows/Highlights

Exposure problems often plague photos. Dark shadows may make a photo seem unusable, but Photoshop offers a powerful command for fixing these problems. The image command Shadows/Highlights is very flexible for solving problems. The command can help salvage images where the subject is silhouetted from strong backlight. You can also use the command to improve subjects who have been washed out by the camera's flash.

The Shadows/Highlights command does more than lighten or darken an image. It makes adjustments by analyzing neighboring pixels. However, when first opened, the tool is very basic. It is important to select the Show More Options check box, which adds significant control. Let's give the command a try.

1. Close any open files, and then open the file Ch10_Shadows_Highlight_1.tif from the Chapter 10 folder.

The Shadow/Highlights command is not available as an adjustment layer. You can still apply it in a nondestructive manner by first converting the photo to a Smart Object.

VIDEO 70:
Shadows/Highlights

2. Choose Layer > Smart Objects > Convert to Smart Object.

3. Choose Image > Adjustments > Shadows/Highlights. The image is brightened automatically because the command boosts the shadowed areas by default.

4. Select the Show More Options check box and be sure to select the Preview check box.

5. Adjust the Shadows and Highlights of the image:

   - **Amount.** This value determines how strong of an adjustment is made to the image.

   - **Tonal Width.** Small values affect a reduced region; larger values include the midtones. If pushed too high, halos appear around the edges of the image.

   - **Radius.** Is a tolerance setting that examines neighboring pixels to determine the affected area.

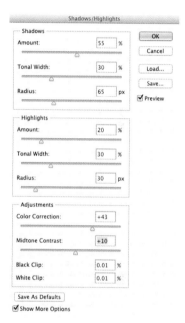

6. Modify the image adjustments to improve image quality:

   - **Color Correction.** This slider modifies the saturation of the adjusted areas. Essentially, it can counterbalance washed-out images.

   - **Brightness.** If you're working on a grayscale image, Color Correction is replaced by a Brightness control.

   - **Midtone Contrast.** This adjustment affects the contrast in the midtones of a photo. Positive values increase contrast, whereas negative values reduce contrast.

   - **Black Clip and White Clip.** This adjustment modifies the black point of shadows and lowers the white point of highlights. This can lower the intensity of the effect.

7. Click Save if you'd like to store the adjustment to use on another photo. When you're satisfied, click OK to apply the adjustment.

If you'd like extra practice, you'll find additional images in the Chapter 10 Extras folder.

Exposure

Starting with Photoshop CS2, support was added for 32-bit images. Generally referred to as high dynamic range (HDR), these images offer great flexibility in exposure. These images can better handle re-creating the wide range of exposures found in outdoor scenes or intense lighting conditions. The Exposure adjustment is usually used on images that exist in 32-bit space and is said to be a 32-bit floating point operation (often shortened to *float*).

Creating an HDR image is a combination of shooting techniques and a Photoshop command. It requires that the camera be secured firmly to a tripod and that you be careful when triggering or adjusting the camera to not move it (or allow anything to move in the shot either). Several photos at various exposures are taken of the same scene (a minimum of three; usually five to seven is adequate). The camera should have its auto-bracket and ISO features disabled. Each shot should be about two f-stops apart. The user then harnesses the Merge to HDR command (File > Automate > Merge to HDR) to create the 32-bit image. You'll create an HDR image later in the book, but for now let's jump ahead to an HDR image that's already built.

1. Close any open files, and then open the file Ch10_HDR1.tif. If you click in your menus, you'll notice that several features are grayed out. Most image adjustments do not work for a 32-bit image. This image was taken in a very low-light environment, but by combining multiple exposures together into the HDR image, I captured a much better photo.

2. Click the Exposure icon in the Adjustments panel. This command makes tonal adjustments by performing calculations in a linear color space (Gamma 1.0) rather than the current color space. This offers extreme flexibility for future changes.

3. Three properties can be modified:

VIDEO 71:
Merge to High Dynamic
Range Pro

- **Exposure.** Modifies the highlight end of the tonal range with little effect on the extreme shadows.

- **Offset.** Darkens the shadows and midtones with little effect on highlights.

- **Gamma.** Adjusts the gamma of the photo.

4. Additionally, three eyedroppers adjust the image's luminance values:

- **Set Black Point eyedropper.** Sets the Offset, which shifts the selected pixel to zero.

- **Set White Point eyedropper.** Sets the Exposure, which shifts the selected pixel to white (1.0 for HDR images).

- **Midtone eyedropper.** Sets the Exposure, which shifts the selected pixel to the middle gray.

5. Make a dramatic adjustment and click OK. Let the image blow out, because this will show you the flexibility of HDR images.

6. Apply a second Exposure adjustment and bring the image back into a more accurate exposure. Notice that the blown-out areas are restored (this is often impossible with 8- or 16-bit images captured in a single exposure because over-exposed or underexposed data is discarded).

VIDEO 72:
Equalize

Equalize

The Equalize command can restore contrast to a washed-out photo. The command attempts to redistribute pixels so that they are equally balanced across the entire range of brightness values. The command works best when you sample a small area that will drive the overall adjustment. The Equalize command takes the

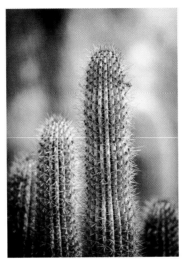

lightest area and remaps it to pure white, and takes the darkest area and remaps it to pure black. Let's give it a try.

1. Close any open files, and then open the file Ch10_Equalize1.tif from the Chapter 10 folder.

2. With the Rectangular Marquee tool, make a selection inside the largest cactus branch.

3. Choose Image > Adjustments > Equalize to repair the image.

4. Make sure the Equalize entire image based on selected area check box is selected, and then click OK.

5. If the image appears overexposed, you can choose Edit > Fade to reduce the intensity of the Equalize command.

Color Lookup

A new option for color grading in Photoshop CS6 is the ability to apply a Color Lookup adjustment layer. The adjustment lets you choose from several different included presets (organized into three categories: 3DLUT File, Abstract, and Device Link). Each method uses a LUT (or lookup table). The benefits of using a LUT are that color changes are absolute and work well across multiple images for consistent adjustments.

NOTE

What's a LUT?

Historically, LUTs have been used by the digital cinema industry to apply color adjustments between different applications. They work by building a new table of colors that completely remap the colors in use.

NOTE

Create Your Own LUTs?

In Photoshop CS6, LUTs are meant to be applied, not created. You can use an application like Adobe SpeedGrade to make custom LUTs or download them from many websites.

1. Close any open files, and then open the Ch10_LUT.tif file from the Chapter 10 folder.

   This image already has a few LUTs applied so you can see the results of the adjustments.

2. Click the visibility icon next to each LUT adjustment layer. Have only one turned on at a time for the best results.

3. To apply a new LUT, click the Color Lookup icon in the Adjustments panel.

4. In the Properties panel, choose a loaded preset from one of the three pop-up menus.

5. Modify the adjustment layer to taste and experiment with opacity and blending modes.

 TIP

Tweak a LUT

Remember that you can adjust the opacity and blending mode for a LUT adjustment layer. This leads to several choices when designing.

Using Camera Raw

The Camera Raw support in Photoshop is enabled by a plug-in (essentially an application that runs inside Photoshop). With Camera Raw you can import and develop raw files, and then pass them on to Adobe Photoshop. Camera Raw is designed to work with the native files recorded by many cameras.

A Camera Raw file contains unprocessed and uncompressed data, as captured by the digital camera's image sensor. These native files contain much more color and exposure information than a JPEG or TIFF file. The camera also includes metadata, such as white balance, exposure, and more, specifying how that information should be treated.

VIDEO 73:
Recovering a Raw File

NOTE

What's the raw extension?

Raw files are not really a file type but rather a description for several manufacturer-specific file formats. You'll find several different file formats in use, and they will vary by camera manufacturer.

NOTE

Can I Use Camera Raw?

Not all cameras work with Photoshop Camera Raw (although the list is very long). Adobe keeps updating the plug-in to support new cameras all the time. To keep track of Camera Raw and for a list of supported cameras, visit www.adobe.com/go/learn_ps_cameraraw.

Opening a Raw File

To process a raw file, you'll need to open it with Photoshop Camera Raw. Essentially, you need to develop the file, deciding during the editing stages which information to include. The Camera Raw software interprets the metadata and raw file information to generate a new image.

The good news is that adjustments you make to a raw file are all stored as metadata. The adjustments essentially reprocess the raw file data. The Camera Raw plug-in writes to a sidecar file, which contains instructions on how to treat the raw data. In fact, you can have multiple sidecar settings for each raw image.

Let's try opening a file.

1. Close any open files, and then choose File > Open.

2. Navigate to the Chapter 10 folder and select Ch10_Mountain. NEF. Do not open the file yet.

   You can choose more than one file at a time to process with the Camera Raw dialog box.

3. Hold down the Command (Ctrl) key and select the Ch10_Recover_Raw.NEF file.

4. Click the Open button to open both images into the Camera Raw window.

   Now that you have something to look at, let's take a quick look at the dialog box and its controls.

An Overview of the Camera Raw Dialog Box

At first glance, the Camera Raw dialog box can be a little over-whelming. It's okay to feel this way, because there truly are a lot of sliders and tabs. What you'll find, however, is that the controls are fairly intuitive and very powerful. Here's a quick overview of what you'll find:

A Filmstrip. If you select more than a single image to open, the images will display here. It is possible to apply star rankings to images in the Filmstrip. You can also synchronize the settings between multiple clips. Just adjust one image, select similar images, and then click the Synchronize button.

B Toggle Filmstrip. If you don't want to see the Filmstrip, just double-click the bar. You can also drag to resize the preview thumbnails.

C Camera name or file format. The camera name and model appears at the top of the window so you know more about the file.

Clipped Warnings

As you make adjustments to the developed image, it's possible to clip data (essentially a loss of detail). In the Histogram display, you'll see two small triangles. You can click the one on the left for shadows and the one on the right for highlights. When enabled, clipped shadows appear in blue, and clipped highlights appear in red. Highlight clipping will warn you if any one of the three RGB channels is clipped (fully saturated with no detail). Shadow clipping will warn you if all three RGB channels are clipped (black with no detail).

VIDEO 74:
Working with Shadows and Highlights in Raw

D Toggle full-screen mode. It is possible to maximize the Camera Raw window to see more details and a larger interface. Click to toggle between the larger and default view.

E Image adjustment tabs. There are ten tabs in total for control-ling the development of Camera Raw files. More on these in the next section.

F Histogram. The Histogram displays the tonal range of the developing image. The left edge shows the shadows, whereas the right shows the highlights.

G Camera Raw Settings menu. Click this submenu to access controls for saving and loading custom settings.

H Zoom levels. You can adjust the magnification level of the image. The most accurate view is 100%, but you'll likely choose to zoom out to see the entire image in full.

I Workflow options. You can specify how images should be saved from Camera Raw and how they should be opened in Photoshop. Clicking the blue hyperlinked text lets you choose a color mode, bit depth, file size, and resolution.

J Navigation arrows. Let you switch between multiple images. These work well if the Filmstrip is hidden.

K Adjustment sliders. For each adjustment tab, you'll find a set of sliders. These controls are essential for developing the image.

Image Adjustments Tabs

The Camera Raw dialog box offers ten tabs to process your raw files. The tabs are organized by task. Normally, you'll use only some of the tabs to adjust each image. For learning purposes, let's take a quick look at each.

Basic

The Basic tab lets you make primary adjustments to white bal-ance, color saturation, and tonality. These are the most important controls and the ones you're most likely to change.

1. Click the White Balance list and choose Auto to have Camera Raw attempt to automatically adjust white balance.

2. Let's set a different white balance. Select the White Balance tool and click on one of the clouds in the sky.

THE RAW TOOLBAR

Across the Camera Raw window is its own toolbar. You'll see several similarities to the Photoshop tools you're already familiar with:

A **Zoom tool (Z).** You can click on an image to zoom into an area. You can also click and drag to make a selection for zooming.

B **Hand tool (H).** When zoomed, you can use the Hand tool to pan across an image. Hold down the spacebar to temporarily switch to the Hand tool.

C **White Balance tool (I).** You can override the white balance settings written by the camera. Just click to select the tool, and then click on an area of the image that should be white or gray.

D **Color Sampler tool (S).** You can add up to eight sample points. These are useful ways to track changes in color as you make adjustments to an image. Many users will place a sampler on a white and black area of an image to track any shifts in color.

E **Targeted Adjustment tool (T).** There are five different tools to choose from. Click and hold to select specific tools.

F **Crop tool (C).** You can crop freely or select from several preset aspect ratios. Remember that any adjustments you make are nondestructive. The cropping will be applied when the image is opened.

G **Straighten tool (A).** If your photo is crooked, just select the Straighten tool. Click and drag with the Straighten tool in the preview image to establish a horizontal or vertical angle.

H **Spot Removal tool (B).** The Spot Removal tool lets you heal or clone imperfections in the raw file. The most typical problem you'll need to tackle is sensor or lens dust.

I **Red Eye Removal tool (E).** If an image has red eye, select this tool and click on the center of the pupil.

J **Adjustments Brush (K).** This powerful tool lets you brush in localized color and exposure adjustments. Click and brush over an area to define it, and then adjust settings with the Adjustment sliders.

K **Graduated Filter (G).** This tool is similar to the Adjustments Brush except it allows you to create a transitioned adjustment gradually between two points. This is most typically used to fix areas like a sky.

L **Open Preferences dialog box (Command+K or Ctrl+K)**

M **Rotate Image Left (L).** Rotates the image 90° counterclockwise.

N **Rotate Image Right (R).** Rotates the image 90° clockwise.

3. In the Basic controls, click Auto to have Camera Raw analyze the image and make adjustments.

4. Drag the Exposure slide to +0.35 to brighten the image.

   The image is now brighter, but some of the highlights are too bright.

5. Drag the Highlights slider to −25 to recover detail in the brightest areas.

   Let's put a little more color into the image.

6. Boost the Saturation to +45 to increase the overall color in the shot.

7. Let's bring the color in the sky out a bit more. Increase the Vibrance slider to +30 to richen the sky without oversaturating the reds in the photo.

   Now that color is correct, let's enhance Contrast. The Clarity slider is best for this. To accurately judge clarity, you'll need to change your view.

8. Double-click the Zoom tool to switch to 100% magnification.

9. Drag the Clarity slider to the right slowly. Stop when you start to notice halos near the edge of details.

   Around +45 you should notice a blooming effect; at this point you have too much clarity.

10. Drag the Clarity slider back to the left until the halos disappear. A value of 30 for this image seems to work well.

11. Click the Zoom Levels presets list and choose Fit In View.

12. Toggle the check box for Preview (near the top of the window) to see the before and after states.

13. Make sure the Preview check box is selected, and then click the Tone Curve tab.

Tone Curve

With the Tone Curve, you can fine-tune tonality in an image with controls similar to Photoshop's Curves adjustment. You can choose to use either a Parametric curve or a Point curve.

1. In the Tone Curve controls, click the Point tab.

2. From the Curve presets list, choose Strong Contrast.

You can also click the curve and make adjustments like the Curves adjustment layer that you learned earlier.

3. Toggle the check box for Preview (near the top of the window) to see the before and after states.

4. Make sure the Preview check box is selected, and then click the Detail tab.

Detail

The Detail tab offers precise control over both sharpening an image as well as reducing noise. All raw images will need some sharpening. Noise, on the other hand, may not appear unless the image was shot with a high ISO setting or under low light.

1. Double-click the Zoom tool to switch to 100% magnification.

It's easiest to accurately judge both sharpening and noise at a 100% view.

2. In the Detail tab, you can adjust sharpening to bring out fine image details:

- **Amount.** Increases definition at the edges of an image. Use a lower amount for a cleaner image. When you open the file, the Camera Raw plug-in calculates the settings to use based on camera model, ISO, and exposure compensation. For this image, enter **35**.

- **Radius.** Use a low number for fine detail and a higher number if the photo lacks much detail. For this image use a lower number like **1.2** to preserve detail in the rocks.

- **Detail.** Controls how much high-frequency information is sharpened in the image and how the edges are emphasized. For this image, try a value of **50** to bring out lots of detail.

- **Masking.** Controls the edge of the mask. Using a value of zero means that everything receives the same amount of sharpening. A higher number limits the sharpening to those areas near the strongest edges.

An easy way to tell how much masking to use is to hold down the Option (Alt) key while dragging. White areas will be sharpened; black areas are ignored (masked). Try this out: Hold down the Option (Alt) key and drag slowly to the right. A value of 50 seems to be the right balance for this image.

3. Noise reduction controls let you remove extra grain from the image:

- **Luminance.** Reduces luminance noise. Set this to **10** for this image (it's not very noisy).

- **Luminance Detail.** Sets a threshold for the noise reduction. Higher values preserve detail but can produce noisier results. Lower values tend to produce cleaner results but likely remove some detail. Use a value of **80** to preserve more details.

- **Luminance Contrast.** Works best for very noisy photos. A value of **80** works well for this image.

- **Color.** Reduces color noise. The default is fine for this image.

- **Color Detail.** Use a higher value to protect detailed edges. A lower value preserves more color but can result in color bleeding. The default is fine for this image.

4. Toggle the check box for Preview to see the before and after states. This image is very subtly changed.

5. Click the Zoom Levels presets list and choose Fit In View.

6. Make sure the Preview check box is selected, and then click the HSL/Grayscale tab.

HSL/Grayscale

The HSL/Grayscale tab offers fine-tuning controls for Hue, Saturation, and Luminance adjustments. The most typical use of this tab is to target a particular color or tone that needs emphasis.

1. Select the Saturation tab.

2. Drag the Red slider to the left to deemphasize the Red tones.

   Try a value of **−10** for this image.

3. Drag the Blue slider to the right to boost the sky further.

   Try a value of **+25** for this image.

   The image on the top is prior to adjustments. On the bottom, the increased saturation comes through.

Before

After

4. Switch to the Luminance tab to change the brightness of a color range.

5. Enter a value of **+15** for both the Red and Orange sliders to lighten the rocky areas of the mountain.

6. Toggle the check box for Preview to see the before and after states.

7. Make sure the Preview check box is selected, and then click the Split Toning tab.

Split Toning

The Split Toning controls are used when you want to color a grayscale image. It only works if you select the Convert To Grayscale in the HSL/Grayscale tab or work with a grayscale image.

Click the Lens Corrections tab.

VIDEO 75:
Lens Correction in Raw

Lens Corrections

The Lens Corrections tab attempts to compensate for defects in lens technology. The first tab lets you automatically compensate for any physical distortion based on a lens profile.

1. Click the option for the Enable Lens Profile Corrections.

Photoshop automatically removes some of the wide-angle distortion from the image. You can refine the adjustment using the third tab (Manual).

2. At the bottom, you can adjust for lens vignetting. This lets you compensate for shadows caused by the lens or hood.

3. Click the second tab (Color) to adjust for common problems like chromatic aberration.

This particular image suffers from neither issue. Chromatic aberration shows as fringing in the color, particularly at the edges of the image. It is easiest to see aberration at 100% magnification.

4. Click the Effects tab.

Effects

The Effects tab can be used to stylize the image. It is used to add photographic imperfections that were more typical with film-based cameras. You can choose to simulate film grain or apply a post crop vignette to the edges.

1. Double-click the Zoom tool to switch to 100% magnification.

It's easiest to accurately judge grain at a 100% view.

2. Set grain to a value of **15** and a size of **35** to create a filmic type noise in the image.

3. Click the Zoom Levels presets list and choose Fit In View.

4. You can use a post crop vignette to stylize the images edges:

- **Style.** You'll find three different options for how the vignette shades the image. The default, Highlight variety, works best for this image.

- **Amount.** Use a negative value to darken the edges or a positive to brighten them. For this image, enter −**25**.

- **Midpoint.** Controls how close the vignette appears to the corner of the image. Enter **60** to push out the edges.

- **Roundness.** A positive value creates a circular effect, whereas a negative value takes on an oval shape. The default is fine for this image.

- **Feather.** Can create a gentler transition between the affected areas. The default is fine for this image.

- **Highlights.** If you're using a very dark vignette, the Highlights slider can be used to protect the brightest tones in your image.

5. Make sure the Preview check box is selected, and then click the Camera Calibration tab.

Camera Calibration

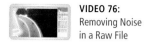

VIDEO 76:
Removing Noise
in a Raw File

The Camera Calibration tab is used to apply specific profiles to raw images. Typically, you'll use it to correct for color cast (unwanted spill) in an image. It can also compensate for unwanted behaviors by a camera's image sensor.

- **Process.** The process list lets you choose a decode technique. The newer 2010 process is a significant improvement that ships with Photoshop CS6. If you're working with raw files you've processed with an older decoder, be sure to switch and update the file for greater control and quality.

- **Camera Profile.** You'll find three types of camera profiles. The ACR options are compatible with older versions of Camera Raw. The Adobe Standard option works best for Photoshop CS6. You'll also find profiles that attempt to match the manufacturer's presets for shooting modes like neutral, standard, and vivid. In most cases (including this one) Adobe Standard is best.

    Make sure the Preview check box is selected, and then click the Presets tab.

Presets

If you like a setting you've created, you can save it as a preset, which makes it easier to reload in the future. Remember that custom presets can serve as a great starting point (especially if you have several images from the same shoot). To make a preset, just click the pad-shaped button at the bottom of the window.

Make sure the Preview check box is selected, and then click the Snapshots tab.

Snapshots

Another way to store a version of your image is to create a snapshot. Each snapshot is essentially a recording of the image's current state. You can in fact create multiple snapshots for a raw file and easily switch between them.

Other Than Raw Files?

You can in fact open TIFF and JPEG files using the Camera Raw plug-in. You need to switch to Adobe Bridge and select the desired files. Then choose File > Open In Camera Raw. You won't see any major benefits to image quality, but you can use the Camera Raw dialog box to adjust the images.

Finish the Process

When you are satisfied with the settings you've entered into the Adjustment sliders, you can decide what to do with the file. Before you open (or close) the file, you should check a few things.

1. Click the Workflow Options text at the bottom of the image.

2. Set the Depth to 16 Bits/Channel for the maximum tonal fidelity.

3. Set the resolution to **300** pixels per inch.

4. Select the Open in Photoshop as Smart Objects check box to ensure future ease in readjusting the raw processing.

5. Click OK to store the settings.

6. Select the Straighten tool (A).

7. Drag across the horizon line at the base of the mountain to straighten the image.

   When you release, you'll see a new crop box drawn on the image. If you need to reset the crop, click the Crop tool in the Tools panel and choose Clear Crop.

8. You now must choose what to do with the file. Clicking the Done button stores the Camera Raw settings in a sidecar file (or database) without opening the image in Photoshop. For this image, click Open Object to develop the raw file and send it to Photoshop.

   A new file opens in Photoshop with the raw file added as a Smart Object.

   You can now use any of the adjustment techniques you've learned in this chapter. Be sure to save the file as a layered Photoshop or TIFF file. If you need to reprocess the raw file, just double-click its thumbnail in the Layers panel to reopen the image into Camera Raw.

The image on the left is unprocessed, whereas the image on the right has had many settings adjusted.

Repairing and Improving Photos

11

Damage, like fashion, is often very subjective. If you show the same set of photos to five people and ask them to comment on mistakes or damage, you'll likely get five very different answers. The reason is that people find different things distracting: A crooked photo may bother some, whereas others may dislike dust on the camera sensor. Several aspects of an image can be "wrong," but it is also impossible to have a "perfect" photo.

Because damage is so subjective, I recommend asking your clients or end customers (if possible) what needs repair. Ask them questions like, would you like anything different or can anything be better? You'll often be surprised by their answers. Sometimes a fix will be as simple

The photo on the right has had several small blemishes repaired, proper contrast restored, and a small "accident" fixed.

as a crop or a color correction, but more often it will involve removing something from (or adding to) the picture. The world has embraced digital enhancement, and you may be surprised at how much Photoshop can do.

This chapter tackles issues like physical damage, such as rips, wrinkles, scratches, and fading as well as digital issues such as overblown skies and noise. It focuses on techniques that you can perform in less than 10 minutes. With practice you can fix 80 percent of the problems in 10 minutes; the other 20 percent you either learn to live with or spend more time on.

Image Selection

Most problems can be repaired, but not every problem is worth trying to fix. Photographers usually shoot many exposures of a subject, so they are willing to discard several that they are unhappy with. It is best to repair images that are close to their desired state; otherwise, you may spend too much time on a project (which could send it over budget in the professional world).

Working with Modern Images

The most common problems in modern photos are color or exposure issues (both of which were addressed in detail in Chapter 10, "Color Correction and Enhancement"). However, modern

photos can still suffer physical damage as well as dust on the camera sensor or lens. If the print is wrinkled or creased, it's always best to use a fresh source (either an alternate print or the negative). If the print is dusty or smudged, gently wipe it with a soft cloth, and then try to scan or rescan it. If you're forced to work with what you have (or there are issues with a digital photo), you can attempt to fix several problems within Photoshop.

Working with Historical Images

Historical photos often have more problems than modern photos. There is a much greater likelihood of physical damage. You may have to repair creases, tears, water damage, or adhesive stains (from scrapbooks). It's likely that the photos will have faded and need a boost in contrast or toning. It is generally easiest to remove color from a historical source while repairing it. The color can then be added back in during the final stages as an overlay or sepia tone.

The Retoucher's Toolbox

The process of making a photo look better is often referred to as *retouching* (while repairing damaged photos is referred to as *restoration)*. Because there are many different problems that can manifest in a photo, Photoshop offers several tools with which to respond. Knowing which tool to use is often a dilemma, but with a little bit of study and practice the process can be greatly accelerated. Let's explore how the tools work and give them a try. But first, realize that most of these tools use a paintbrush behavior. Be sure your painting tools are set to Brush size and your other tools to Precise in the Preferences dialog box (Edit > Preferences). This will allow you to better see your tools as you move them in your image.

VIDEO 77:
Cloning

Clone Stamp Tool

The Clone Stamp tool works by replacing unwanted or damaged pixels with good pixels that you target. It's a popular tool that is relatively easy to use and achieves accurate results. The Clone Stamp tool allows you to set a sample point (where the good pixels are taken from), and then paint into bad areas (to cover up damage or blemishes). This technique is very powerful, because the Photoshop paint engine can use soft brushes, which can soften the stamp's edge, making the strokes more believable as they blend together better.

1. Open the Ch11_Clone.tif file from the Chapter 11 folder. You'll notice a distracting dark area in the upper-right corner.

2. Activate the Clone Stamp tool by pressing S. Roll over the tool's icon and be sure you have not accidentally activated the Pattern Stamp tool.

3. Select a soft-edged brush from the Options bar or Brush panel. If needed, modify an existing brush. A brush around 200 pixels wide works well.

TIP

Clone Across Layers

If you're working with a layered image, you can clone from all visible layers by selecting Sample All Layers. This method can be used to clone to an empty layer, which makes the cloning nondestructive. If the Sample All Layers option is deselected, only the active layer is used.

4. In the Options bar, you need to specify the alignment for the clone:

- **Select Aligned.** The sample point and painting point move parallel as you move. If the user clones and moves the cursor to the right, the sample point moves as well. This ultimately creates more variety in the cloning, which is desirable. However, it can lead to the unwanted material being repeated into the stroke.

- **Deselect Aligned.** If Aligned is not selected, the initial sample point is used (even after you stop and resume cloning). This option ensures that you are always sampling from the same pixels when starting a new stroke.

Choose the Aligned option for this image.

5. Option-click (Alt-click) within the current document (or even another open document set to the same color mode). This defines the source point for sampled pixel data. Click in the large, tan area in the upper corner.

6. Click and paint as if you were using the Brush tool. You can also try small dabs and short strokes to get a blended look. The sampled pixels are taken from the sample point and cover the unwanted pixels. Continue cloning until the entire shadow is painted over. You may need to select a new sample point to get a realistic clone. Try blending multiple strokes together and lower the opacity of the brush for the best results.

TIP

For Better Results When Cloning

- Try cloning at a low opacity and build up strokes.
- Try sampling from several different places to fill in an area.
- Experiment with blending modes.
- Clone to an empty layer by setting the Sample method to use All Layers.

Healing Brush Tool

The Healing Brush tool (J) is an innovative and powerful tool that can be used to repair blemishes in a photo. The Healing Brush tool operates much like the Clone Stamp tool. However, instead of just moving pixels from one area to another, the Healing Brush tool clones pixels while also matching the texture, lighting, and shading of the original pixels.

Because the Healing Brush samples surrounding areas, you may want to make an initial selection around the damaged area and feather it. This will give you better results on an area with strong contrast. The selection should be slightly bigger than the area that needs to be healed. It should follow the boundary of high-contrast pixels. For example, if you're healing a blemish on a subject's face, make an initial selection of the skin area to avoid mixing in the adjacent background or clothing. The selection will prevent color bleed-in from outside areas when painting with the Healing Brush tool.

VIDEO 78:
Healing Brush

1. Close any open files, and then open the file Ch11_Healing_Brush1.tif from the Chapter 11 folder.

   The photo is of a wall texture that will be used as a background layer for a composite. There is a distracting element that needs to be removed.

2. Activate the Healing Brush tool by pressing J. (Be sure to closely examine the icon and not select the Spot Healing Brush tool.)

3. Select a soft brush from the Options bar or the Brush panel.

4. Set the blending mode to Replace. This option preserves noise and texture at the stroke's edges.

5. Specify a source for repairing pixels in the Options bar. The standard option is to use Sampled. This takes pixels from the area surrounding the sample point. As the brush moves, the sample point also moves to ensure variety in the sampled source.

6. Specify the alignment option. If Aligned is selected, the sample point and painting point move parallel as you move the stroke. If Aligned is deselected, the initial sample point is Always. The Always option ensures that you are always sampling from the same area.

7. If you want to heal to an empty layer, select the Sample All Layers check box. This allows you to sample one layer, and then apply the healing to a new empty layer above. This will provide greater flexibility in your workflow. If the Sample All Layers box is deselected, only the active layer is used.

8. Add a new, empty layer above the *Background* layer.

9. In the middle of the wall, Option-click (Alt-click) on the clear brick texture.

10. Click and start to paint as if you were using a brush. Because the sampled pixels are drawn from before you click, it may be necessary to release and start over occasionally to avoid sampling the problem area.

11. After several short strokes, release the mouse to merge the sampled pixels. Before the pixels blend, you will have a visible stroke. Afterward, the stroke should gently blend.

12. Continue to heal the remaining unwanted pixels. To improve the overall blend, you can sample from a few different areas.

Spot Healing Brush Tool

The Spot Healing Brush tool was added to Photoshop as a way to harness powerful blending technology with less work (although the Healing Brush is pretty labor-free to begin with). It can quickly remove blemishes and imperfections in photos without requiring a sample point to be set. The Spot Healing Brush tool automatically samples pixels from the area around the retouched area. Let's give the tool a try.

VIDEO 79:
Spot Healing Brush

1. Close any open files, and then open the file Ch11_Spot_Healing.tif from the Chapter 11 folder.

   Look closely at the image; you'll see some acne on the child's forehead and a wet spot on her shirt. Both are easy fixes with the Spot Healing Brush tool.

2. Activate the Spot Healing Brush tool from the Tools panel.

3. Choose a soft-edged brush from the Options bar. Make the brush only slightly larger than the problem areas. For this image, a brush size of 25 pixels and a hardness of 25% will work well.

4. Set the blending mode in the Options bar to Replace to pre-serve noise, grain, and hair texture at the edges of the stroke.

5. Choose a Type of repair in the Options bar:

   - **Proximity Match.** Pixels from the edge of the selection are used as a patch for the selected area. This should be the first attempt at repair; if it doesn't look good, switch to the Create Texture option.

   - **Create Texture.** Pixels in the selection are used to create a texture to fix the damaged area. If the texture doesn't work, try dragging through the area one more time.

6. Click once on an area you want to fix. You can also click and drag over a larger area. After fixing the acne, touch up the wet spot on the child's shirt. If you are unhappy with the spot healing stroke, simply undo and try again with a smaller brush. You can also try stroking in different directions to modify your results.

Upon close examination, you should notice that you have healed several blemishes in the photo. If only life were so easy.

Patch Tool

The Patch tool uses the same technology as the Healing Brush tool, but it is better suited to fix large problem areas. Start using the Patch tool by selecting the area for repair and then dragging to specify the sampled area. For best results, select a small area.

The Patch tool can be used two different ways:

- **Source.** Make a selection in the area that needs repair, and then drag to an area of good pixels.

- **Destination.** Make a selection in an area of good pixels, and then drag that selection on top of the unwanted pixels.

Let's give it a try.

1. Close any open files, and then open the file Ch11_Patch1.tif from the Chapter 11 folder.

2. Select the Patch tool by pressing J to cycle through the tools. (It's in the same well as the Healing Brush tool.)

3. Set the Patch tool to Content-Aware. This does a superior job of removing the patched area and seamlessly blending it. The feature is new to CS6; if you're using an earlier version of Photoshop, choose Source.

4. Set the Adaptation method to Very Strict for the highest-quality patch.

5. Make a selection around the discarded cigarette butt under the cat's arm.

6. Drag into the clear area of the brick street.

7. Release and let the Patch tool blend.

8. Repeat for the remaining trash or blemishes in the shot.

> **TIP**
>
> **Making Selections**
>
> Although you can make a selection with the Patch tool, you can always make a selection using any other selection tool (such as Marquees or Lassos), and then activate the Patch tool. The Patch tool behaves just like the Lasso tool (as far as selections go), but it may not offer the level of control you need.

Red Eye Tool

Red eye is caused when the camera flash is reflected in a subject's retinas. This happens frequently in photos taken in a dark room, because the subject's irises are open wide. There are two solutions to fixing red eye in the field:

VIDEO 80:
Content-Aware Patching

- Use the camera's red eye reduction feature. This will strobe the flash and adjust the eyes of your subject. This strobing will increase the time from when you click the camera's shutter and the photo is taken.

- Use a separate flash unit that can be held to the side or increase the distance between the lens and the flash.

Getting it right in the field is important, but you can fix it in Photoshop as well. Photoshop offers a powerful Red Eye tool that can fix flash problems. It effectively removes red eye from flash photos of people and white or green reflections in the eyes of animals.

1. Close any open files, and then open the file Ch11_Red_Eye.tif from the Chapter 11 folder.

2. Zoom into the red eye area. An easy way is to take the Zoom tool and drag around the problem area.

3. Select the Red Eye tool from the Tools panel or press J repeatedly to cycle through the tools.

4. Click in the red eye area to remove it. If you're unsatisfied with the results, choose undo and modify the two options in step 5.

5. In the Options bar, adjust the Pupil Size to a smaller number to convert a more constrained area (30% works well for this image). Adjust the Darken Pupil setting as desired to modify how dark the pupil will be after the conversion.

VIDEO 81:
Content-Aware
Fill/Scale/Heal

Content-Aware Fill

The Content-Aware fill option provides the ability to automatically generate new textures to fill a selected area. What happens is that Photoshop randomly synthesizes similar content to fill the area based on the source image. This is a great way to remove an object or blemish from a scene. In some cases it completes the job in one step; in others it offers a great jump start and can be touched up with a little cloning or healing.

1. Close any open files, and then open the file Ch11_Content_Aware.tif from the Chapter 11 folder.

   Before you remove the distracting items, let's straighten the image first.

2. Press C to invoke the Crop tool, and then click the Straighten button in the Options bar.

   Find a surface you think should be horizontal (or vertical). The edge of the sand is a good reference point.

3. Click and drag along a line to measure the angle.

4. In the Options bar, click the commit button to apply the new crop.

5. With the Lasso tool, make a rough selection around the woman and seaweed on the beach. Make a selection slightly larger than the woman.

6. Choose Select > Modify > Feather and enter a value of **5** pixels to blend the selection.

7. Choose Edit > Fill or press Shift+Delete to bring up the Fill dialog box.

8. From the Use menu, choose Content-Aware fill and click OK.

9. Press Command+H (Ctrl+H) to hide the selection.

   Try removing the beach chair in the lower-left corner and clean up any blemishes with the Content-Aware Fill command, Clone Stamp, or Spot Healing Brush.

![TIP]

Try, Try Again

If you don't like the first attempt Content-Aware fill generates, just choose Edit > Undo and apply another Content-Aware fill.

This image was finished with a little additional cloning, a Levels adjustment, and a Vibrance adjustment layer.

Content-Aware Move

The Content-Aware Move tool is the latest extension of the capabilities of cloning, healing, and Content-Aware technology in Photoshop CS6. With the Content-Aware Move tool, you can select an object, and then drag it into a new position. The original object is extracted, and its background is filled generating a new texture with Content-Aware fill technology; then the repositioned copy is blended into the image. This tool can be quite effective, especially if you adjust the Adaptation property in the Options bar to a stricter setting.

1. Close any open files, and then open the Ch11_Content_Aware_Move.tif file from the Chapter 11 folder.

   The image has some blue guides to help with composition that should be visible in the image.

2. Select the Content-Aware Move tool (J), which is in the same well as the Patch and Heal tools.

3. Drag a loose selection around the bird.

VIDEO 82:
Content-Aware Move

4. Choose the Very Strict Adaptation method in the Options bar to produce the most accurate blend.

5. Choose the Move mode in the Options bar to reposition the object.

   The Extend mode method can be used on other images to change the apparent width or depth of an object while preserving key details.

6. Drag the bird to a new position based on the rule of thirds guides and release.

   The rule of thirds guides were manually added to the image.

   The image may take a few seconds to blend. Feel free to refine the blend using additional cloning or healing tools.

VIDEO 83:
Blur and Sharpen

Blur and Sharpen Tools

Often, a photo will need a focus adjustment. Although global changes are often implemented through blur or sharpen filters, it's frequently necessary to lightly touch up an area by hand. To do this, you can use the Blur tool (to defocus) or the Sharpen tool

(to add focus or detail). Both tools are driven by brush-like settings, which allow you to change size, hardness, strength, and blending mode. Remember that if the Caps Lock key is down, brush previews are disabled.

1. Close any open files, and then open the file Ch11_Blur-Sharpen.tif from the Chapter 11 folder.

2. Select the Blur tool from the Tools panel (it looks like a water droplet).

3. Specify a brush size of approximately **120** pixels and a Strength of **50**%. The Strength settings modify how quickly the tool alters the image. Sometimes several built-up strokes are better for a subtle look.

VIDEO 84:
Blur Gallery Explored

4. Paint over an area of the edge of the white bowl to deemphasize it.

5. Choose one of the tool's blending modes. The Darken and Lighten modes are particularly useful for isolating the blurring effect to darken or lighten areas, respectively. Try the Darken mode and blur the dark floor.

6. Switch to the Sharpen tool and try enhancing parts of the image. Enable the Protect Detail option in the Options bar. The duck's bill is a good choice as well as the eyes and edges of feathers. Experiment with the Mode and Strength settings.

7. Be careful not to oversharpen the image, because it will quickly introduce visible noise and distortion.

TIP

Blur Gallery

Are you looking for another way to blur your images? You'll find three great filters for creating Field, Iris, or Tilt Shift blurs included with Photoshop CS6. Don't miss the in-depth video.

TIP

Nondestructive Tools

Both the Blur and Sharpen tools can be used nondestructively. Simply create a new layer to hold modified pixels. Then in the Options bar, select the Sample All Layers check box. The blurring or sharpening will be isolated to the selected layer.

Smudge Tool

The Smudge tool simulates dragging a finger through wet paint. The pixels are liquid and can be pushed around the screen. With the default settings, the tool uses color from where you first click and pushes it in the direction in which you move the mouse. This

tool is useful for cleaning up dust specks or flakes in a photo. Set the tool's blending mode to Lighten or Darken (depending on the area to be affected), and you'll have digital makeup to touch up the problem.

1. Close any open files, and then open the file Ch11_Smudge.tif from the Chapter 11 folder.

2. Select the Smudge tool from the Tools panel (it looks like a finger painting icon).

3. Zoom into the model's flyaway hair.

4. Experiment with the Darken and Lighten modes. These are particularly useful for isolating the smudge by pushing only dark or light pixels.

5. Smudge the edges of the hair pixels. Experiment by switching blending modes: You can always undo the smudge, and then change the tool's mode and resmudge. To quickly cycle blending modes, press the Shift+= or Shift +- shortcut keys.

Using the Smudge tool's Darken mode lets you push darker pixels over lighter pixels.

TIP

Smudge Tool for Historical Images Too!

The Smudge tool also works great for touching up blemishes in historical photos. Rips, tears, and cracks can easily be filled in using the Smudge tool's Lighten and Darken modes. You can also try the Blur tool in a similar fashion.

Dodge and Burn Tools

The Dodge and Burn tools are known as toning tools. They allow you finer control over lightening or darkening your image. These tools simulate traditional techniques used by photographers. In a darkroom, the photographer would regulate the amount of light on a particular area of a print. These tools are particularly helpful when touching up faded photos, especially when repairing water damage. Let's try out both tools.

VIDEO 85:
Dodge and Burn

1. Close any open files, and then open the file Ch11_Dodge_Burn.tif from the Chapter 11 folder.

2. Duplicate the current layer because the Dodge and Burn tools are destructive. Closely examine the four faces. You should notice that the two on the right look washed out, and the two on the left are a bit dark.

3. Select the Dodge tool from the Tools panel. Adjust the brush to be soft and large (approximately 80 pixels). Set the tool to adjust the Midtones.

4. Paint over the shadowed faces on the left half of the picture to bring out the darkest areas a bit.

5. Select the Burn tool from the Tools panel. Adjust the brush to be soft and large (approximately 80 pixels). Set the tool to adjust the Highlights and set an Exposure setting of **20%**.

6. Paint over the washed-out faces on the left half of the picture to restore the contrast a bit.

7. Continue to touch up areas in the photos as needed. Lower exposure settings are generally more desirable.

TIP

Protect Those Tones

If you are working on color images, be sure to use the Protect Tones option for the Dodge and Burn tools. Simply select the check box in the Options bar to get more natural-looking results.

PHOTO BY JAMES BALL

Sponge Tool

The Sponge tool is very elegant and efficient. This toning tool can be used to make subtle adjustments in color saturation or grayscale contrast. It can also be used during conversion processes to prepare images for commercial printing or television. The Sponge tool allows you to gently desaturate (or saturate) areas by brushing over them.

1. Close any open files, and then open the file Ch11_Sponge.tif from the Chapter 11 folder.

2. When converting RGB images into CMYK, there is often a shift in colors. This is because RGB has a wider color gamut than CMYK, and it can display more colors. Photoshop allows you to highlight the areas that are "out of gamut" or will shift when you convert modes. Choose View > Gamut Warning. The gray areas represent out-of-gamut areas.

3. Select the Sponge tool by pressing O to cycle through the tools, or choose it from the Tools panel.

4. Adjust the brush to a large size and set it to have soft edges.

5. Set the tool to Desaturate and adjust the flow to a lower value. It is generally better to use a slower flow and make several applications.

6. Paint over the gray gamut warning areas with the Sponge tool until they disappear.

7. If needed, you can switch the Sponge tool to Saturate to boost areas. If you see a gray gamut warning, you've gone too far.

8. When you're done, you can convert the image to CMYK by selecting Image > Mode > CMYK. CMYK conversion is covered again in Chapter 16, "Printing, PDF, and Specialized File Types."

9. To complete the image, choose File > Save As, pick a new destination, and rename the file to **Ch11_Sponge_CMYK.tif**.

TIP

Gamut Warning Color

If you'd like to change the gamut warning color so it stands out more, open your Photoshop Preferences. In the Transparency & Gamut controls, click the swatch next to Color to set a new warning color.

Lens Correction

The Lens Correction filter is designed to fix common flaws in an image (such as barrel distortion, lens vignettes, and chromatic aberration). The filter can be run on 8- or 16-bit-per-channel images that use the RGB or Grayscale image mode. The filter can also correct perspective problems caused by camera tilt.

1. Close any open files, and then open the file Ch11_Lens_Profile.tif from the Chapter 11 folder.

2. Choose Filter > Convert for Smart Filters to ensure flexibility in editing.

3. Choose Filter > Lens Correction.

    A new window opens. Look in the bottom-left corner for information about the camera and lens used for the shot (this is included in the metadata the camera wrote to the original file).

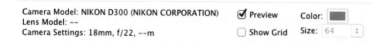

4. Choose a manufacturer from the Camera Make menu. In this case choose Nikon Corporation.

5. From the Camera Model menu, choose the correct camera model. In this case just choose Nikon D300s.

6. From the Lens Model menu, choose the correct lens. The closest match is the 17.0-70.0 mm f/2.8-4.5.

7. Switch to the Custom tab for advanced controls.

8. Click the Show Grid option at the bottom of the window.

    Let's compensate for the low angle, which is causing some keystoning.

9. Set the Vertical Perspective to **−50**.

TIP

Create Your Own Profiles?

If you want to create your own lens profiles, Adobe has a great utility. Visit http://labs.adobe.com/technologies/lensprofile_creator/ for full details.

VIDEO 86:
Lens Correction

10. Set Vignette Amount to **20** to further brighten the edges.

11. Click OK to apply the correction.

You can double-click the Lens Correction filter in the Layers panel to open the Smart filter for future edits.

Adaptive Wide-Angle Correction

A common flaw caused by wide-angle lens is distortion. If you shoot with a very large field of view (wide-angle rectilinear or full-frame fisheye), the photo will often show a bending of straight lines and other distortion near the edges of the photo. The Adaptive Wide Angle Correction plug-in (new to CS6) can fix perceptible distortion. The plug-in requires only a small amount of input from a user to know which lines should be straight.

Let's try using the command on a very distorted image.

1. Close any open files, and then open the Ch11_Adaptive_Wide_Angle.tif file from the Chapter 11 folder.

2. Choose Filter > Convert for Smart Filters to ensure flexibility in editing.

3. Choose Filter > Wide-Angle Correction.

4. Choose a correction method from the pop-up menu. You can choose among Fisheye, Perspective, Full Spherical, or Auto.

   Try out the different methods to see their different approaches. For this project, Auto works well.

VIDEO 87:
Adaptive Wide-Angle
Correction

5. Select the Constraint tool in the upper-left corner of the new panel.

6. Hold down the Shift key to define a horizontal or vertical anchor.

   Draw in the center of the image to start; then you'll work your way out wider.

7. Click and drag to define a straight line along the edge of one of the buildings.

   The image updates to minimize distortion.

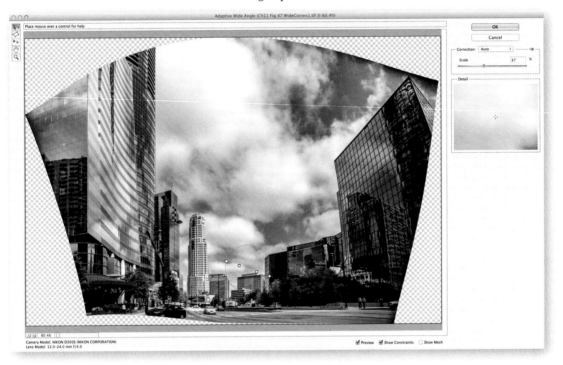

8. Continue dragging with the Constraint tool to define vertical and horizontal surfaces.

   Hold down the Shift key when dragging. The line should properly help define a portion of the image as perpendicular or vertical. You can also drag the center control points to rotate a constraint option.

9. Adjust the Scale slider to minimize the presence of gaps in the image.

10. Click OK to apply the effect.

11. Crop the image or use the Clone Stamp tool to fill in the gaps.

Restoration in Action

Learning how to fix damaged areas in photos is not a step-by-step process. Rather, it is learning how to identify problems and make strategic decisions about which techniques to employ to fix the image. Practice is the best path to becoming a skillful retoucher. However, you can expect good results if you know which tools to use. I have personally seen students become proficient using Photoshop's rich suite of tools in just a few weeks.

Soft Focus

Cameras are much more likely to generate a soft focus under low light. The Smart Sharpen filter has the most options of any sharpening filter built into Photoshop. It allows you to choose the sharpening algorithm as well as control the amount of sharpening in shadow and highlight areas. This filter can produce dramatically better quality, but do not expect results like you see in a TV police drama.

1. Close any open files, open the Ch11_ Sharpen1.tif file, and zoom the document window to 100%. This will give you the most accurate view of the sharpening.

2. Choose Filter > Sharpen > Smart Sharpen and select the Advanced radio button.

3. Click and drag the image in the preview window so you can better see the wood texture.

4. Adjust the controls in the Sharpen tab:

   - **Amount.** Sets the amount of sharpening. A higher value increases contrast between edge pixels, which gives the appearance of more sharpness.

   - **Radius.** Determines the number of pixels surrounding the edge pixels that will be affected by the sharpening. A greater radius value means that edge effects will be more obvious, as will the sharpening.

TIP

Oversaturated Colors

If you sharpen a color photo and you get oversaturated colors, switch to the Lab image mode. Apply the filter only to the Lightness channel.

- **Remove.** Allows you to set the sharpening algorithm to be used:

  - **Gaussian Blur.** Is used by the Unsharp Mask filter. It works well on images that appear slightly out of focus.

  - **Lens Blur.** Detects edges and detail in an image. It provides finer sharpening of detail and can reduce halos caused by sharpening.

  - **Motion Blur.** Attempts to reduce the effects of blur caused by camera or subject movement. You will need to set the Angle control if you choose Motion Blur.

- **Angle.** Set this to match the direction of motion. It's only available when using the Remove control's Motion Blur option.

- **More Accurate.** Allows Photoshop to spend more time processing the file. It generates more accurate results for the removal of blurring.

5. You can refine the sharpening of dark and light areas—try using the Shadow and Highlight tabs. These controls should be used if you start to see halos in light or dark areas:

- **Fade Amount.** Adjusts the amount of sharpening in the highlights or shadows regions.

- **Tonal Width.** Controls the range of tones in the shadows or highlights that are modified. Smaller values restrict the adjustments to smaller regions.

- **Radius.** Controls the size of the area around each pixel that determines if a pixel is considered a shadow or a high-

light. Moving the slider to the left specifies a smaller region; moving the slider to the right defines a larger region.

6. When you're satisfied, click OK to apply the filter.

Faded Historical Photos

VIDEO 88:
Restore a Damaged Photo

A common problem with old black-and-white or sepia-toned photos is that they fade over time. You can use a Levels or Curves adjustment, but both commands often introduce color artifacts into the image. A few extra steps are needed to get the best results.

1. Close any open files, and then open the file Ch11_Fading_Historical.tif from the Chapter 11 folder.

2. With the Eyedropper tool, sample the color tint if you want to retain it in the finished piece.

3. Leave the photo in RGB mode but strip away the color. Choose Image > Adjust > Desaturate or press Shift+Command+U (Shift+Ctrl+U).

4. Perform a Levels adjustment and restore the white-and-black points. Drag the black Input Levels slider and the white Input Levels slider toward the center.

5. Add a Solid Color fill layer by choosing Layer > New Fill Layer > Solid Color. Click OK. The Foreground color you previously sampled will load automatically.

6. Set the Color Fill layer to use the Color blending mode. Adjust the Opacity slider as desired.

TIP

Colorize Another Way

You can use a Hue/Saturation adjustment layer to tint the image. Just click the Colorize option and adjust the sliders to taste.

VIDEO 89:
Replacing Skies

Blown-out Skies

A professional photographer can spend a good part of a day waiting for the perfect sky and weather conditions. You, however, may not be as lucky. Skies will often be washed out and appear missing due to overexposure. One solution is to take pictures of

the sky when it looks its best, and then use a few techniques to combine two or more images into a new composite.

1. Close any open files, and then open the file Ch11_Fix_Sky.tif from the Chapter 11 folder.

2. Use the Color Range command (Select > Color Range) to choose the sky region.

3. Subtract any stray selections in the lower half of the photo by using the Lasso tool and holding down the Option (Alt) key. Alternatively, switch to Quick Mask mode for more detailed touch-up of the selection.

4. Double-click the *Background* layer to float it. Name the layer **Boat** and click OK.

5. Invert the selection by choosing Select > Inverse or by pressing Shift+Command+I (Shift+Ctrl+I).

6. Use the Refine Edge command to improve the selection and add a layer mask to the image.

7. Click the Add layer mask button to mask the sky area.

Let's now add a new sky. You'll find a diverse collection of skies in the Chapter 11 folder in a subfolder named Skies. Match one that has the right color and time of day for this photo (try DSC_2197.jpg). Feel free to use the others for future projects.

8. Choose File > Place and select the file DSC_2197.jpg. Press Return (Enter) to apply the placed photo.

9. Drag the sky photo behind your masked image. Use the Free Transform command to scale and position the clouds. There may be fringe on the edges that will need touching up.

10. Select the Layer Mask thumbnail in the Layers panel.

11. Open the Properties panel and click the Mask Edge button to refine the mask as desired.

12. Touch up any problem areas on the Layer Mask. Use the Smudge tool set to Darken mode to touch up the area around the trees on the right of the frame. You can also touch up the Layer Mask by using a paintbrush and black set to 20% Opacity. Brush over areas that need to be blended.

13. Blur the sky slightly so it better matches the depth of field in the image. Use the trees for guidance. You can use the Gaussian blur filter (Filter > Blur > Gaussian Blur) set to a value of 4–6 pixels.

TIP

Shooting Skies

The desert or the ocean is the best place to shoot the sky. This is often because the amount of environmental and light pollution is greatly reduced. Don't worry if this isn't an option for you; just keep your eyes out for a great day with beautiful skies and remember to shoot some still plates for your collection.

14. To make the colors match better, you can place a second copy of the sky on top. Be sure just the blue sky is covering the photo. Set the blending mode to Overlay or Soft Light and lower the Opacity of the layer.

The completed image, Ch11_ Fix_Sky_Completed.tif, is on the DVD if you'd like to examine it more closely.

Remove Grain/Noise

Often, distracting noise or grain will appear in your image. This is typically caused by shooting photos with a high ISO setting on a digital camera, but it can also be caused by underexposure or a long shutter speed. A lower-quality consumer camera is also more likely to exhibit noise problems. Additionally, film grain can be picked up by a scanner and cause problems as well.

The most common type of noise is luminance (grayscale) noise where the noise does not have varying colors. This noise is usually more pronounced in one channel of the image, usually the blue channel. By adjusting for noise on a per-channel basis, higher-image quality can be maintained. Let's give it a try:

1. Close any open files, and then open the file Ch11_Remove Grain.tif from the Chapter 11 folder.

2. Activate the Channels panel and view each channel separately. Click the channel's name to isolate it. Do this for each channel.

   You should notice a large amount of noise in the Blue channel.

3. Activate all three channels by clicking the RGB composite channel.

4. Choose Filter > Reduce Noise.

5. Select the Advanced radio button to enable per-channel corrections. This allows for additional correction to be added at the channel level.

TIP

Remove Noise from a Raw File

You learned how to remove noise and grain from a raw file in Chapter 10. Go back and watch video #76 if needed.

6. Switch to the Blue channel within the filter's dialog box and adjust Strength and Preserve Details as desired.

Adding Lens Blur

Selectively blurring an image can help your viewer find a focal point. Photoshop offers a realistic lens blur that also produces depth-of-field blurring. This allows some objects to be in focus while others fall out of focus. You can be very specific in regard to the blurring if you make an accurate alpha channel to serve as a depth matte. The depth matte defines how far away things are from the camera. Black areas in the alpha channel are treated as being the foreground, whereas white areas are seen as being in the distance.

VIDEO 90:
Lens Blur

1. Close any open files, and then open the file Lens Ch11_Lens Blur.tif from the Chapter 11 folder.

   An alpha channel has already been added to the image. It was created using the Calculations command and Quick Mask mode (see Chapter 5, "Selection Tools and Techniques").

2. Make sure the RGB composite channel is selected.

3. Choose Filter > Blur > Lens Blur to run the Lens Blur filter.

4. Choose the alpha channel from the Source menu. You can click the Invert box if you need to reverse the blur. For faster previews, choose Faster. When you're ready to see the final appearance, select More Accurate.

5. Adjust the Iris shape to curve or rotate the iris. Photoshop mimics how a traditional lens operates. Even if you are not an experienced photographer, you can twiddle and adjust as desired.

6. Move the Blur Focal Distance slider until the desired pixels are in focus. Additionally, you can click inside the preview image to set the Blur Focus Distance.

7. You can add Specular Highlights by adjusting the Threshold slider. You must set the cutoff point for where highlights occur. Then increase the highlights with the Brightness slider.

8. Finally, it's a good idea to add a little noise/grain back into the image. Normally, the blur obscures this, but putting it back in makes the photo seem more natural as opposed to processed.

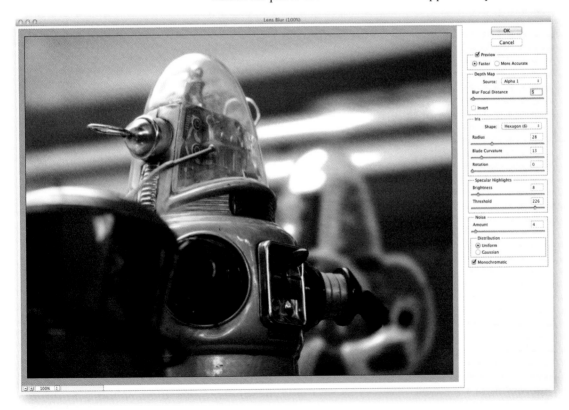

Using Vanishing Point

Vanishing Point is a special plug-in that allows for perspective cloning. Essentially, a user can identify perspective planes (such as sides of a building), and then apply edits such as painting, cloning, copying or pasting, and transforming. All the edits to the image honor the perspective of the plane you are working on; basically, you are retouching the image dimensionally. This produces significantly more realistic results, but it does take some time to set up.

VIDEO 91:
Vanishing Point

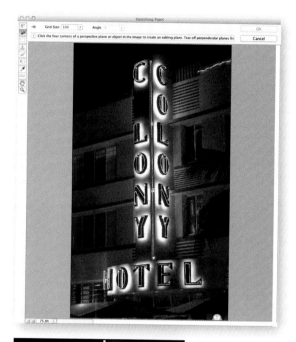

1. Close any open files, and then open the file Ch11_VP.tif from the Chapter 11 folder. This photo of a sign is marred because one of the letters is burned out. With Vanishing Point you can clone or repair the sign.

2. Invoke the Vanishing Point dialog box by choosing Filter > Vanishing Point. This will bring up a custom interface for defining the perspective planes, as well as tools for editing the image.

   You must first specify planes to define perspective in the image. For this photo, you want to replace the burned-out letter O.

3. Choose the Create Plane tool and define the four corner nodes of the plane surface. You can use the edges of the sign for guidance when creating the plane. See the figure for guidance.

4. After creating the four corner nodes, Photoshop allows you to move, scale, or reshape the plane. An accurate plane means accurate vanishing point effects, so take your time. If there's a problem with a corner node's placement, the bounding box and grid turn red or yellow. You must then move a corner node until the bounding box and grid turn blue or green. This means that the plane is valid. A plane that is yellow or red is a problem plane and needs to be adjusted.

5. Grab the left edge of the plane and extend it to the left, and then repeat for the right edge. This gives you more room for cloning. Strokes can be painted only onto the grid.

6. Zoom in so you can make a more accurate selection.

7. Select the Stamp tool in the Vanishing Point window. Option-click (Alt-click) on the illuminated letter O that is on the front of the sign. You can also experiment with the Heal option to improve the blending.

8. Position your painting cursor (using the preview for guidance) and clone the illuminated letter over the burned-out letter.

9. When you're satisfied with the perspective cloning, click OK.

Table 11.1 shows the keyboard shortcuts to make Vanishing Point easy to use.

Table 11.1 Vanishing Point Shortcut Keys

Result	Mac OS	Windows
Zoom tool	Z	Z
Zoom 2x (temporary)	X	X
Hand tool	H	H
Switch to Hand tool	Spacebar	Spacebar (temporary)
Zoom in	Command+=	Ctrl+=
Zoom out	Command+- (minus)	Ctrl+- (minus)
Increase brush size	]	] (Brush, Clone tools)
Decrease brush size	[	[(Brush, Clone tools)
Increase brush	Shift+]	Shift+] (Brush, Clone tools) hardness
Decrease brush	Shift+[	Shift+[(Brush, Clone tools) hardness
Undo last action	Command+Z	Ctrl+Z
Deselect all	Command+D	Ctrl+D
Hide selection	Command+H	Ctrl+H and planes
Repeat last duplicate	Command+Shift+T	Ctrl+Shift+T and move
Fill a selection	Option-drag	Alt-drag under the pointer with image
Create a duplicate of	Command+Option-drag	Ctrl+Alt-drag a floating selection
Render plane grids	Option-click OK	Alt-click OK
Exit plane creation	Command+. (period)	Ctrl+. (period)

Using the Type Tool

Although Photoshop initially had *very* primitive type tools, its capabilities have grown significantly because many people choose to create and stylize type within Photoshop. This flexibility allows many designers to start (and even finish) designs inside Photoshop.

For many tasks, like multimedia and web graphics, Photoshop plays an important role. In fact, if raster graphics are the intended output, Photoshop offers a full suite of typographic controls. Even if you intend to use other tools for text layout, it's worth spending time learning Photoshop. With support for precision layout as well as the use of text and paragraph styles, the Photoshop CS6 upgrade takes typography to a new level.

The Photoshop text engine is the standard that Adobe uses throughout its software products. Working with type might seem foreign at first, but you'll find that type is fairly easy once you understand a few key areas of the interface.

Open the file Ch12_Colonial_Postcard. psd to explore using type in a finished design. In this case Photoshop was used to design a postcard.

Role of Type

Many people rely on pictures to tell a story, but there's just no getting around the use of type. Sure, a picture of a bus on a street sign would clue most into realizing they were standing at a bus stop, but you couldn't stop there. Without accurate use of a few letters and numbers, you'd have little confidence in the route or timing of the service. It is proper use of type that designers must rely on to communicate vital information to audiences. If you can combine this functional purpose with a better sense of style and control, you can improve the professional appearance of your designs.

Choosing Fonts

Font choice can be a very tough decision for you if you are a new designer. You can easily become overwhelmed with the sheer quantity of options. To simplify the process, you need to approach this decision with a triage mentality and consider a few guiding questions:

- **Readability.** Is the font clear to read at the size you are using it? Are all the characters in the line readable? If you look at it quickly and then close your eyes, what do you remember about the text block?

- **Style.** Does the font convey the right emotion for your design? The text on an action movie poster is very different from that advertising the latest romantic comedy. Type is a like wardrobe; picking the right font is essential to the success of the design.

- **Flexibility.** Does the font mix well with others? Does it come in various weights (such as bold, italic, and book) that make it easier to convey significance when using that font?

These are my three guiding principles, but there are other constraints at play as well that require much more analysis. It's a good idea to formally study typography if you want to work in a design field professionally. At the bare minimum, you can at least read a few books. I strongly recommend *The Mac Is Not a Typewriter* (Peachpit Press, 2003) by Robin Williams and *Stop Stealing Sheep & Find Out How Type Works* (Adobe Press, 2002) by Erik Spiekermann and E.M. Ginger. But for now, let's go over the essentials.

Serif vs. Sans Serif

A font has many characteristics, but the presence or lack of serifs is one of the easiest to identify. Serifs are the hooks that distinguish the details of letter shape. Sans serif fonts tend to be more uniform in shape. Choosing which type of font to use will greatly depend on your needs.

Table 12.1 shows the pros and cons of serif versus sans serif fonts.

Table 12.1   Comparison of Serif vs. Sans Serif Fonts

	Pros	Cons
Serif	• Increased readability • More traditional • More options available due to longer history	• Thin lines can cause problems for low-resolution printing or applications like video and Internet
Sans Serif	• More modern • Can compress more information into a smaller space • Optimal for onscreen usage	• Letter shapes not often as unique • Can be harder to read if too stylized

X-Height, Ascenders, and Descenders

You'll quickly notice that point size for fonts is a very relative measurement. The apparent size of your text will depend on which font you choose and what resolution your document is set to. Most designers look at the height of a lowercase *x* when deciding which font to use, because a lowercase *x* is a very clean letter with a distinct top and bottom. By comparing the *x* characters, you can quickly compare and contrast fonts. This measurement is combined with ascenders (strokes that go above the top of the *x*) and descenders (strokes that go below the bottom of the *x*, or the baseline). These three aspects provide a visual clue to the font's purposes. Heavily stylized fonts (such as those used for titles or logos) often have greater variety than those intended for a page layout, where the text must take up little space yet remain easy to read.

Font Weight/Font Families

If a font comes in several weights (such as bold, condensed, book, italic), it offers increased flexibility. These different versions of a font are called a font family. When choosing a font to use in a design, pros often look to font families. Some of the best designs use a single font family but mix weights. This allows a consistent look with the added benefit of a consistent style throughout. You'll find font families listed next to the font name in the Options bar and in the Character panel.

Using Vector Type

Now that you have a clear understanding of the basics, you can start to use text in Photoshop. Your goal should be to keep your fonts as vector type as much as possible. Type will be created as a vector if you use the Horizontal or Vertical Type tools. Vector type uses curved lines, not pixels, that can be scaled and transformed infinitely without quality loss. This allows you to make last-minute changes, like scaling the headline bigger on your print advertisement when the client requests it, and allows greater flexibility for changes throughout the design process.

Type Tool

Photoshop has two kinds of type tools that use vectors: the Horizontal Type tool and (the much less used) Vertical Type tool.

Let's try adding some text using the Horizontal Type tool.

1. Create a new document by pressing Command+N (Ctrl+N). From the Preset list choose 800 × 600 and click OK.

2. Press T (for Type) to select the Horizontal Type tool or click the Text icon (a black letter T). You can then press Shift+T to cycle through the four Type tools as needed. As an alternative, you can click and hold on the T in the Tools panel to see a flyout list of tools.

3. Notice that several options related to type are now available in the Options bar. These options are discussed in the following sections. For now, click the color well in the Options bar and specify a color that will contrast with your background.

VIDEO 92:
Formatting Text

4. Click once inside your document; a new type layer is added. Type a few words to practice. Good? OK, now you'll learn what all those newly available options mean.

5. Click the Commit button in the Options bar and leave this document open as you experiment with other typographic controls.

Point Text vs. Paragraph Text

When adding text to a document, you have two options that determine how that text behaves. Point Text adds text beginning at the point where you click and continuing from there. Paragraph Text constrains the text to a box and will wrap when it hits the edge. To create a Paragraph Text block, click and drag using the Type tool to define the paragraph area first. Which option you choose depends on your design needs.

Table 12.2 shows the pros and cons of using Point Text and Paragraph Text.

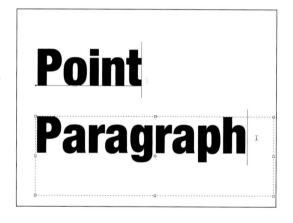

Table 12.2   **Point Text vs. Paragraph Text**

	Pros	Cons
Point Text	• Instant results • Good for small amounts of text • More flexible when using Warped Text (see "Warped Text" later in the chapter)	• Can lead to manual reformatting, including inserting manual hard returns
Paragraph Text	• Adds column-like behavior to page layout • Allows for use of hyphenation and Adobe Every-line Composer for smoother layout (more on this option in the "Paragraph Panel" section of this chapter)	• If text is too large at the start, you may not see the text entry • Can require designer to resize text block to accommodate copy or font changes

Number of Fonts

There are no hard and fast rules about how many fonts to use on a page, but here are a few "basics":

- Using a font family (with mixed weights/styles) is best.
- Using two fonts is good.
- Using three fonts is OK.
- Using four fonts—are you sure?
- Using five fonts or more— you're in trouble!

Character Panel

The bulk of your control over type lies in the Character panel. This panel gives you access to options that allow you to control the characters in your text block including basics such as font, size, and weight, as well as important advanced controls like kerning and baseline shift. If you don't see the Character panel icon in the Options bar, choose Window > Character. There are several controls here—all of them are essential, so let's take a look at each one.

Font Family

Setting the font family simply means picking the font you want to use. Nothing too complex, but navigating hundreds of fonts in your Font Family menu can be time-consuming. Here are a few tips to help you choose a font quickly:

- You can click in the Font Family field and just start typing the font name to jump through the list.

- If a text layer is active or even just selected, you can click in the Font Family field. Use the up and down arrows to cycle through loaded fonts.

- To make selection easy, you can see the fonts in their actual face. Just click the Font Family down arrow to see a font preview.

Name That Font

Are you trying to match a particular font for your design? A useful website is www.WhatTheFont.com, which offers visual recognition for type. Simply load a JPEG file with a text sample, and it will try to match the font to an extensive database.

Font Style

Certain fonts have multiple styles or weights—just look at the Font Style menu, which is to the right of the Font Family menu. Click the triangle to access the menu and choose variations like bold, italic, and condensed (as long as the font was designed to include them). This is a *much* better option than using the Type Enhancements buttons at the bottom of the Character panel. The Type

Enhancement buttons simply thicken the character (for faux bold) or skew it (for faux italic). This can produce text that is much harder to read and is generally not very elegant. It is always best to use the true bold or italic versions created by the font's designer.

Font Size

Traditionally, type is measured in points. The PostScript standard (which was developed for use by commercial and laser printers) uses 72 points per inch. However, this principle doesn't hold up very well, because different fonts will have different x-heights.

Instead of worrying about point size, just use it as a "relative" measurement. Increase the point size to make text appear larger, decrease it to reduce the size of the text. If you need to be more precise, such as designing text for the web, you can measure text in pixels.

To switch text measurement to pixels:

1. Press Command+K (Ctrl+K) to launch the Preferences dialog box.

2. Choose the Units & Rulers category.

3. In the Units area, switch Type to be measured in Pixels if you want a more precise measurement.

Leading

Pronounced "*led*-ing" as in the metal, not "*lead*-ing" as in sheep, leading is the space between lines of type. The name comes from when strips of lead were used on a printing press to space out lines of text. Adjust your leading value to improve your text's readability. Leading works best when you are using Paragraph Text. By default, the leading should be set to Auto; however, adjust as needed to fit text into your design. Just be careful to avoid setting leading too tight; otherwise, your ascenders and descenders will collide, resulting in a negative impact on readability.

NOTE

Finding Fonts

Here are a few of my favorite websites that offer free and affordable fonts:

- **Chank**
  www.chank.com

- **Fonthead**
  www.fonthead.com

- **DincType**
  www.GirlsWhoWearGlasses.com

- **Font Bros**
  www.FontBros.com

- **Acid Fonts**
  www.AcidFonts.com

- **1001 Free Fonts**
  www.1001freefonts.com

- **FontSpace**
  www.fontspace.com

NOTE

Spell Check?

Ewe betcha! Starting with version 7, Photoshop includes a Check Spelling command (it's in the Edit menu).

Welcome

improper kerning

Welcome

proper kerning

Kerning

Adjusting the space between individual letter pairs is called kerning. So what, you say, why bother? Design pros *always* check their kerning. Adjusting the space between letter pairs produces a better optical flow. Think of each word as existing in a stream; you are trying to balance out the spacing between each letter so the water flows evenly between each letter pair.

Taking the extra effort to kern letters will produce text that is easy to read. This is especially true as your text block gets bigger. Inexpensive fonts and freeware fonts usually have the most kerning problems because it takes a lot of effort for a fontmaker to set proper kerning for every possible letter combination. Cheap or free fonts are just that–cheap or free and may have kerning issues. Although you can adjust kerning using the Character panel, here's a more "organic" method:

1. With the Type tool, click between two letters in the file you created earlier.

2. Hold down the Option (Alt) key and use the left arrow key to tighten the spacing between a character pair, or use the right arrow key to loosen spacing.

3. Release the Option (Alt) key and then use the arrow keys to move to the next pair.

4. Hold down the Option (Alt) key and repeat kerning as desired.

For a more artistic example of good kerning, open the project file Ch12_Surf_Card.psd to examine its construction.

tracking

loose tracking

tracking

tight tracking

Tracking

Kerning adjusts the space between pairs of letters, but tracking affects all letters in the text block or the selection. Tracking can be adjusted to fit text into a smaller space, for example, if you must fit a certain number of characters on a line without reducing point size.

Conversely, you might choose a loose track to improve readability (especially if you're using all caps). Tracking, like kerning, is subjective and can be learned best by studying professional examples and looking for inspiration and guidance.

Vertical Scale

Do you need to make the text a little taller? Perhaps you want to make the text look skinnier, or you are trying to create a stretched look. Well, you can adjust the vertical scale from 0–1000% if you are so inclined. Normally, this causes unintentional fluctuations in font appearance. If you are working on a shared computer, be sure to inspect this option and make sure it's set to 100% before designing to avoid unintentional scaling.

Horizontal Scale

You can use horizontal scale to compress (or expand) the width of text. By scaling down text, you can pack more text on a line. Increasing horizontal scale can make the text appear "fatter." Normally, this kind of scaling is less desirable than trying to find a font that better matches your design goals. Be sure to check to see if scaling is applied before designing with the Type tool.

Baseline Shift

Earlier, baseline was discussed when you learned about x-height. This is the virtual line that the characters sit on. If you need to reposition elements such as quote marks or apostrophes for design purposes, this property is useful.

Text Color

By default, text in Photoshop is black. Although black is a very functional color (a third of my wardrobe is black or a shade of black), it won't always work for your designs. Click the Color Swatch to load the Color Picker window. Click a radio button for the color model you want to work with, and then adjust the Color slider as desired. Click in the Color Field to choose the color you want. If you need to use a Pantone color (or at least a close equivalent), click the Color Libraries button (selecting colors is covered in depth in Chapter 6, "Painting and Drawing Tools").

Type Enhancement Buttons

Herein lies a collection of treasures as well as several booby traps. Some of the Type Enhancement buttons are truly useful, but others are just plain bad design and should only be used in a pinch:

- **Faux Bold.** Faux is French for *fake*. Do not use a faux bold if a true bold is available within the font style you are using. This button just makes the text thicker and harder to read.

- **Faux Italic.** Same deal here: Skewing the text to the right does not make it italic. Always choose an italic version of the font you are using from the Font Style field.

- **All Caps.** Formats the text in all uppercase letters; just click this button instead of retyping.

- **Small Caps.** Works well for titles and in certain layouts. It replaces all lowercase text with a smaller version of the capital letter.

- **Subscript.** Used for scientific notation and other specialty purposes where a character is reduced in size and lowered below the baseline.

- **Superscript.** Used for specialty purposes such as showing mathematical power. This reduces the character's size and moves it above the baseline.

- **Underline.** Draws a line below the text. You may choose to manually add a line on another layer for better control.

- **Strikethrough.** Places a line through the characters to indicate text for removal.

italic
faux italic

Notice the dramatic differences between choosing italic from the Font Style menu as opposed to choosing the Type Enhancement button.

H_2O
subscript

$E=mc^2$
superscript

Ligatures

Some fonts contain additional ornamental elements. These characters can be difficult to access because they are not on standard keys. To make it easier to find them, the Character panel has special buttons near the bottom. Which options are available depends on the chosen font. These can include ligatures, fractions, swashes, ornaments, ordinals, titling and stylistic alternates, superior and inferior characters, old-style figures, and lining figures. For more details on ligatures, see the Photoshop Help menu.

Language Selection Menu

Computers should help make the design process easy, so in this vein, recent versions of Photoshop ship with a built-in spell check. Not every country is represented, but you do have obscure options like Nynorsk Norwegian and Turkish.

1. In the Character panel, select the language you are using.

2. Choose Edit > Check Spelling to invoke the spell check for all visible layers. The language chosen in this setting will also affect the hyphenation of words.

Anti-alias Menu

When designing text at low resolutions, adjusting your Anti-alias settings can improve readability. Anti-aliasing blends the edge pixels of text. This option is most needed when working with complex character shapes. You have five methods to choose from:

- **None.** No anti-aliasing
- **Sharp.** Makes text appear its sharpest
- **Crisp.** Makes text appear somewhat sharp
- **Strong.** Makes text appear heavier
- **Smooth.** Makes text appear smoothest

Smooth   None

Paragraph Panel

To complete your control over text, you'll need to visit the Paragraph panel. Even though there are not as many choices as the Character panel, you will still need these controls. The Paragraph panel, as its name implies, works best with Paragraph Text.

Use of the Paragraph panel results in precisely aligned text on this poster. Open the project Ch12_Concert_Sign. psd file to examine its construction.

Alignment/Justification Buttons

The Alignment buttons attempt to align text left, right, or centered. They also add support for justification, which forces the text to align to both margins through the adjustment of spaces between words.

Indent Fields

The three Indent fields allow for the indentation of the left or right margins, as well as the first line of text. If you will have multiple lines of text, be sure to use the first line indentation to improve readability.

Spacing Fields

To further improve readability when multiple paragraphs are involved, use the Spacing option. You can specify how much space to add before or after a paragraph (either really works the same). This is a much better option than adding extra hard returns at the end of a paragraph.

Enable Hyphenation

At the bottom of the Paragraph panel is a Hyphenate check box. If selected, it allows lines to break mid-word. Photoshop uses the selected dictionary from the Language Selection menu in the Paragraph panel. Although the Hyphenate option better fills out a text block, it is not always the best for large type. It is more acceptable for a multicolumn layout or body copy. Be sure to try the Adobe Single-line and Every-line Composer options, which you can access from the Paragraph panel submenu:

- **Adobe Single-line Composer.** Determines line breaks on a line-by-line basis. It is the default option, but it can often lead to strange hyphenation or line breaks.

- **Adobe Every-line Composer.** Examines the entire block of text and makes line breaks based on all lines of text. This option can often create a better visual flow and is generally preferable to the Single-line Composer.

What's the Order?

Type styles have a *hierarchical* relationship. The paragraph style affects all of the text for a paragraph, whereas a character style can override it and modify individual letters or words within. Both can be replaced by formatting individual characters using the Character panel.

Styles allow you to quickly format your text. A style can contain formatting for individual characters (such as bold or italic) or for an

Applying Styles

Styles allow you to quickly format your text. A style can contain formatting for individual characters (such as bold or italic) or for an entire paragraph (like hyphenation or alignment). They are typically used in page layout applications, but have made their way into Photoshop CS6. If you find yourself working with text a lot, using styles can add consistency and save time.

Character Styles

The Character Styles panel can be accessed by choosing Window > Character Styles. The panel is used to specify the

look of individual characters or words. To create a character style, simply select a character or word and modify its style using the Character panel. Then click the Create New Character Style button at the bottom of the Character Styles panel. If you want to closely see the content of the style, just double-click it in the list. You can then name the style as well as see all the properties that have been applied.

Paragraph Styles

The creation and use of Paragraph Styles is nearly identical to Character Styles. A paragraph style has all of the same styles as a character except it applies a style to an entire paragraph (regardless of what's selected). The paragraph style also allows for options to control line indents, alignment, and hyphenation. To properly use the Paragraph Styles options, be sure to double-click a style and view all of its properties (updating where needed).

Clear Overrides

If you've modified text after you've applied a style, it is considered an override. In this case, you can use it as is or click the Clear Override button at the bottom of the Character Styles or Paragraph Styles panel (both are a curved arrow pointing backwards). This will remove the additional style and reset the text to the state specified by the originally applied style.

Modifying Text

If you need to tweak your text a little more, you're in luck. Photoshop has even more options for typographic effects. The next five options discussed can truly enhance your typographic treatments.

Free Transform

Because the text you're using is vector-based, it can be sized and modified using the Free Transform command with no loss of quality. The text will "redraw" itself after the command is applied. The Free Transform command lets you rotate, scale, skew, distort, and add perspective in one continuous operation, which ensures the highest quality of your text. Let's experiment with this command.

1. Select your text layer and press Command+T (Ctrl+T) or choose Edit > Free Transform.

2. Do one or more of the following options:

   • To scale by dragging, drag a handle.

   • Press Shift while dragging a corner handle to scale proportionately.

   • Press the Option (Alt) key while dragging a corner handle to scale from the center.

Reuse Styles

If you want to permanently store a style to reuse in a different document, just click the panel submenu button (in the upper-right corner of the panel). This allows you to save styles to a common library that can then be reloaded with another document.

NOTE

Simple Design Rules

- Limit total number of fonts used.
- Use heavier fonts if designing for onscreen display (web, presentations, or video).
- Make sure text is readable. Print it out or at least move a few feet away from the computer screen and take a fresh look.
- Be consistent with capitalization and justification.
- Do not overuse Layer Styles.

- To rotate by dragging, move the pointer outside the bounding border. Notice that the pointer changes to a curved, two-sided arrow. Click and drag.

- To distort freely, press Command (Ctrl) while dragging a handle.

- To skew, press Command+Shift (Ctrl+Shift) while dragging a handle.

- To apply perspective change, press Command+Option+Shift (Ctrl+Alt+Shift) while dragging a handle. You may also need to combine this option with Scale to achieve a believable perspective change.

- If you forget how to do any of the preceding options, right-click (Ctrl-click) a corner of the transform box to display a pop-up list of options.

3. Click the Commit button (the check mark in the Options bar).

Text on a Path

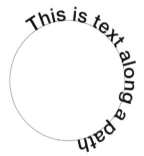

Originally a job for Illustrator, placing text along a vector path allows you to make text follow a curved line or other geometric shape. Starting with Photoshop CS, this ability could be achieved in Photoshop.

1. Add a path to your document using the Pen tool or Shape tool.

2. With the Horizontal Type tool selected, move over the path until your cursor changes to a new icon (an I-bar with a curved path).

3. Click and start typing.

4. Use the Direct Selection tool to move the margin of the text for repositioning. You can also pull up or down to move the text to the inside or outside of the path.

5. Adjust the baseline and tracking as needed for improved readability.

6. Click the Commit button or press Return (Enter).

Warped Text

With names like Flag, Fish, and Wave, the Warp Text dialog box doesn't scream *useful*. However, a lot of powerful (and useful) distortions are available. These vector distortions allow you to reshape text, which is particularly helpful for advertising-style type effects:

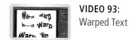

VIDEO 93:
Warped Text

1. Select an existing text block.

2. Click the Create warped text button in the Options bar.

3. Choose a Style for the warp and specify Horizontal or Vertical.

4. Additionally, experiment with the Bend, Horizontal Distortion, and Vertical Distortion properties.

5. Click OK when you're satisfied.

6. To modify the text effect after you've closed the Warp Text dialog box, simply click the Create warped text button again.

Using Layer Styles

Text often needs a little style, and Layer Styles allow you to add a stroke, shadow, bevel, or even texture to your text. At the bottom of the Layers panel you'll see a small *f*x. This is the easiest way to access Layer Styles. But be sure to show good taste and not go wild with effects. Let's work with some prebuilt styles to see the possibilities available to you.

1. Select or create a text layer.

2. Select the Styles panel or choose Window > Styles to open the Styles panel.

3. From the panel's submenu (the triangle in the right corner), choose Text Effects.

4. Click a style's thumbnail to apply the effect; just click another to apply an additional effect.

Some of these effects are attractive and useful; many are gaudy (but that is my personal taste). The best approach is to create your own styles. Be sure to see Chapter 13, "Layer Styles," for more information.

System Performance

Having too many fonts active can impact the performance of your system by hogging RAM and slowing system boot and application launch times. Instead, use a font manager like FontBook or Suitcase to better manage your font collection.

VIDEO 94:
3D Text

Filters on Text

If you want to run a filter on text, Photoshop will rasterize the text. This process converts the text from being vector-based (and scalable) into pixel data (which cannot be enlarged without visible softening of the edges due to blowing up pixels). When you have a text layer selected and you want to apply a filter, Photoshop will warn you that it will rasterize the type and leave it uneditable. Click OK if you are sure you want to do this. I recommend making a duplicate text layer as a backup (with the visibility icon turned off) before filtering text, or try to create the effect using Layer Styles and warped text instead. Open the file Ch12_Light.psd to see an effect that combines the Radial Blur–Zoom filter with Layer Styles.

Layer Styles 13

Photoshop comes with several built-in effects: shadows, glows, bevels, textures, and strokes. These effects allow for quick changes to a layer's appearance. Layer Styles are "live" effects, which is to say that as the content of a layer updates, so does the effect. For example, if you have a bevel and shadow applied to a type layer and you change the text, the effect will be applied to the new characters. Because they update so quickly, Layer Styles have grown in popularity and are widely used by all kinds of designers.

This flower was created from two basic shapes. The beveling, textures, and colorization were done with Layer Styles. Open the file Ch13_Flower_Style. psd from the Chapter 13 folder on the DVD to explore the effects.

The effects that are applied to a layer become the layer's custom style. You can tell that an effect has been applied if an *f* icon appears to the right of the layer's name in the Layers panel. A layer style can be expanded by clicking the triangle icon next to the *fx* icon to reveal the layer effects in the panel. This makes it easier to edit the effects to modify the style. Let's start exploring the many options of Layer Styles and how they will impact your overall designs.

NOTE

New Order

The Layer Styles in Photoshop CS6 have been reordered. They now match the Z-order style in which they are actually applied (for example, drop shadow is at the bottom, below the other effects).

Adding a Layer Style

Photoshop offers ten effects to choose from. Each offers several options for customization and can be used to create unique and dynamic layer styles. Each effect has its own interface with many shared commonalities; however, each deserves close exploration.

1. Create a new document and choose the Photo category and the Portrait, 2×3 preset.

2. Select the Type tool and add the letter **T**. Use a thick sans serif font and set the point size large enough to fill the canvas. If you are not yet familiar with the Type tool, open Ch13_Layer_Style_Start.psd from the Chapter 13 folder.

3. At the bottom of the Layers panel, click the *fx* icon and choose the first effect, Drop Shadow.

4. The Layer Style dialog box opens and provides you with control over the effect.

Bevel and Emboss

The Bevel and Emboss effect is very versatile, but you'll need to be careful not to overdo it. You can use bevels in combination with other effects to create realistic depth. This effect has five different kinds of edges:

- **Outer Bevel** effect adds a three-dimensional beveled edge around the outside of a layer. This bevel is created by adding a clear edge.

- **Inner Bevel** effect generates a similar effect inside the edge. Instead of a clear edge, it uses the layer's pixels.

- **Emboss** effect combines inner and outer bevels into one effect.

- **Pillow Emboss** combines the inner and outer bevel effects, but it reverses the outer bevel. This causes the image to appear stamped into the layer.

- **Stroke Emboss** must be used with the Stroke Layer Style. These two effects combine to create a colored, beveled edge along the outside of the layer.

The Bevel and Emboss effect allows significant control over the edges. You can change the lighting source and direction of the bevel, as well as the bevel's thickness, softness, and depth:

- **Depth.** Specifies how thick the bevel is.

- **Direction.** Indicates whether the bevel goes up or down to change the look of the bevel.

- **Altitude.** Allows you to set the altitude of the light source between 0° and 90°. The higher the number, the more the bevel appears to go straight back.

- **Gloss Contour.** Creates a glossy, metallic appearance. The Gloss Contour is applied after shading the bevel or emboss.

- **Highlight Mode and Opacity.** Specify the blending mode and opacity of the highlight.

- **Shadow Mode and Opacity.** Specify the blending mode and opacity of the shadow.

Bevel Overuse

Don't over-bevel. A slight bevel helps a text or logo element lift off the page or screen and adds subtle depth. Overuse, however, looks amateurish.

Like a Style?

You can easily store a custom style as the default by clicking the Make Default button below the style. To reset an applied style for the default, just click the Reset to Default button.

THE FLEXIBLE POWER OF CONTOUR SETTINGS

The least understood option of Layer Styles is the Contour setting. Most users leave Contour set to the default linear slope setting. The easiest way to grasp the Contour setting is to think of it as a cross-section of the bevel (it represents the shape of the bevel from a parallel point of view).

The basic linear contour reflects light with predictable results. However, irregularly shaped contours can generate metallic highlights or add rings to the bevel. The Contour setting is extremely powerful and unlocks many looks. Be sure to choose the Anti-aliased option for smoother results.

You have a few options available to modify a contour:

- Click the menu and select a preset.

- If you don't like the 12 included contours, you can load additional contours. Loading contours is similar to loading styles—just click the submenu triangle.

- You can make your own contours by defining the shape of the curve. Click the curve and add points. If the Preview check box is selected, the curve will update in near real time. This is the best way to learn how the Contour controls work. You'll find Contour controls on glows, shadows, and bevels.

You'll find an extra set of contours called UAP contours.shc in the Chapter 13 folder.

- **Contour.** Provides flexibility of the Contour controls and is the bevel effect's best option. There are two Contour settings: the first affects the bevel's lighting; the second, the specialized Contour pane, alters the shape of the edge.

- **Texture.** Allows you to add texture to the bevel. You'll find several textures available in the Pattern Picker, and additional textures can be added by loading them from the Picker's submenu.

Deselect the Bevel and Emboss check boxes to remove the bevel, and then select the Stroke check box.

Stroke

The Stroke effect places a colored border around the edge of a layer. You can choose from inner, outer, or center strokes, as well as advanced controls such blending modes, textures, and gradients. If you'd like to emboss the stroke, combine it with the Stroke Emboss effect (within the Bevel and Emboss options).

Deselect the Stroke check box to remove the stroke, and then select the Inner Shadow check box.

Inner Shadow

The Inner Shadow effect casts a shadow in front of the layer. This effect can be used to create a "punched-out" or recessed look. It looks best when the shadow is set to a soft setting. Inner shadows look good when used in combination with other layer styles but are distracting when overused.

The controls of this effect are nearly identical to the Drop Shadow; the only new setting is Choke. The Choke slider shrinks the boundaries of the Inner Shadow prior to blurring.

Deselect the Inner Shadow check box to remove the shadow, and then select the Inner Glow and Outer Glow check boxes.

Inner Glow and Outer Glow

The Inner Glow and Outer Glow effects create a glow on the outside and inside edges of an object. Both effects allow you to set the color, amount, and shape of the glow. If you choose a dark glow, you might need to change its blending mode to see it.

The key difference between the two is that Inner Glow lets you set the glow's emanation, either from the edges of the layer or from the center of the layer. Inner Glows signify light coming from behind the layer. It is unlikely that you would need to apply a Drop Shadow and a glow simultaneously. Tweak Contour and Quality add a variety of shapes to your glows. Use these options to further fine-tune the effect:

- **Technique.** You can choose the Softer option, but it does not preserve as many details. Choose Precise if the source has hard edges (like text or a logo).

- **Source.** Determines where an Inner Glow emanates from— either the edges or the center of a layer.

- **Range.** Helps target which portion of the glow is targeted by the contour.

- **Jitter.** Varies the application of the glow's gradient. It affects color and opacity.

Deselect the Outer Glow and Inner Glow check boxes to remove the glows, and then select the Satin check box.

VIDEO 95:
Type Effects

Easy Bake Effects

If you'd like to permanently apply a layer style, simply highlight the layer and choose File > Scripts > Flatten All Layer Effects.

Satin

You can use the Satin effect to add irregular ripples or waves in your layer style or to create liquid effects and subtle highlights. This effect requires experimentation because its controls are very sensitive. To create different looks, experiment with different colors, contour settings, and blending modes. The Satin effect works well in combination with other effects.

Deselect the Satin check box to remove the satin, and then select the Color Overlay check box.

Color Overlay

The Color Overlay style replaces the contents of your layer with a new fill color. This can be a great time-saver and allows for fast design of text effects or web buttons. Additionally, you can use blending modes to create tinting effects.

Deselect the Color Overlay check box to remove the color, and then select the Gradient Overlay check box.

NOTE

Adding Soft Highlights

Satin is an underused effect that can add soft highlights to a layer.

Gradient Overlay

The Gradient Overlay allows you to overlay a gradient on top of a layer. You can harness the full power of the Gradient Editor. For more on gradients, see Chapter 6, "Painting and Drawing Tools." The Dither option makes a cleaner gradient and should typically be selected for best results.

Deselect the Gradient Overlay check box to remove the gradient, and then select the Pattern Overlay check box.

Pattern Overlay

A Pattern Overlay uses photo-realistic patterns or seamless tiles. To create more believable effects, combine patterns with blending modes. Photoshop ships with several seamless patterns, and you can find several more online.

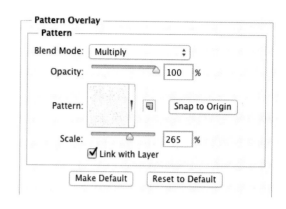

Deselect the Pattern Overlay check box to remove the pattern, and then select the Drop Shadow check box.

Drop Shadow

The Drop Shadow effect is straightforward and useful, and it serves as an introduction to the Layer Styles. Several of the Drop Shadows' interface elements appear in other effects. Let's examine its window closely:

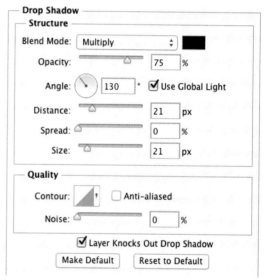

- **Blend Mode.** Specifies the blending mode for the shadow. This allows the shadow to more realistically blend with lower layers. The Multiply blending mode is the most common for shadows. This mode causes the darkness of the shadow to mix with background colors, which more closely simulates a natural shadow.

- **Color.** By default, color is set to black for the shadow. But shadows often pick up the color of the light source or background. To change the color of the shadow, click the color rectangle to load the Adobe Color Picker.

- **Opacity.** Adjusts the opacity of the effect. Opacity is the opposite of transparency: the higher the number, the less you can see through the layer.

VIDEO 96:
Photo Effects

- **Angle.** Sets the direction of the shadow.

TIP

Change the Color of Several Layers at Once

1. Apply a Color Overlay Layer Style.
2. Copy the layer style by right-clicking (Ctrl-clicking) the small *fx* icon and choosing Copy Layer Style.
3. Select multiple layers that you want to change.
4. Right-click (Ctrl-click) and choose Paste Layer Style.

TIP

Make Up Your Mind... Or Change It

At the bottom of the Layer Styles controls are two buttons. You can click Make Default to have the current settings carry forward to new instances of layer styles. In the future, just click the Reset to Default button to change the current style to the stored default.

- **Use Global Light.** Allows you to use a consistent light source for all layer effects. It's a good idea to leave the Use Global Light check box selected so that your designs have realistic (and consistent) lighting.

- **Distance.** Affects how far the shadow is cast. You can also click in the window and manually drag the shadow into position.

- **Spread.** Affects how much the shadow disperses.

- **Size.** Modifies the softness of the shadow.

- **Contour.** Most users skip the Contour settings. This is a terrible mistake. The contour is essentially a curve; it is representative of how Photoshop fades transparency. There are several presets to try, and you'll explore this setting more later on.

- **Anti-aliased.** Gives you a smoother onscreen appearance. This is important if you are creating titles for screen usage (such as Internet or video).

- **Noise.** Places noise in the shadow, which adds random dispersion to your style.

- **Layer Knocks Out Drop Shadow.** Is selected by default (and should probably stay that way). It ensures that the shadow does not bleed through partially transparent text.

LAYER STYLE SHORTCUTS

Adobe created a few useful shortcuts that increase the efficiency of Layer Styles:

- Double-click a layer in the Layers panel (except on the name) to open the Layer Styles dialog box.
- To edit a specific effect, double-click its name in the Layers panel.
- Turn off an effect's visibility by clicking the eye icon next to it in the Layers panel.
- Copy and paste layer styles by right-clicking (Ctrl-clicking) the effect icon in the Layers panel and choosing Copy Layer Style. You can then paste layer styles to other layers by right-clicking (Ctrl-clicking) and choosing Paste Layer Style.
- Move a layer style from one layer to another by dragging it.
- Option-drag (Alt-drag) a layer style from one layer to another to copy it.

Working with Layer Styles

Using Layer Styles is an important part of a professional user's workflow. The efficiency and flexibility offered by Layer Styles are huge time-savers. They can also add consistency to a designer's techniques. Be sure to fully explore all the ways Layer Styles can be useful to you.

Using Prebuilt Layer Styles

Adobe Photoshop includes some very attractive Layer Style presets to work with. Using these presets is an excellent way to learn the potential of Layer Styles. By seeing the possibilities, you can learn how to combine effects to create your own custom looks.

1. Open the file Ch13_Style_Practice.psd from the Chapter 13 folder.

CREATING DUOTONES AND TREATED PHOTOS WITH LAYER STYLES

The Color, Gradient, and Pattern Overlays are very useful when working with photos. If you're working with groups of historical sources or grayscale photos, you can use Layer Styles to create consistent tinting effects. Often, it is easiest to strip out all the color data of a historical photo before restoring it. You can then add the duotone or sepia tone effect back in as the last step.

1. Open the file Ch13_Photo_ Styles_Practice.tif from the Chapter 13 folder.

2. Load the Layer Styles set UAP Photo-Styles.asl from the Chapter 13 folder as well.

3. Double-click the *Background* layer to float it. Name the layer *photo*.

4. Click the different styles to try them out.

5. Open the effect window and examine how blending modes and textures can be harnessed for powerful effects.

2. Activate the Styles panel by choosing Window > Styles. Each swatch represents a layer style. To apply a style, highlight any layer (other than the *Background* layer or a locked layer) and click a swatch.

3. If you need more looks, click the Styles panel submenu. You'll find several options built into Photoshop. When you select a new set of styles from the Preset list, you are presented with a choice:

   • **Append.** Adds new styles to the bottom of the current list

   • **Cancel.** Does not load anything new

   • **OK.** Replaces the current list with new presets

   You can also load styles that don't appear in the Preset list. Choose Load Styles from the Styles panel submenu. You'll find a collection of styles called UAP Styles.asl in the Chapter 13 folder. If you'd like these new styles to appear in your Preset list, locate the Presets folder inside your Photoshop application folder. Any Layer Style library copied into the Styles folder will appear as a preset the next time you launch the application.

You'll find these presets and 31 other styles in the UAP Styles set on the DVD.

Creating Your Own Layer Styles

It's a pretty straightforward process to create your own layer styles. You simply add one effect at a time and experiment with different combinations. Options like Contour and blending modes go a long way toward creating appealing layer styles. The Layer Styles feature is quick to learn and easy to master; just continue to experiment with many options.

Saving Layer Styles

Once you've created an original style (or even modified an existing one), you may want to save it. There are two ways to save a style:

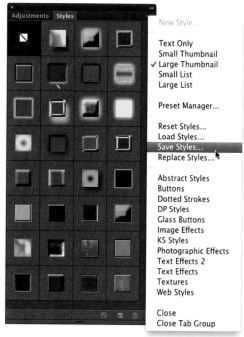

- **Embed.** Photoshop embeds the layer style information into the layered files. Be sure to save the document in a layered format (such as Photoshop Document, Layered TIFF, or Photoshop PDF). Three months from now, when your project comes back to life, you can open your source files and start making changes. Remember that layer styles will automatically update as you make edits to the layer.

- **Save as a Library.** After creating a layer style, you can add it to the open style library by clicking an empty space in the Styles window. A new thumbnail swatch is created, and you are prompted to name the swatch. It is then available to you until you load another style library.

If you want to permanently save styles, you must save a Styles library (or set) from the loaded swatches. It's a good idea to create a personal set in which to store your styles. There is no "new set" option. Simply create new styles and then delete any styles you don't want by dragging them onto the trash icon at the bottom of the panel or Option-clicking (Alt-clicking) an unwanted style. When you're ready to save, choose Save Styles from the Styles panel submenu.

You should store styles in <*Photoshop Application folder*> > Presets > Styles. Styles placed in this default location will appear in your menu when you restart Photoshop.

TIP

Scaling Styles

When you're changing the image size (Image > Image Size), specify that you'd like styles to scale proportionately.

Maximizing Filters

14

Filters are among Photoshop's most popular features. These specialized add-ons can be used to boost productivity or add special effects. Photoshop ships with over 100 built-in filters, and there is a rich array of others available from third-party developers. Filters are so popular that you'll find more tutorials online than you could ever make through in a lifetime.

Photoshop almost did not ship with filters, because many at Adobe thought they were too "gimmicky." However, John Knoll, co-creator of Photoshop, managed to "sneak" them in. Those early executives were partially right, though: When used improperly (or too often), filters can be gimmicky. Think of filters like spices: When used properly, they can add to a meal, but if they're overused, they can ruin it—and no one can live on spices alone.

Filters Defined

The proper use of filters can significantly extend Photoshop's capabilities. There are filters that perform important image-enhancement tasks for removing grain or damage. Additionally, filters can be used for tasks like blurring and sharpening image details.

Both built-in and third-party filters were run on this image. You would not normally run as many filters on a single image, but you can see just how diverse filters can be.

Filters allow you to achieve more quickly what otherwise would be time-consuming results; they can unlock options that could not be done with standard tools. Filters can often create stylized looks as well as enhance the lighting of a photo.

Gaussian Blur	⌘F
Convert for Smart Filters	
Filter Gallery...	
Adaptive Wide Angle...	⇧⌘A
Lens Correction...	⇧⌘R
Liquify...	⇧⌘X
Oil Paint...	
Vanishing Point...	⌥⌘V
Blur	▶
Distort	▶
Noise	▶
Pixelate	▶
Render	▶
Sharpen	▶
Stylize	▶
Video	▶
Other	▶
Digimarc	▶
Browse Filters Online...	

By definition, a filter must reside in Photoshop's Plug-ins folder. Besides the bundled filters that are installed with Photoshop, you'll find a few specialty filters on the Photoshop installer DVD or in the Support area of Adobe's website.

Preparing to Use Filters

Filters can save time and can be fun to use. But before you rush in and try out every filter in Photoshop, you need to make sure the image is ready to be processed. Many filters are render-intensive, so there's no reason to spend extra time on pixels you may be throwing away.

Fix Major Errors

Filtering mistakes only draws further attention to them. Most importantly, make sure the image is properly exposed with natural-looking contrast. This can be accomplished easily using a Levels adjustment (Image > Adjustments > Levels). For more on Levels, see Chapter 10, "Color Correction and Enhancement."

The original image (left) lacks contrast. Proper contrast (center) creates an image that's ready for filtering (right).

Set Your View

Filtering an image is easiest when you can see all your pixels (otherwise, resampling occurs). For best results, zoom in 100% or choose View > Actual Pixels. You can also double-click on the magnifying glass in the Tools panel or press Command+Option+0 (Ctrl+Alt+0). The Navigator panel is useful to get a global overview and to move quickly around an image that is zoomed in. Some filters also offer the ability to view a 100% preview in the filter interface.

Check the Color Mode

You'll want to be sure that you are working in RGB mode whenever possible (Image > Mode > RGB). This will ensure that you have the most filters available. Very few filters work in CMYK mode because CMYK conversion is supposed to be the last step in processing an image. Only filters that are meant for print work have been optimized to work in CMYK mode.

If you have a CMYK image and you need to convert it back to RGB mode for filtering, go ahead. You do not have to worry about color shift when converting from CMYK to RGB. Because CMYK has fewer colors than RGB, no information will be lost.

Check the Bit Depth

It's also important to keep an eye on bit depth when working with filters, or your filter options will be limited. The vast majority of filters only run on images in the 8-bit mode. In fact, as of Photoshop CS6, only 43 of the built-in Photoshop filters will work in 16-bit mode, and only 23 of them work in 32-bit mode.

The filters designed to work at higher bit depths are primarily for image enhancement (as opposed to stylization). These filters are targeted for use with digital photography applications. Although a 16-bit image can be processed more without showing banding or posterization, you may need to work in 8-bit mode. If you can work in 16-bit mode, do so, but be prepared to lose some functionality with filters and image adjustments. If a filter is grayed out, it doesn't work in the selected bit depth.

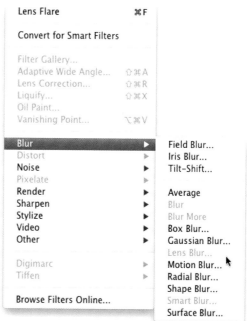

Depending on the Color Mode or Bit Depth, some filters will be unavailable. If the filter is grayed out, you'll need to choose another.

NOTE

Color-correct Before Filtering

An image should be color corrected properly before filtering. Remember: GIGO (garbage in = garbage out).

VIDEO 97:
Smart Filters

VIDEO 98:
Fading a Filter

Understanding Filter Interfaces

Because filters are designed for specialty purposes, the interface you use to control filters will vary. A few filters have no user interface (for example, Average, Despeckle, Facet). If a filter does not have an ellipsis (…) after its name, it has no user interface. These filters are fairly limited and will likely fall off your favorites list.

Most filters, however, will have some form of user interface. Some filters have their own window; others use the Filter Gallery. No matter which interface you use, consider selecting the Preview option. This allows you to see the filter's changes to your canvas before you actually apply the filter.

Here are a few more tips about using a filter's interface:

- Click in the preview window and drag your view to change the preview area.

- Use the + or - button under the preview window to zoom in or out. Additionally, you can zoom into the preview by pressing Command+= (Ctrl+=) and zoom out with Command+- (Ctrl +-).

- Click in the image window to adjust the center point of the preview window. (This may not work in all cases.)

- When you're in a dialog box, fully explore it. Try adjusting all the variable sliders one at a time. If there's a Load button, try loading presets that shipped with the product.

- To see the "before" state, click and hold inside the preview window. When you release, the filter preview is shown again.

Depending on the filter chosen, Photoshop will use a different interface. Newer filters like Oil Paint have a very large preview area while older filters like Diffuse have a much smaller preview area. The Gallery Effects filters have a unique user interface that allows multiple effects to be combined into a single operation.

Getting the Best Results

Many people simply "slap" filters on their images and expect great results. This bandage approach does not usually create award-winning results. With a little bit of care, you can achieve significantly better looks.

Using Smart Filters

If you'd like maximum flexibility, you can choose to apply filters to a Smart Object. Any filter applied to a Smart Object is applied as a Smart Filter. The names of the Smart Filters appear in the Layers panel directly below the Smart Object they have been applied to. Smart Filters can be adjusted, masked, or removed at any time (even after a document has been closed and reopened). This makes using Smart Filters essentially nondestructive but can slow down your system if you're working on high-resolution images.

Let's practice with Smart Filters:

1. Open the Ch14_Well.tif file from the Chapter 14 folder on the DVD.

2. Choose Filter > Convert For Smart Filters, and click OK. If an item is already a Smart Object, there is no need to convert it.

3. Choose Filter > Sharpen > Smart Sharpen, and adjust the filter as desired.

4. Click OK to apply the filter. The Smart Filter appears below the Smart Filters line in the Layers panel beneath the Smart Object layer.

   Let's modify the Smart Filter's results.

TIP

Is There an Interface?

If a filter name is followed by an ellipsis (...), it has a dialog box that will open. If not, the filter is as-is and cannot be tweaked before application (but you can still use the Fade command afterward).

NOTE

Graphics Card Dependent

Some filters like the new Oil Paint and Blur filters may require a specific category of graphics card. This is because some new features are heavily dependent on your computer's GPU (graphics processing unit). See http://www.adobe.com/products/photoshop/tech-specs.html for more details.

VIDEO 99:
Blur Tools Combined

TIP

What Is Smart?

Almost Every filter in Photoshop (except for 4 blurs, Liquify, and Vanishing Point) can be used as a Smart Filter. Even more useful, you can apply the Shadow/Highlight adjustment as a Smart Filter.

VIDEO 100:
Masking Smart Filters

5. Double-click its name, Smart Sharpen, in the Smart Filter list. Reduce the amount of sharpening for the filter, and then close its dialog box.

6. Choose Filter > Blur > Gaussian Blur, and apply a blur at a high value, such as **15** pixels. Click OK to apply the filter. The filter appears at the top of the Smart Filters list.

   Smart Filters can also use blending modes, which opens many options.

7. Double-click the Edit Blending Options icon next to the filter in the Layers panel.

   A Blending Options window opens to adjust the filter.

8. Set the filter's blending mode to Soft Light, and adjust the Opacity to **80%**.

9. Click OK to close the Blending Options window and update the Smart Filter.

   The blended Gaussian Blur filter has nicely intensified the color in the image but has also softened the image a little too much. This can be fixed easily by adjusting the Smart Filters stacking order.

10. Drag the Smart Sharpen filter so it appears at the top of the Smart Filter list. Remember that Photoshop applies Smart Filters from the bottom up.

11. Continue to experiment with Smart Filters and add additional effects.

12. When you're satisfied, close the photo. You can save it if you'd like to a local drive.

> **TIP**
>
> **Smart Filters Only Where You Want Them**
>
> Smart Filters automatically have a Layer Mask attached. If you make a selection before applying a Smart Filter, the Layer Mask will hide the filter's results. If you need to alter the Smart Filter after the fact, you can use standard masking techniques to paint on the Smart Filter mask. The mask applies to all the Smart Filters applied to a layer. If you need to disable the Layer Mask, hold down the Shift key and click its thumbnail.

Better Define the Target Area

You spent a lot of time attaining accurate selections in Chapter 5, "Selection Tools and Techniques" (if you skipped it, reviewing it now will help you get the most out of this chapter). For the best results, you'll want to accurately select the area to be filtered. Depending on what you want to achieve, filters can be run on the entire image, a

small portion of the image, or even a single channel. Also, it's not a bad idea to test a filter first by running it on a small area.

Smooth the Edges

A hard-edged selection creates a visible border where the filter processed the image. It is absolutely essential to soften your selections. Two techniques work well (and can be combined):

- Choose Select > Modify > Smooth to round out hard corners in your selection.

- Choose Select > Modify > Feather to create a gradual edge. This is similar to the difference between a line drawn by a ballpoint pen and a line drawn by a felt-tip pen.

- Choose Select > Refine Edge to improve the overall selection intuitively.

Fade and Blend

The Fade command is a little-known secret in Photoshop. It allows you to further modify filters by harnessing the power of blending modes. Use this command to access all 24 blend modes besides Normal. It makes your filter collection 24 times larger.

You must choose the Fade command immediately after the filter has run (even before you deselect the active selection). Let's try it out:

NOTE

Smart Fade?

The Fade command is not available for Smart Filters (for that functionality, use the Blending Options icon).

VIDEO 101:
Oil Paint

1. Open the file Ch14_Butterfly.tif from the Chapter 14 folder.

2. Choose Filter > Stylize > Glowing Edges.

3. Adjust the sliders as desired until you have an image that looks much like a black velvet painting.

4. Click OK.

5. Invoke the Fade command by choosing Edit > Fade <name of filter>, or press Command+Shift+F (Ctrl+Shift+F). To remember this shortcut, think of it as though you want to command (or control) the shifting (fading) of the filter.

6. Try different blending modes and Opacity settings to modify the look of the filter.

TIP

Using the Fade Command

If you forget to invoke the Fade command, step backward through your History panel until the filter is removed. Then run the last filter again (with the same settings) by pressing Command+F (Ctrl+F). You can then invoke the Fade command.

The Guide to Standard Filters

Do you want to know more about filters? You'll find a detailed filter guide included in the Chapter 14 folder. The guide examines every standard filter included with Photoshop CS6.

Filters are often surprising, so the guide will help you explore them in depth. Be sure to examine the official uses for each filter as well as recommendations for new techniques. The guide is richly illustrated to help inspire new ideas.

Actions and Automation

15

Photoshop is an extremely efficient program, but you're truly missing out if you don't learn how to use its automation features. Automation is one of the key differences between Photoshop and its sibling Photoshop Elements. You'll find three categories of technology that can streamline your workflow and save you hours of work per week. These powerful commands can take the most repetitive tasks and automate them completely:

- **Actions** record a series of commands for playback on future images. They can be used to generate extremely complex results. You can also use batch processing to run an action on an entire folder of images.

- **Automate commands** perform complex production tasks (like creating panoramic or high dynamic range [HDR] images) with minimal effort.

- **Scripts** can perform tasks that are more complex than actions. Scripts have made a strong impact on complex workflow issues.

Along with automation commands in Photoshop, a few additional tasks can be easily completed using Adobe Bridge. You can use Bridge as a powerful image browsing and organization tool. Bridge also makes it simple to batch rename files or create contact sheets and Web galleries.

Actions

Photoshop's actions technology lets you record nearly every command (or better yet, a series of commands), and then play them back on another image. You can use basic actions, such as a resize or file format change, to quickly convert files at a push of a button. These simple actions can be recorded and then mapped to empty

TIP

Actions as F keys

Actions can be assigned to F keys for easy access. Just double-click to the right of an action's name in the standard view of the Actions panel and pick an F key. You can also add modifier keys to extend the number of F keys.

NOTE

F keys = System Keys?

Your OS may be using the function keys for controlling things like volume and screen brightness. You may need to disable or modify this system behavior in your control panel settings for the OS. You could also rely on modifier keys inside Photoshop.

function keys at the top of your keyboard. By using combinations of Shift and Option (Alt) as modifiers to the function key, a standard keyboard can have 48–60 customizable keys (depending on the size of your keyboard).

Meet the Actions Panel

If your Actions panel looks something like this figure, you're using Button mode. This is a useful way to access actions, but you cannot create or modify actions when using Button mode.

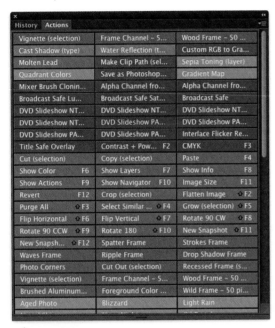

To use actions, let's take a closer look at the Actions panel. To toggle the visibility of the Actions panel, press Option+F9 (Alt+F9). If the panel does not look like a list, go to the panel's submenu (in the panel's upper-right corner) and make sure that Button mode is not selected.

The interface has fairly clear controls. The Stop, Record, and Play buttons behave as you might expect. The folder icon creates a new set (place) to store actions, and the page icon creates a new (empty) action. Click the trash icon to delete the highlighted items, or you can drag actions or sets onto it.

Let's practice with actions by using some of the built-in actions.

1. Open the file Ch15_Bike.tif from the Chapter 15 folder.

2. From the Actions panel submenu, choose Image Effects. This menu item adds a set of actions that will process the image to a different look using a combination of filters and adjustments.

TIP

Tools of Action

With Photoshop CS6, you can record the relative position of tools, allowing for some very complex actions.

3. Click the triangle next to the Image Effects set to display the actions contained within.

4. Choose the action Sepia Toning (layer) and click Play. The action should take very little time to process the image. The end result is a nice sepia tone effect.

5. Choose File > Revert, and then try other actions from this set to see the diversity of those actions.

You can explore the steps in an action by clicking the triangles in the Actions panel to look at how elaborate some actions are. You may be thinking that these are interesting, but they will get stale quickly because they create the same look each time.

This does not have to be the case. It's very easy to modify an action. The easiest way to do this is by turning on dialog boxes. Normally, an action will play all the way through using the original values assigned to the filters or image adjustments. However, if you click in the column next to each step, you can enable dialog boxes for a filter or adjustment (click a second time to disable dialog boxes). These dialog boxes let you enter variables and influence an action's outcome. Let's try this out:

1. Choose File > Revert, and then go back to the Sepia Toning (layer) action in the Actions panel. Click the triangle next to the action so you can expand it and see all of its steps. You may find it useful to expand individual steps to better see what command they perform.

2. The final step, Make, creates a new adjustment layer for the tinting. Click next to its name to enable the dialog box.

3. Run the action again. This time a dialog box opens for the final step so you can customize the tint effect. Click OK to create the adjustment layer. Modify the tint effect, and then click OK to finish the action.

This exercise has only scratched the surface of what's possible with actions. Actions open all sorts of options, for creative and technical outcomes.

NOTE

Different Is Good (When It Comes to Actions)

By modifying an action, several different outcomes are possible. Expand the triangle next to the action's name to see the list of steps. It is possible to turn on only some of the dialog boxes by clicking next to a specific step.

Working with Third-Party Actions

An innumerable amount of actions are available on the Internet. The Adobe Studio Exchange website (www.adobe.com/exchange)—mentioned in an earlier chapter—is an excellent starting point. Most actions are available for free; some of the most creative and useful actions are sold by small and large developers. Let's try out some third-party actions and learn how to load and use them:

1. Open the file Ch15_Spacesuit.tif from the Chapter 15 folder.

2. In the Actions panel, click the submenu to choose Load Actions.

3. Navigate to the Chapter 15 folder where you'll find a folder named PanosFX Actions. The folder contains four sets of actions from the creative mind of Panos Efstathiadis (www.PANOSFX.com). Load the action "Stamp v2 by Panos.atn."

4. Select the README first! Action, and click Play to run the action. Follow the onscreen instructions.

5. Select the !!! STAMP !!! round stamp action, and click Play.

6. Follow the detailed onscreen instructions. You can substitute the Return (Enter) key for clicking the Commit check mark if you want.

7. When the action gets to the very end, it asks you to make a choice. You can stop and preserve the high-res version or click Continue to reduce the image to a very small size for screen resolution. I recommend clicking Stop.

8. All the important layers are in a group already. You can drag this group into a new document or save it to use later.

Three more sets and a total of nearly 20 actions are available to explore in the Lesson folder. These are some wonderful samples of how powerful and devoted the Photoshop community is.

VIDEO 102:
Creating an Action

Creating Actions

By now, actions should seem pretty appealing. You've explored using built-in actions as well as loading (and finding) third-party actions. Now it's time to create your own.

You must first create a set to hold your personal actions (think of it as a folder). Sets hold actions, and there's no limit to how many actions can be placed into a set or how many sets you can load. Let's give it a try:

1. Close the previous files, and then open the Ch15_Desert.tif file.

2. Call up the Actions panel and click the folder icon to create a new set. Give the set a name of your own choosing, and click OK.

3. Click the New Action icon. You can give the action a name now or rename it later. In this case, name it **Cartoon Look**, and click Record to start recording.

4. Choose Filter > Convert for Smart Filters to make the layer a Smart Object, and if necessary click OK.

5. Run the Find Edges Filter by choosing Filter > Stylize > Find Edges. There is no dialog box for this effect.

6. To achieve the look you need to fade the filter, click the Blending Options icon for the Smart Object (it looks like a double arrow next to the effect's name).

7. In the new window, try the Overlay blending mode and adjust the Opacity slider as desired. Depending on the source image, you may need to try different blending modes. You can always remove steps from a recorded action afterward by dragging individual steps into the trash can in the Actions panel.

8. To enable flexibility, turn on the dialog box for the Set Filter Effects step.

9. In the Actions panel, click Stop.

Congratulations; you've created your first action from scratch. The preceding recipe is one of my own, but the technique works with most filter recipes. Let's try making one more:

1. Open the Ch15_Desert.tif file from the Chapter 15 folder or if it is still open from the last action, choose File > Revert.

2. Click the New Action button. You can give the action a name now or rename it later. In this case, name it **Zoom Blur**, and click the Record button. The action is now recording.

3. Duplicate the *Background* layer by selecting it and pressing Command+J (Ctrl+J).

4. Desaturate the color from the duplicate layer by pressing Command+Shift+U (Ctrl+Shift+U).

5. Now you'll make the image zoom from a center point. Choose Filter > Blur > Radial Blur. Set the Method to Zoom and use an Amount of **100** at Good Quality. Move the center point by dragging within the Blur Center area in the dialog box to place it relative to the subject, and then click OK.

6. Repeat the Blur filter by pressing Command+F (Ctrl+F).

7. On the topmost layer, make a Levels adjustment by pressing Command+L (Ctrl+L). Bring the black and white Input sliders toward the center. Move the gray slider until the midtones are brighter. Click OK.

8. Change the blending mode of the top layer to Screen mode, and set it to 80% Opacity.

9. Press Option+[(Alt+[) to select the previous layer.

10. Press Command+Option+F (Ctrl+Alt+F) to run the Zoom filter again with options.

11. Set the amount to **30**, and click OK.

12. To achieve the look you need to fade the filter, choose Edit > Fade Radial Blur. Lower the Opacity of the effect to **30%**, and click OK.

13. In the Actions panel, click Stop.

Experiment and create your own looks. Virtually every menu command or button can be recorded. Starting with Photoshop CS6, even tools can (just be sure to set your rulers to percentages to get relative results—see the "Tips for Creating Better Actions" sidebar). Actions can be duplicated, modified, and deleted. Be sure to explore all the options in the Actions panel submenu. Be sure to dissect actions made by others to get ideas of what is possible. With a little practice and imagination you'll be amazed at what you can accomplish.

If you want to check out the actions you just created, compare them to a set I've saved in the Chapter 15 folder.

Saving Actions

Actions are stored in a temporary cache. If you delete the set, load a replacement, or experience an application crash, your new actions could be overwritten. Therefore, it's important to save your actions so they can be backed up and reloaded in the future.

1. Click an action set. You can use the one created in the previous exercise. You must click the whole set, not just an action in that set.

2. Go to the Actions panel submenu, and choose Save Actions.

3. The Photoshop Actions folder (inside the Presets folder) will be chosen by default. If it isn't, manually locate it in your Presets folder.

4. If you add to the set later, just be sure to resave it to the same location with the same name.

TIPS FOR CREATING BETTER ACTIONS

Making great actions from scratch can be a bit of a challenge. You need to come up with great design ideas or useful time-savers. You also need to make sure the action is technically solid so it runs without errors. Here are a few tips to make your actions a little more tech-savvy:

- Run actions on a duplicated image or folder to preserve your originals.

- Brush strokes, cloning, and most manual tools from the Tools panel may not record properly with actions. Photoshop CS6 improves this, but realize that strokes are based upon a relative percent-based position.

- As an alternative to tools, try using options such as a Gradient Fill layer (Layer > New Fill Layer > Gradient) instead of the Gradient tool. Fill layers are easier to modify after running an action as well.

- To play a single step of an action, double-click it.

- If you make a mistake in an action, click Stop. Delete the incorrect steps by dragging them into the Actions panel's trash can. Choose Edit > Step Backward as many times as needed. Then click Record and start again from the last good point.

- Button mode lets you launch actions quickly—just click an action and it runs. You can access the command from the Actions panel submenu. You'll need to disable Button mode to access recording and editing features.

- Choose Playback Options from the Actions panel submenu. Specify that you want the actions to play back an action accelerated. Photoshop can process faster than it can redraw the screen.

- Be sure to back up your custom actions to two locations: the default location and a secondary backup location. This way a reinstall or upgrade won't blow away your custom actions.

- To create an action that will work better on all files, set the rulers to measure using percentage.

- Choose File > Automate > Fit Image to resize an image for a specific height or width.

- Photoshop records the names of layers as you select them. This may cause playback issues, because the action will look for specific names. Use keyboard shortcuts to select layers and such so that the action won't look for a specific name for that step. For more on layer shortcuts, see Chapter 8, "Compositing with Layers."

Outcome	Mac	PC
Choose layer above	Option+]	Alt+]
Choose layer below	Option+[	Alt+[
To Move the Current Layer		
Up the layer stack	Command+]	Ctrl+]
Down the layer stack	Command+[	Ctrl+[
To the top	Shift+Command+]	Shift+Ctrl+]
To the bottom	Shift+Command+[	Shift+Ctrl+[

VIDEO 103:
Batch Processing

Automate Commands

Photoshop offers several commands for speeding up profes-sional imaging workflow. You'll explore several options available throughout this chapter. If you are working with an older version of Photoshop, you might not have some of these automation tools. Each is a significant time-saver, and you should attempt to inte-grate them into your workflow as often as is feasible.

Batch

If you liked actions, you'll love the Batch command. The Batch command allows you to apply an action to a group of images. This is a huge time-saver, especially for mundane tasks like resiz-ing. You can also use it to batch process an entire roll (or card) of images and run the same Levels adjustment on each image. Let's give it a try.

Let's start by making the action "batchable":

1. Open a JPEG image from the Batch folder in the Chapter 15 folder.

2. Choose File > Save As, and save a copy to the desktop. This is a temporary copy to prepare the action and can be thrown away when you're finished.

3. Call up the Actions panel.

4. Create a new action in your custom set named **Zoom Blur Batch**, and start to record.

5. Click the Zoom Blur action, and click Play (an action can record the running of another action).

6. When the action completes, choose File > Save As. Navigate to your desktop and save the file. Select a TIFF file format, deselect the Layers box, and click Save.

7. Choose a compression option: In this case LZW is very efficient.

8. Click Stop.

9. Close the open image.

10. Discard the two temp images from your desktop now (or later).

The action is now ready to be applied to a folder of images.

1. Choose File > Automate > Batch to invoke the Batch window.

2. Specify a set and an action from the set that you'd like to use. The action must be currently loaded in the Actions panel to appear in this list. In this case, use the Zoom Blur Batch action that you created earlier.

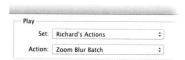

3. Choose the files that you want to process from the Source menu:

- **Folder.** This option processes all items in a specified folder. Click Choose to navigate to and select the folder. A folder can include additional subfolders as well. For your images, choose Folder. Click Choose and navigate to the folder called Batch in the Chapter 15 folder.

- **Import.** This option processes images from a digital camera, scanner, or a PDF file. A useful batch and action would be to create an action that sets a document's resolution to 300 pixels per inch without resampling. You could then run this action on all items you import from a digital camera.

- **Opened Files.** This option processes all open files.

- **Bridge.** This option works on all selected items in Adobe Bridge. You would first select several images in Bridge, and then choose Tools > Photoshop > Batch.

4. Set processing options that guide what is and is not processed as well as how to handle errors or files:

- **Override Action "Open" Commands.** If your action contains an Open command that refers to specific filenames rather than the batched files, you'll want to deselect the Override Action "Open" command.

- **Include All Subfolders.** This option applies the action to all files in the subdirectories of the specified folder.

- **Suppress File Open Options Dialogs.** This option hides File Open Options dialog boxes. It's a good idea to use this when batching actions on Camera Raw image files. Photoshop will then use the latest settings. For maximum compatibility, select this option.

TIP

Batch Multiple Folders

You can batch multiple folders at once. Create aliases or shortcuts within one folder that point to the desired folders. Be sure to select the Include All Subfolders option.

NOTE

Filenaming Compatibility

For filenaming compatibility, be sure to choose Windows and Mac OS to ensure that filenames are compatible with the OS.

TIP

Converting File Formats

The Batch command cannot convert file formats. This can easily be done in advance using the Image Processor script that ships with Photoshop. In fact, you can even add an action to the Image Processor script. It is a good idea to convert a JPEG file to TIFF or PSD before running an action. More on the Image Processor later in the chapter.

VIDEO 104:
Create a Slideshow in Photoshop

- **Suppress Color Profile Warnings.** This option ignores color profile warnings, which can cause an action to hang and wait for user interaction. For maximum compatibility, select this option.

5. Specify a destination for the processed files by choosing one from the Destination menu:

   - **None.** This option leaves the files open without saving changes.

   - **Save And Close.** This option saves the files in their current location. This is a destructive edit because it will overwrite the original files.

   - **Folder.** This method saves the processed files to another location (this is the safest option). Click Choose to specify the destination folder. For this batch, navigate to the desktop and create a new folder named **Batch Processed**.

6. If the action you're using includes a Save As command, choose Override Action "Save As" Commands. Otherwise, the image may write to the wrong folder. For maximum compatibility, select this option.

7. If you chose Folder as the destination, you'll need to specify a filenaming convention. Several pop-up fields are available for easy filenaming. These fields make it very easy to rename files from a digital camera or to specify a serial number. Photos from multiple digital cameras often end up with the same name, so this is a very good idea because you can create more accurate and descriptive names for each image. In this case, choose the following settings:

   - **Field 1.** Dinosaur Exhibit_ (manually type in)

   - **Field 2.** mmddyy (date) (from pop-up list)

   - **Field 3.** _ (manually type in)

   - **Field 4.** 3 Digit Serial Number (from pop-up list)

   - **Field 5.** extension (from pop-up list)

   These settings will result in a name like Dinosaur Exhibit _052612_001.tif.

8. Set an option for error processing from the Errors menu:

- **Stop For Errors.** This option suspends the process until you confirm the error message. Choose this option only if you will be monitoring the batch process closely.

- **Log Errors To File.** This option records each error into a file without stopping the process. After processing, a message appears indicating if any errors occurred. For this batch, choose Log Errors To File. Save a file named **Error Log.txt** on the desktop.

9. Set the file compatibility for Mac OS and Windows.

10. Click OK to run the batch. Photoshop will batch process the images. Depending on the speed of your computer, this may take a few minutes. You can abort a batch by pressing Esc at any time.

Crop and Straighten Photos

When scanning images, it's often possible to fit more than one image on the scanner bed. Scanning multiple images at once can save input time when you are loading images into Photoshop. Fortunately, the Crop And Straighten Photos command picks up and keeps the efficiency going. Let's give it a try.

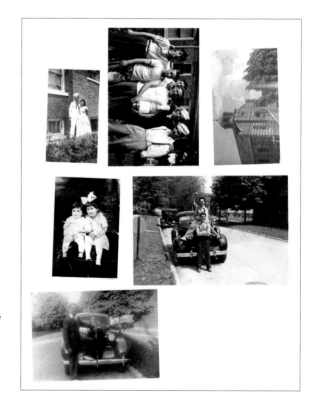

NOTE

Hidden Menu Items

It's possible to customize menus and actually hide commands. If you don't see a particular command, be sure to choose the Show All Menu Items command at the bottom of each menu or submenu.

1. Open the Ch15_Crop_and_Straighten.tif file from the Chapter 15 folder. If you would rather, just scan in a few images on your own scanner.

2. Choose File > Automate > Crop And Straighten Photos.

   Each image should be cropped, straightened, and moved into its own document window.

TIP

Crop and Straighten Best Results

For best results, you need to keep 1/8 inch between the images in your scan. If the Crop And Straighten Photos command does not succeed (which is rare), you should process the individual images using the Crop tool. If images are dramatically different exposures, scan them separately.

Conditional Mode Change

The Conditional Mode Change command is meant to be used within an action. It allows you to specify conditions for a mode change to occur during an action. Recording a mode change into an action can result in an error if the action is run on an image that has a different image mode. For example, if one step of an action were to convert an image from a source mode of RGB to a target mode of CMYK, applying this action to an image in Grayscale mode would result in an error. The command allows you to specify one or more source modes and a mode for the target mode.

Fit Image

The Fit Image command is also meant to be inserted into an action. It allows you to specify a maximum width and height (in pixels) that the image cannot exceed. This is useful when sizing images for the screen or Internet. If you intend to use it for print resolution, you'll need to know your resolution setting and multiply by your desired print size to convert inches to a pixel-based measurement.

Photomerge

The Photomerge command allows you to merge several (adjacent) photographs into one continuous image. This command is used to make panoramic images, which was covered in depth back in Chapter 8. If you skipped that hands-on activity, flip back to Chapter 8. If you'd like another set of practice images, you'll find a folder called Photomerge in the Chapter 15 folder.

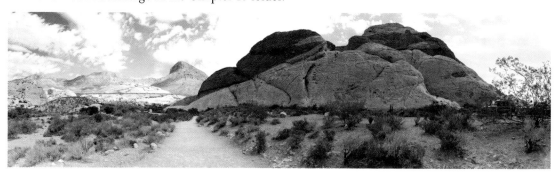

Merge to HDR Pro

The Merge to HDR command was introduced in Photoshop CS2 as a way to create technically accurate 32-bit images. It allows you to take multiple exposures (with different values) of a subject (shot from a locked tripod or camera mount) and merge them into a new image that better displays highlights and shadows. The resulting image is also a 32-bit image that allows great flexibility for adjusting exposure.

With Photoshop CS5, the Merge to HDR command got a major overhaul for stylistic purposes, and it can now create tone-mapped images that display a wider range of exposure than a traditional photo. HDR images were initially discussed in Chapter 10, "Color Correction and Enhancement." Let's create another HDR image:

1. Choose File > Automate > Merge to HDR Pro.

2. In the Merge to HDR dialog box, click Browse to navigate to the source images. You'll find a folder named Merge to HDR in the Chapter 15 folder. In the folder, Shift-click images 1–5 to select them. Select the Attempt to Automatically Align Source Images check box, and then click OK.

3. After a few moments, a second Merge to HDR dialog box opens. You'll see thumbnails for each of the images used as well as a resulting image.

4. From the Preset list, choose Photorealistic High Contrast to get a punchier image.

5. Select the "Remove ghosts" check box to remove the trailing image details caused by wind blowing items in the scene.

6. Adjust the exposure with the following values: Exposure: **–1.0**, Shadow: **50%**, and Highlight **–80%**.

7. Boost the Saturation to **30%** for richer colors.

8. Click OK to create a new HDR image.

9. Try adjusting the Exposure settings to different values to see the results of the HDR image.

The image on the left exhibits ghosting caused by slight movement between exposures. Selecting the "Remove ghosts" check box compensates for variables like wind.

Scripts

Photoshop scripting offers a more powerful automation technology than actions. Scripts allow for the execution of more elaborate tasks than what actions can do because scripts recognize conditional states like image mode and orientation. Scripting was introduced in Photoshop CS, and powerful built-in scripts automate the processing of multiple layers or layer comps.

Creating original scripts requires you to use a scripting language such as AppleScript, JavaScript, or Visual Basic. Photoshop includes a script editor and debugger for JavaScript. JavaScript is the preferred language because the scripts are cross platform. Scripting is complex; it's essentially computer programming. Plenty of resources are available for those who want to learn scripting, but be prepared to spend some time. You'll find a folder called Scripting Guide in the Photoshop application folder. In it you'll find sample scripts and a PDF with detailed information.

Fortunately, some wonderful examples of scripting are available at the Adobe Studio Exchange website (www.adobexchange.com). Be sure to look for scripts by Photoshop guru Russell Brown on his site (www.RussellBrown.com). Load new scripts by choosing File > Script > Browse. To permanently add a script to the Script menu, copy it into the Scripts folder inside your Presets folder. For now, let's explore the built-in scripts.

VIDEO 105:
Image Processor Script

Image Processor

You can use the Image Processor command to convert and process multiple images. The Image Processor differs from the Batch command in that you don't have to first create an action. The Image Processor can be used for any of the following tasks:

- To convert a set of files to JPEG, PSD, or TIFF format. You can also convert files simultaneously to all three formats.

- To process a set of Camera Raw files using the same Camera Raw options.

- To resize images to fit within a specified pixel dimension.

- To embed a color profile into images or convert files to sRGB and save them as JPEG images for the Web.

- To include copyright metadata within the processed images.

NOTE

Batch Processing

The Image Processor is another way to batch process images (and you don't need to go through the extra step of using the Save As command). The Image Processor script can be more flexible than the Batch command. The Image Processor works with PSD, TIFF, JPEG, or Camera Raw files.

TIP

Saving Settings

You can click Save to save the current settings in the Image Processor dialog box. These settings can be reloaded for a later job if needed.

1. In the Actions panel, click the submenu and load the Image Effects actions.

2. Choose > File > Scripts > Image Processor.

3. Choose the images you want to process. You can use open images or navigate to a folder to choose images. Click Select Folder and navigate to the folder named called Batch in the Chapter 15 folder. Highlight the folder and click Choose.

4. Select a location in which to save the processed files. You should make and then choose a Script Exports folder on the desktop.

5. Select the file types and options you want to convert to:

   - **Save as JPEG.** Sets the JPEG quality between 0 and 12. You can also resize the image and convert it to the sRGB color profile.

   - **Save as PSD.** Sets the PSD options. You can also resize the image and select Maximize Compatibility.

   - **Save as TIFF.** Saves images in TIFF format with LZW compression. You can also resize the image.

   For this example, choose JPEG and choose to resize to **800 × 800** pixels with a compression of **10**.

TIP

Apply One Setting to All

If you need to process a group of Camera Raw files taken under the same lighting conditions, you can open and adjust only the first image to your satisfaction. In the Image Processor dialog box be sure to select the "Open first image to apply settings" check box. You can then reuse the same settings for the other images.

6. You can choose other processing options as well:

   - **Run Action.** If an action is loaded into Photoshop, you can run it on the image during the process.

   - **Copyright Info.** This includes any text you enter in the IPTC copyright metadata for the file. Text overwrites the copyright metadata in the original file.

   - **Include ICC Profile.** This embeds the color profile with the saved files.

   For this example, choose the Aged Photo action from the Image Effects set to run on the processed images.

7. Click Run. Photoshop processes the images to the specified folder.

Layer Comps to Files

You may remember layer comps, which were covered in depth in Chapter 8. This useful design tool allows you to save different arrangements of layer visibility, position, and effects. Layer comps are very useful when experimenting with designs. Photoshop makes it easy to create an individual file for each layer comp.

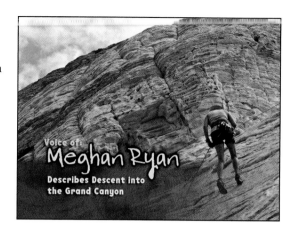

1. Open an image that uses layer comps. You can use your own or the file named Ch15_Script_Sample.psd from the Chapter 15 folder.

2. A warning dialog box about the display of nonsquare pixels appears with pixel aspect ratio preview. This is a graphic intended for use in a digital video project; therefore, it uses a special pixel designed for video technology. Click OK to close the dialog box.

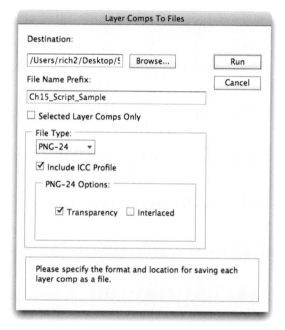

3. Choose File > Scripts > Layer Comps To Files to export all layer comps to individual files, one for each comp. You can choose to create BMP, JPEG, PDF, PSD, Targa, TIFF, PNG-8, or PNG-24 files.

4. Click Browse to specify a target destination. Select the Script Exports folder you created on your desktop.

5. Specify PNG-24 files as the File Type output (this will automatically embed the transparency of each layer into the file).

6. Click Run.

If desired, you can create a PDF file using an additional script. For even more control, use Adobe Bridge to share these files for review (these techniques are discussed later in the chapter).

VIDEO 106:
Export Layers to Files Script

TIP

Mini Bridge

A welcome addition to Photoshop is Mini Bridge. Mini Bridge lets you quickly browse and organize files. You can also click the Tools button and choose Photoshop and a list of automated tasks. Be sure to try it out by choosing Window > Extensions > Mini Bridge.

NOTE

Complex Names

If you need to do a complex batch rename, you can click the plus button (+) to add descriptive information. A preview of the new filename appears at the bottom of the dialog box. Be sure to keep the total character length low to avoid conflicts with different operating systems.

Automation with Adobe Bridge

Longtime Photoshop users will notice that certain Automation commands have gone missing. You will no longer find the Picture Package command as part of the application, and you will have to perform some tasks in Adobe Bridge. These changes were due in part to some core technology changing within the application and an effort to streamline tasks. Let's take a look at a few useful commands you'll find in Adobe Bridge.

Batch Renaming Files

One of the key functions of Adobe Bridge is organizing your digital images. As part of that organization, you'll likely rename files. This is particularly true since most digital cameras progressively number their files, which is great for counting but not organizing. Bridge makes it easy to rename several files or folders at one time; this process is called a batch.

1. If it's not running already, launch Adobe Bridge CS6 (you can also launch Bridge from within Photoshop by choosing File > Browse in Bridge).

2. Navigate to the folder named Batch in the Chapter 15 folder. Double-click to open the folder and view the nine images contained within it.

3. Press Command+A (Ctrl+A) to select all the files within the folder.

4. Choose Tools > Batch Rename. A new dialog box opens.

5. You must specify a destination for the renamed files. You can choose to keep them in their current folder, move them to another folder, or copy them to another destination. For this example, choose to "Copy to other folder" and specify a target folder on your desktop (you cannot resave files to the DVD-ROM drive).

6. Specify New Filenames using a combination of menus and a text field. For this example, choose Text and enter **Dinosaur_ Exhibit_**. Then add a sequence number of **1** and specify Two Digits.

7. In the Preview section, check the New filename for accuracy.

Bridge from the Start

If you'd like Bridge to launch automatically when you log in to your computer, open Bridge's preferences and select the Advanced category. Simply select Start Bridge at Login to make Bridge readily available.

8. Specify that you want the files to be compatible in Mac and Windows.

9. In the Options section, select the "Preserve current filename in XMP Metadata" check box.

10. When you're ready, click the Rename button to complete the batch rename. The Batch command is a useful way to improve the organization of your files.

PDF Contact Sheet and Presentation Output

Another useful function of Bridge is its ability to quickly generate PDF files for selected images. Bridge CS6 includes a workspace called Output that uses the Adobe Output Module script. In just a few clicks, you can generate Adobe PDF contact sheets and presentations.

- **Contact sheet.** A contact sheet is a useful catalog of a group of images. You can place multiple, small thumbnail images on a large page along with caption information.

- **PDF Presentation.** The PDF presentation output lets you quickly create a multipage PDF file that you can use to display images as a slide show presentation. The PDF output also offers options for image quality, security settings, and display preferences. You can also add text overlays at the bottom of each image in the PDF presentation.

Let's go ahead and create a PDF file from a folder of images:

1. If it's not running already, launch Adobe Bridge CS6.

2. Choose Window > Workspace > Output. The Bridge interface rearranges to show the Output panel at the right side of the screen. The Content panel appears at the bottom of the screen (nested with Preview); this is where you see thumbnails for the images you choose to use. The left column contains a list of folders.

3. Navigate to the Chapter 15 folder.

Contact Sheet

The Output Module offers several contact sheet templates as starting points. You can modify these presets as needed to serve your unique needs.

1. Select all the images in the Contact Sheet folder, and then press Command+A (Ctrl+A).

2. Click the PDF button in the Output panel.

3. Click the Template menu and choose a layout option. For this example, choose the 4*5 Contact Sheet option, and click the Refresh Preview button. Bridge creates a preview layout of the first page for the PDF file. Let's customize the appearance a bit more.

4. In the Document controls, change the Page Preset to U.S. Paper and set the Background to White.

5. Select the Open Password check box, and enter **raster-vector**. A password provides security to keep a document private for only its intended recipient.

6. In the Layout controls, change the Columns to **3** and Rows to **4** to place a larger image on the contact sheet.

7. In the Overlays controls, increase the Size menu to **12 pt** and set the style to Bold.

8. Click the Refresh Preview button to see how the PDF contact sheet will look.

9. Click the Save button to create the contact sheet. Name the file and store it on your desktop. When Bridge is finished creating the file, it will open by default in your system's PDF viewer application.

Slide Show

The Output Module also offers presets for generating a PDF slide show. This is a useful way to present several images in one document. The PDF file can be emailed, posted to the Web, or used as part of a live presentation.

1. Switch back to Bridge and select all the images in the PDF Presentation folder.

2. In the Template menu, choose Maximize Size.

3. In the Document controls, change the Page Preset to the Web category and select the size of 1280 × 1024. Also, set the Background color to Black.

4. In the Layout controls, deselect the Rotate for Best Fit option. Images will then all remain oriented to the screen.

5. In the Overlays section, deselect Filename overlays.

6. Adjust Playback controls to your liking (scroll to the bottom of the list). You may want to use a longer duration such as Advance Every 10 Seconds. Feel free to modify the Transition and Speed controls.

7. Click the Refresh Preview button to see how the PDF slide show will look.

8. Click the Save button to create the PDF slide show. Name the file and store it on your desktop. When Bridge is finished creating the file, it will open by default in your system's PDF viewer application.

9. When you are finished viewing, press the Esc key to exit the full-screen slide display.

Web Gallery Output

The Web Gallery component of the Adobe Output Module is a very easy way to quickly build a website for displaying photos. A Web photo gallery uses a home page with thumbnail images and several gallery pages with full-size images. Power users and amateurs alike have discovered the power and flexibility of creating entire galleries within Bridge.

Without knowing any HTML or Flash, users can quickly create online galleries for their images. Bridge offers several customizable templates, which are well suited for different tasks like client review or online portfolios.

1. If it's not running already, launch Adobe Bridge CS6.

2. Choose Window > Workspace > Output. The Bridge interface rearranges to show the Output panel at the right side of the screen. The Content panel appears at the bottom of the screen (nested with Preview); this is where you see which images you've selected to use. The left column contains a list of folders.

3. Navigate to the Web Gallery folder inside the Chapter 15 folder.

4. Press Command+A (Ctrl+A) to select all the photos contained within the Web Gallery folder.

5. Click the Web Gallery button in the Output panel.

6. Choose the Lightroom Flash Gallery from the Template list.

7. Choose Paper White option from the Style menu.

8. Customize the gallery by entering Site Info. This information helps the site's visitors understand the photos presented (such as when and where the photos were captured). For this exercise, enter your own information into some of the fields.

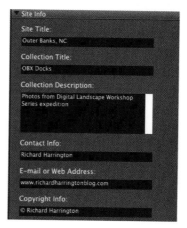

9. You can change the Color Palette controls to further stylize the site. Try changing the Header color to a dark orange by clicking its swatch and using the Color Picker.

10. Customize the design of the page using the Appearance controls:

   - Set the Slideshow Size to **800** pixels.

   - Set the Gallery Image Size to **650** pixels.

   - Set the Thumbnail Size to **100** pixels.

11. Specify a destination for the generated Web Gallery (the folder will contain several pages and images). If you have a Web site, you can use the built-in Bridge FTP features to upload the Web Gallery to your server. For this exercise, click the Save to Disk button, and then click Browse and specify your Desktop.

12. Click the Preview in Browser button to simulate the site (this will only load the first ten images). Browse the Web site and try its many controls. The Web Galleries are truly versatile and elegant.

13. When you're satisfied with the preview, close the Web browser and return to Bridge.

14. Click the Save button in the Create Gallery controls to generate the Web Gallery.

Printing, PDF, and Specialized File Types

16

At some point, you'll need to send your images to an output device. Several different devices are available, including paper and film printers, plates, or a digital printing press. Whether you are printing on a desktop inkjet printer or sending your images to prepress, there are some essentials you should know. In the digital age, preparing a photo for web or video has become just as important with many devices like tablets and digital signage growing in popularity.

Understanding the core technology will ensure that your jobs go smoothly and that your images turn out as desired. The material in this chapter serves as a primer on printing and PDF technology. Additionally, you'll explore screen delivery techniques.

Professional Printing Options

Depending on the type of image you've processed, you'll need to determine the right type of printer for output. This will be a balance of

PHOTO BY ISTOCKPHOTO.COM

Professional printing is a trade that requires a lot of experience and specialized knowledge.

budget and availability. The simplest images, such as line art, use only one color. An illustration may use several colors, and those can be printed using CMYK inks to create the different colors or spot inks that exactly match. The most complex images are photographs because they use varying colors and tones to simulate the image. These types of images are generally referred to as *continuous-tone images*.

Color Separation

If your multicolored image is intended for commercial output (printing on a large press), it will need color separation. This process allows for a master plate to be created for each color. Generally, the plates created are for cyan, magenta, yellow, and black—also called key—(CMYK) inks.

These plates can be created in several ways. Usually, the process is handled by a printing professional. However, let's take a quick look at how these separations can be created in Photoshop.

1. Open the file Ch16_Color. tif from the Chapter 16 folder.

2. Check to make sure that your document is in CMYK Color or Multichannel mode.

3. Choose File > Print.

4. Choose Separations from the Color Handling menu.

5. Click Print. Your printer will print separations for each color in the image.

Separations in Multiple Locations

Depending on the printer you are using, the separation options may also appear in the Print dialog box. Under the Mac OS, use the pop-up menu in the second Print dialog box that appears. With Windows, click the Print Settings button to access additional printer driver options.

Halftoning

To simulate continuous tones in images, commercial printers break down images into dots. For those images printed on a press, this process is referred to as *halftoning*. By varying the size of the dots, the halftone screen creates the optical illusion of variations in tone.

An inkjet printer also uses dots, but it's not the same. An inkjet printer's dots are very small and uniform in size.

Quality of Detail

How clear an image prints depends on its resolution and screen frequency. Professional printing devices are often capable of high resolution. As such, they require a finer screen ruling (lines per inch). For more on resolution, you can revisit Chapter 3, "Acquiring Digital Images." It's a good idea to discuss resolution requirements with your service provider or vendor before starting a job.

TIP

How Do Laser Printers Work?

For more information on laser printing, be sure to read the information article at http://computer.howstuffworks.com/laser-printer1.htm.

Desktop Printing Options

The majority of Photoshop users print their images on desktop printers most of the time. These printers generally fall into three categories:

- **Inkjet.** These printers are the most popular and widespread. They offer relatively affordable printing. For best results, look for inkjet printers with separate cartridges for each color.

- **Dye sublimation.** These printers allow for printing of lab quality prints. Recently, the price of these printers has plummeted. These printers do not use dots; rather, transparent film (using CMYO dyes–Cyan, Magenta, Yellow, and Overcoating) is heated and transferred to the paper. The vaporized colors are absorbed into the printer paper. This method is less vulnerable to fading over time if it uses a laminated overlay.

- **Laser printer.** Laser printers use static electricity to affix powder to the page to form the image. These printers are generally more expensive than inkjets but can usually print faster and at a higher quality.

©ISTOCKPHOTO

RGB vs. CMYK

Inkjet printers use CMYK inks, but they prefer to ingest RGB images. If the image is in RGB mode, there is no reason to convert it if you're using an inkjet printer. Desktop printers are designed to do their own CMYK conversion using internal software. Sending a CMYK image to an inkjet printer will usually result in a second (and unpredictable) color

TIP

A Better Print Needs More Data

If you're printing from a Mac, you'll have the option to print using 16 bits of information. This option is best when working with a 16-bit image because it will give you the highest possible quality. The extra information really helps reproduce subtle tones like skies and shadows.

conversion. It is important to realize that the computer screen can display more colors than the printer can print. You might want to use the Gamut Warning command (View > Gamut Warning) to identify areas that need to be toned down with the Sponge tool before printing.

Printing Paper

Several specialty papers are available for desktop printers. You will not get good results trying to print on plain white copy paper. These specialty papers must be selected in the printer window. It's a good idea to identify the paper you are using so the printer driver can adjust the density of the ink coverage to match the paper stock. To conserve paper, you might want to create and print a contact sheet with several smaller images first. It is a good idea to stick with the ink and paper recommended for your particular printer. Remember that different papers and different printers will warrant very different output.

VIDEO 108:
Printing Dialog Box

Printing Commands

Several commands are associated with printers. Those specific to your printer are controlled by the printer driver, which can be clearly explained by visiting the printer manufacturer's website. Many different drivers are available, so instead of focusing on the multitude of manufacturers and hardware options, let's focus on what can be controlled within Photoshop.

Print

Photoshop offers a powerful Print command with great flexibility when printing in Photoshop. The command allows you to adjust the size of an image and its position on the page, and to specify color management policies. Learning to control the Print window will help you produce the best results.

1. Open the file Ch16_Print.tif from the Chapter 16 folder.

2. Choose File > Print or press Command+P (Ctrl+P). The Print window is divided into three areas of functionality.

3. The left side of the Print window shows you how the image will print on the current page. Notice how the photo is currently clipped because it is too large for the selected paper. To fix this, adjust the settings in the Print window.

4. Choose a Printer from the Print menu. The setting you choose will depend on which printer is attached to your computer. If the printer supports it, choose the 16-bit Data option.

5. In the Scaled Print Size section, select the Scale To Fit Media check box. Photoshop adjusts the print resolution so the image fits on the page. If you want to permanently change the image, you'll need to exit printing and choose Image > Image Size.

6. If needed, you can click the Print Settings button to access the printer driver controls. These allow you to adjust options like ink coverage, print quality, and paper size.

7. In the Color Management area, click Color Handling and choose Printer Manage Colors. This is generally the best option for consumer-quality printers because it lets the printer use its specialty software to get the most accurate color.

8. In the Color Management area, you need to specify the Rendering Intent. This is how the colors will be converted for the destination color space. This option is useful for high-end printers that offer PostScript support; however, most consumer-oriented printer drivers ignore this option and use the Perceptual rendering intent, but there are four options to choose from:

   • **Perceptual.** This method attempts to present color so it is natural to the human eye, even though the color values may change.

TIP

Your Image Is Larger than the Paper's Printable Area

When you choose to print, you might get a warning that the image is larger than the printable area of the paper. If this happens, click Cancel, choose File Print, and select the Scale to Fit Media check box.

- **Saturation.** This method tries to produce vivid colors in an image; however, it may sacrifice color accuracy.

- **Relative Colorimetric.** This method compares the highlights of the source color space to the destination and shifts all colors accordingly.

- **Absolute Colorimetric.** This method leaves colors that are in gamut untouched while clipping those colors that are out of gamut for the destination color space.

9. If needed you can select different output options, like Labels and Crop Marks, in the Printing Marks area. These are often used for separations or to identify prints by filename and additional info embedded in the file (like exposure information). For this image, the default settings are fine.

10. Once you have the print settings properly configured, you have three choices:

- To print the image, click Print.

- To close the dialog box without saving the settings, click Cancel.

- To save the printer options for later use, click Done.

COLOR MANAGEMENT CHOICES

When printing, you have to keep color management in mind. This process determines how color accuracy is maintained.

Photoshop Manages Color
In the Photoshop Manages Color software workflow, Photoshop does all the color conversion. This method works best when you have a custom ICC profile for each specific printer, ink, and paper combination. This method is more commonly used in professional printing environments when working with higher-end devices that have been professionally calibrated.

Printer Manages Color
The Printer Manages Color workflow approach lets the printer hardware handle the color conversion. Instead of performing the color management, Photoshop sends all the necessary details to the printer. This method is the best method when printing to inkjet photo printers because each combination of paper, printing resolution, and additional printing parameters requires a different profile. Using this option is generally best, but it does require you to set printing options and turn on color management in the printer driver.

If you're working with a PostScript printer, you can harness powerful options. PostScript color management allows for color separations and complex color management.

Print One Copy

If you are in a rush and don't need to make any additional changes in the Print dialog box, you can print one copy with your current options. Choose File > Print One Copy to output a single print using the latest settings you have loaded.

PDF Essentials

The Portable Document Format (PDF) is a file format invented by Adobe and was intended to be an extension of PostScript. A PDF can describe any combination of text, images, multimedia, and layout. It is independent of the device it was created on and can be viewed on virtually every operating system and portable media player or phone.

The PDF is an open standard, which means that the computer industry is able to create applications that can read or write PDFs without paying Adobe additional fees. This openness led to the quick adoption of PDF, and it is utilized online extensively.

The most powerful PDF authoring tool is Adobe Acrobat, which is bundled with Photoshop in the Adobe Creative Suite or sold as a standalone product. However, Photoshop has the ability to create PDFs. The PDF file format is an excellent way to send files to a service bureau or print shop because the file can be stored at print resolution with embedded vector files and high-quality output options.

Compression Options for Adobe PDF

When you choose to save artwork as a Photoshop PDF, you are presented with the Save Adobe PDF dialog box. You can choose to compress text and line art as well as downsample bitmap images. Depending on the settings you choose, you can significantly reduce the size of a PDF file with little or no loss of detail. Let's open the Save Adobe PDF dialog box.

1. Open the image Ch16_PDF.tif from the Chapter 16 folder.

2. Choose File > Save As.

3. From the Format menu choose Photoshop PDF.

4. Target the Desktop for saving, and then click Save to open the Save Adobe PDF dialog box.

5. A warning dialog box opens to caution you that the settings you choose in the Save Adobe PDF dialog box will override settings in the Save As dialog box. Click OK to dismiss the warning.

6. In the Save Adobe PDF dialog box, you can choose an Adobe PDF Preset.

   This is a fast way to specify that the newly generated PDF file is intended for commercial printing or to be distributed via email. You can also choose to Preserve Photoshop Editing Capabilities to save layers and editable text for future changes. At this point, you can click Save PDF to generate the file right away or keep modifying the settings for special purposes.

ADOBE PDF STANDARDS

You can choose to create a PDF that matches the most widely used standards for print publishing. There are three different types of PDF/X formats:

- **PDF/X-1A (2001 AND 2003).** PDF/X-1a is an industry-recognized standard for graphic exchange. Choosing PDF/X-1a requires all fonts to be embedded and for the appropriate PDF bounding boxes to be specified. PDF/X-compliant files must contain necessary information describing the condition for which they were prepared to be printed. PDF/X-1a-compliant files can be opened in Acrobat 4.0 and Acrobat Reader 4.0 and later.

- **PDF/X-3 (2002 AND 2003).** The main difference in this newer version of PDF is that it allows for the use of color management. Additionally, it supports device-independent color as well as CMYK and spot colors. Also, ICC color profiles can be used to specify color data later on in the workflow. PDF/X-3-compliant files can be opened in Acrobat 4.0 and Acrobat Reader 4.0 and later.

- **PDF/X-4 (2008).** The newest format of PDF is designed to support newer features like printing artwork with live transparency and layers. This format is designed to work within the existing Adobe PDF Print Engine. The major benefit is that PDF/X-4 jobs can print without flattening artwork or converting the file to PostScript.

For more information on PDF/X, see www.adobe.com/products/acrobat/standards.html.

Compression

The Compression area of the Save Adobe PDF dialog box offers several options for reducing file size. You do not need to downsample, but you might want to if you want to better match the output resolution of a particular printer or to reduce file transfer times.

The interpolation method you choose determines how pixels are deleted:

- **Average Downsampling.** This method averages the pixels in a sample area and replaces the entire area with the average pixel color.

- **Subsampling.** This method chooses a pixel in the center of a sample area and replaces the entire area with that color.

- **Bicubic Downsampling.** This method uses a weighted average to determine pixel color. It generally yields better results than Average Downsampling. This is the slowest but most accurate method.

The Compression setting offers three compression methods:

- **ZIP.** This works well for images with large areas of single colors or repeating patterns.

- **JPEG.** This is suitable for grayscale or color images. JPEG compression eliminates data, so it usually results in much smaller file sizes than ZIP compression.

- **JPEG2000.** This is the new international standard for image data compression. Like JPEG compression, JPEG2000 compression is suitable for grayscale or color images. It also provides additional advantages, such as progressive display.

The Image Quality setting determines how much compression is applied. The settings will vary based on the compression method you choose, but they are clearly labeled.

You can select the convert 16 Bit/Channel Image to 8 Bits/Channel check box if you're working with a 16-bit image. This can significantly reduce file size but is not a good option if you're creating a PDF for professional printing. This option is grayed out if the image you are working with is already in 8-bit mode.

Output

The most common way to create accurate color when creating a PDF is to stick with the PDF/X standard. However, you can choose to modify settings in this area and embed color profiles. Be sure to check with your printer or service bureau regarding color profile settings.

Security

The PDF format supports several different security options, which can be useful to protect the document from unauthorized viewers or to preserve copyright by blocking copying or printing functions. Here are two of the most important security options:

- **Require a password to open the document.** The viewer must enter a password to view the PDF document.

- **Use a password to restrict printing, editing, and other tasks.** Several options can be placed on the document. You can restrict printing and block modifications to the page. This is a good idea if you are posting a PDF for review purposes but do not want people to be able to print the file.

It is important to note that the security in PDF files is very strong but can be breached. These security options are useful and work well for most users. You'll also find additional modifiable options that allow the copying of text or access to screen readers for the visually impaired.

Summary

The Summary area provides a single pane view of all the settings you have used. This is a quick way to verify the options you've enabled.

When you're finished, you can click Save PDF to create the PDF file. You can also click Save Preset if you want to save the settings you've modified for future PDF creation.

Specialized File Formats

Photoshop is a feature-rich and truly enjoyable program, but it is frequently not the end of the road for a designer or artist. Most often, professionals (and even hobbyists) will need to save their files for use in other software packages and environments. Whether it's a JPEG for a website, an EPS for a professional printer, or a PNG file for video editing, Photoshop can create it. In fact, Photoshop supports more than 20 file formats by default. Additional formats used by cameras or other software packages can be added via plug-ins. Not all formats will work with every color space or image type, but each has a special purpose. Let's explore some of the most common formats you'll encounter. Bold items in the following tables are supported features.

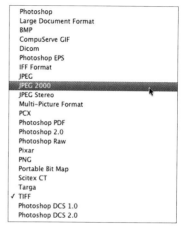

From the Save As dialog box, you can select from several file formats. Certain ones may be unavailable due to bit depth or image mode.

Photoshop (.psd)

Layers	**8-bit**	**16-bit**	**32-bit**
Bitmap	**Grayscale**	**Duotone**	**Indexed Color**
RGB	**CMYK**	**Lab**	**Multichannel**

Note that not all color spaces work in 16- and 32-bit modes.

Photoshop format is the default file format. This format supports all Photoshop's features. It's a good idea to save your design files in this format for maximum editability. Additionally, many other software packages recognize Photoshop layers.

CompuServe GIF (.gif)

Layers	**8-bit**	16-bit	32-bit
Bitmap	**Grayscale**	Duotone	**Indexed Color**
RGB	CMYK	Lab	Multichannel

The online service provider CompuServe originally developed the Graphics Interchange Format (GIF). This format displays 8-bit or indexed-color graphics and images in HTML documents on the Internet. You'll hear the file called both "giff" and "jiff"; both are

NOTE

Many Formats to Choose From

If you need to explore additional formats, you'll find further information in the Photoshop Help menu.

acceptable. GIFs use a color table (with no more than 256 colors total, not per channel) to represent the image. This can lead to a small file size but also banding in the image. If you need transparency in a web graphic, GIF is one of two choices (the other is PNG). There are also animated GIFs, which are GIF frames displayed one after the other to create animation. Unless you need transparency or animation, JPEG is a better option for web delivery.

Compare a JPEG (left) and a GIF (right). Notice how the GIF uses fewer colors. This format can reduce file size but often creates banding or color shifts.

Photoshop EPS (.eps)

Layers	**8-bit**	16-bit	32-bit
Bitmap	**Grayscale**	**Duotone**	**Indexed Color**
RGB	**CMYK**	**Lab**	Multichannel

EPS Options

| Preview: | TIFF (8 bits/pixel) | ⇕ | OK |
| Encoding: | ASCII85 | ⇕ | Cancel |

☐ Include Halftone Screen
☑ Include Transfer Function
☐ PostScript Color Management
☐ Include Vector Data
☐ Image Interpolation

The Encapsulated PostScript (EPS) language file format can contain both vector and bitmap graphics. It is nearly universal and is supported by virtually all graphics, illustration, and page-layout programs. EPS format is used to transfer PostScript artwork between applications. When you open an EPS file that contains vector graphics, Photoshop rasterizes the image.

You can embed an image preview into an EPS file, which makes previewing your image easier in a page-layout program.

JPEG (.jpg)

Layers	**8-bit**	16-bit	32-bit
Bitmap	**Grayscale**	Duotone	Indexed Color
RGB	**CMYK**	Lab	Multichannel

The Joint Photographic Experts Group (JPEG) format is most often used to display continuous-tone images (such as photos) on the Internet. Most digital cameras use JPEG because it provides excellent compression; the maximum set-

ting provides comparable image quality to much larger file formats like TIFF. Occasionally, the print industry (especially newspapers) will use JPEGs.

The JPEG format supports RGB, CMYK, and Grayscale color modes but does not support alpha channels. JPEG is a lossy compression, which means that some data is discarded during compression of the image. JPEGs should not be used as an archive or production file format. You should generally only save JPEG files once, because resaving continues to discard data and lower image quality. If you have acquired an image as a JPEG in your camera, be sure to save the edited document as a PSD or layered TIFF file.

If you are using JPEG as a source format, be sure to set the digital camera to Maximum quality. The best way to create JPEGs for the Internet is with the Save For Web command (discussed in depth at the end of this chapter).

Notice the difference in file-size savings between the two formats. The JPEG (even at maximum quality) is almost four times smaller. File savings make JPEG a popular format for mobile phones, consumer digital cameras, and the newspaper industry.

Large Document Format (.psb)

Layers	8-bit	16-bit	32-bit
Bitmap	Grayscale	Duotone	Indexed Color
RGB	CMYK	Lab	Multichannel

FORMATS THAT SUPPORT SPOT COLOR CHANNELS

Do you need spot color channels for special printing jobs? Then you'd better stick to these file formats:

- Photoshop
- Photoshop Large Document Format (.psb)
- JPEG2000
- Photoshop PDF
- Photoshop Raw (not Camera Raw)
- TIFF
- Photoshop DCS 2.0

TIP

Large Document Format Doesn't Automatically Mean Larger Files

When comparing a file saved as a standard .psd file versus the large format .psb file, the two file sizes are virtually identical. Using the Large Document Format does not increase file size, it just allows a larger-sized file to be saved.

FORMATS THAT SUPPORT ALPHA CHANNELS

Do you need embedded transparency for use in printing, multimedia, video, or animation programs? Then you might want to stick with file formats that support alpha channels. Be sure to check your software program's manual to see which of the following formats are compatible:

- **Photoshop**
- **BMP**
- **JPEG2000**
- **Large Document Format**
- **Photoshop PDF**
- **Photoshop 2.0**
- **Photoshop Raw**
- **Pixar**
- **SGI RGB**
- **Targa**
- **TIFF**

There is normally a 2 GB file size limit in older versions of Photoshop and most other computer applications. To respond to the need for larger file sizes, Adobe launched the Large Document Format (PSB). It supports documents up to 300,000 pixels in any dimension (up to 100 inches at 300 ppi). All Photoshop features, such as layers, effects, and filters, are supported.

Additionally, 32-bits-per-channel images can be saved as PSB files. It's important to remember that files saved in the PSB format can be opened only in newer versions of Photoshop.

PNG (.png)

Layers	**8-bit**	16-bit	32-bit
Bitmap	**Grayscale**	Duotone	**Indexed Color**
RGB	CMYK	Lab	Multichannel

The Portable Network Graphics format provides lossless compression. It is increasingly common on the Internet, but not all browsers support it. The PNG format was created to be a patent-free alternative to GIF. Its major advantage is the PNG-24 file, which allows for 24-bit images (8 bits per channel) and embedded transparency. It is technically superior to GIF.

The file on the left is a PNG-24. Notice how the transparency is handled perfectly (even in the soft glowing areas). On the right is a GIF, which is an 8-bit image. Transparency is not handled as cleanly, and you will notice a white edge outside of the glow.

Targa (.tga)

Layers	**8-bit**	16-bit	32-bit
Bitmap	**Grayscale**	Duotone	**Indexed Color**
RGB	CMYK	Lab	Multichannel

The Targa format was originally designed for use on systems using the Truevision video board. The name is in fact an acronym meaning Truevision Advanced Raster Graphics Adapter. The Targa format predates Photoshop. It is a common format in the video industry (because it supports alpha channels), especially for PC users.

TIFF (.tif)

Layers	**8-bit**	**16-bit**	**32-bit**
Bitmap	**Grayscale**	**Duotone**	**Indexed Color**
RGB	**CMYK**	**Lab**	Multichannel

The Tagged-Image File Format is one of the most common and flexible formats available. It is widely used to exchange files between applications and computer platforms, and has a long legacy of compatibility. One benefit of TIFF is that it acts as a layered file within Photoshop but is treated as a flattened file by other applications. Additionally, TIFF is one of the few formats to work in a bit depth of 8, 16, or 32 bits per channel. High dynamic range images can be saved as 32-bits-per-channel TIFF files.

Adobe Digital Negative (.dng)

Layers	**8-bit**	**16-bit**	32-bit
Bitmap	Grayscale	Duotone	Indexed Color
RGB	CMYK	Lab	Multichannel

There are several competing raw file formats for digital cameras (most are proprietary to a particular manufacturer.) Adobe released the Adobe Digital Negative (DNG) file format to unify things. The concern is that proprietary formats will become obsolete more quickly due to company changes. Adobe hopes the DNG format will be the open-standard model. The specs for this format are available to camera and software manufacturers, and Adobe has had relative success getting others to adopt it. For more information, visit www.adobe.com/dng.

The DNG format offers a unified solution for camera raw images. In Photoshop you can only save a DNG file from the Adobe Camera Raw dialog box. You can also download a standalone DNG Converter for free from Adobe's website. This format is also used by many Adobe Lightroom users to store raw files.

Specialized Processes

Creating files for specific devices often requires special processing. The techniques discussed in this section are fairly elaborate, so the short overviews are meant for a clearer understanding of possibilities. The creation of specialized formats for the Internet, professional printing, or video requires a mastery of several interconnected skills. Let's take a quick look at converting to special purpose files.

VIDEO 109:
Save For Web

Save For Web

Preparing images for the web or mobile devices is all about compromise. You must learn to balance appearance with file size. If a web page takes too long to load, people will leave—which defeats the purpose of running the site. Fortunately, Photoshop provides a powerful command for compressing images and previewing the results: the Save For Web command.

Let's give the Save For Web command a try.

1. Open the file Ch16_ Surfboards.tif from the Chapter 16 folder.

2. Choose File > Save For Web.

3. The Save For Web dialog box offers several important options for optimization and preview:

- **Tools.** If you can't see the entire image, you can use the Zoom tool to make the image more visible. Additionally, you can use the Hand tool (or hold down the spacebar) to drag and navigate around the image. Alternatively, you can click the Zoom Level menu in the lower-left corner and choose a magnification level.

- **Optimization tabs.** By clicking the four tabs at the top, you can choose to view the Original image, an Optimized view, 2-Up for two versions of the image side by side, or 4-Up for four versions of the image side by side. Being able to compare optimized images helps you choose the right format and compression settings. For this image, choose 2-Up.

- **Image Optimization Info.** The area below each image in the Save For Web dialog box gives you optimization infor-

```
JPEG                                    60 quality
51K
10 sec @ 56.6 Kbps   ▾≡
```

mation. You can see the current optimization applied, the projected file size, and the estimated download time based on a selected modem connection speed. Choose the JPEG High preset, and you'll notice that the file has been reduced from 32 MB to 1.055 MB (a significant savings). However, the download time is 196 seconds on a 56K modem (you can right-click the time to choose another speed).

4. You need to further reduce the file size for Internet delivery. The first area to tackle is the actual image size in pixels. In the Image Size field you'll see that the image is more than 4,000 pixels tall (which is much taller than a typical web page that can be displayed on most monitors). Type in a Height of **600** pixels, so the image can integrate easily into the web page (even with a screen resolution of 1024 × 768, a height of 600 would allow the image to display without scrolling up and down). Press the Tab key to exit the file and apply the resize value.

```
Image Size
W:  398    px ⌐
H:  600    px ⌐⌐  Quality: Bicubic ⌄     Percent: 14.6  %
```

5. The file size has been significantly reduced, but it's difficult to see the effects of the compression. Set the image magnification view to **100%**.

6. Change the amount of Compression by either changing the preset (from High to Medium, for example) or adjusting the Quality amount. You can manually enter a number or click to access a slider (you will need to release the slider for the image to refresh). Try a setting of **45** to see the results. The image is now at just over 32K, which is more than a 99.9 percent reduction in file size and a fundamental change for web delivery.

7. Toward the lower-right corner you have the ability to choose to preview the image in a web browser. If you don't see your browser of choice, just choose Edit List, and then choose Find All to add all web browsers on your computer.

8. Click Save to specify a location for the saved file. Choose your desktop and click Save in the new dialog box to process the image and save a compressed web-ready version. The original file will remain untouched, and its resolution and quality will be identical to its state when you launched the Save For Web command.

9. Experiment with other file formats such as GIF and PNG to see their benefits and limitations.

Convert to CMYK

Although CMYK conversion is an everyday process for many users, several authors and trainers have developed some useful techniques. What I offer here is a proper workflow that will work for most users, on most images, in most environments. I encourage you to continue to explore prepress production through further reading. CMYK conversion can be a very tricky process, and it is essential that you have access to the color profile used by your output device. Additionally, be sure to discuss the process with your service bureau that will do the professional printing. With all of these caveats said, let's take a look at the process.

1. Check your color management settings by choosing Edit > Color Settings or by pressing Shift+Command+K (Shift+Ctrl+K). Choose North America General Purpose 2.

2. Open the file Ch16_Gamut.tif from the Chapter 16 folder.

3. Choose View > Gamut Warning or press Shift+Command+Y (Shift+Ctrl+Y). Areas that are too bright or saturated for CMYK printing will be highlighted in gray. This is because

the RGB space can represent a wider ranger of visible colors based on the additive method of color. CMYK printing instead uses the subtractive model, and it has a narrower range. The warning is useful because it lets you identify areas that are subject to color shifting when printing or converting to the CMYK color mode.

4. Select the Sponge tool (O) from the Tools panel. Adjust the brush to a large size with soft edges. Set the flow to a lower value such as 30% and the mode to Desaturate. Deselect the Vibrance option to have greater impact on the saturated color areas. These settings will gently soak up the color in the oversaturated areas.

5. Carefully paint over the oversaturated areas with the Sponge tool. It may take multiple strokes or adjusting the Flow setting, but you'll see the gamut warning go away as you reduce the oversaturated areas. Repeat for other problem areas in the photo.

6. When all of the gamut warning has been removed, choose Image > Mode > CMYK. There should be no visible color shifting. By taking the time to manually touch up the out of gamut areas, you'll get a better CMYK conversion with less posterized edges or color clipping.

7. Save the image in a print-ready format such as TIFF.

Add an Alpha Channel

You explored saving selections as channels much earlier in the book (Chapter 5, "Selection Tools and Techniques"). The alpha channel can be used to store transparency information, and it is particularly useful for video and multimedia users. In Photoshop's Actions panel, you'll find the Video actions that I co-wrote with Daniel Brown (a Photoshop expert). These can speed up certain tasks for a video workflow. Two of these actions can create an alpha channel for multi-layered graphics with transparency.

1. Make sure the Logo layer is selected in the Layers panel.

2. Call up the Actions panel and load the Video Actions by clicking the submenu. Choose the Video Actions set.

3. Choose the Create Alpha Channels from Visible Layers action. You must see Photoshop's transparency grid for it to work.

4. Click the Play Selection button to run the action. A dialog box appears with instructions. Read it and click Continue. A new alpha channel is added to the document.

5. Choose File > Save As and save the file as a PSD, TIFF, or Targa file, and then choose to embed the transparency by including the alpha channel.

There are many other issues related to creating graphics for use in video. I invite you to check out my "other" Photoshop book, aptly titled *Photoshop for Video* (Peachpit, 2010).

Include a Clipping Path

If you are preparing an image to import into a page layout program (such as Adobe InDesign or QuarkXPress), you may want to embed a clipping path. The clipping path embeds the transparency information into the file.

It's important to note that paths are vector based; therefore, they have hard edges (and do not preserve softness or a feathered edge). Features like a drop shadow cannot be preserved when creating a clipping path (but can often be added in the page layout program). An alternative to clipping paths is to use an alpha channel (which can include a feathered edge).

Photoshop offers a few ways to create accurate clipping paths; let's explore the easiest. Photoshop has a built-in wizard to help you create clipping paths.

1. Open the file Ch16_Clipping_Path.psd from the Chapter 16 folder.

2. Choose Selection > Load Selection, and then click OK to use the default properties. Photoshop loads a selection based on the transparency in the document.

3. Switch to the Paths panel and click the Make work path from selection icon.

4. Double-click on the work path to open the Save Path dialog box. Name the path Logo Edge and click OK.

5. Click the Paths panel submenu and choose Clipping Path.

6. Select the new path Logo Edge from the Path pop-up menu.

7. Leave the flatness value empty to print the image using the printer's default value.

8. Convert the file to CMYK by choosing Image > Mode > CMYK.

9. Choose File > Save As and store the file as a Photoshop EPS, DCS, or PDF format for PostScript printing or as a TIFF for use in Adobe InDesign or QuarkXPress.

This path is functioning as a clipping path. When the path's name appears outlined, it is being used as a clipping path.

End of the Road

Have you reached the end of the road? Hardly. Photoshop contains a wealth of tools. But you have now gained a firm foundation of knowledge. Many more techniques and specialized uses are worth exploring. And there is a plethora of Photoshop websites and books available to further your knowledge. A great place to start is at my blog at www.richardharringtonblog.com. You should also explore the National Association of Photoshop Professionals; be sure to check out its website at www.PhotoshopUser.com. You can also subscribe to the free Understanding Adobe Photoshop podcast on iTunes or check out advanced classes at Lynda.com. Photoshop will be a core tool as you grow into other software applications. Continue to expand your Photoshop knowledge and the investment in time will pay back greatly.

Index